Spirituality in Daily Life

EXPERIENCING GOD EVERYDAY

Published by:
GITA PUBLISHING HOUSE
Sadhu Vaswani Mission,
10, Sadhu Vaswani Path,
Pune - 411 001, (India).
gph@sadhuvaswani.org

Spirituality in Daily Life
© 2012, J.P. Vaswani
ISBN: 978-93-80743-67-7

DADA VASWANI'S BOOKS
Visit us online to purchase books on self-improvement, spiritual
advancement, meditation and philosophy. Plus audio cassettes, CDs,
DVDs, monthly journals and books in Hindi.
www.dadavaswanisbooks.org

Printed by:
MEHTA OFFSET PVT. LTD.
Mehta House,
A-16, Naraina Industrial Area II,
New Delhi - 110 028, (India).
info@mehtaoffset.com

Spirituality in Daily Life

EXPERIENCING GOD EVERYDAY

J. P. Vaswani

GITA PUBLISHING HOUSE
PUNE, (India).
www.dadvaswanisbooks.org

Books and Booklets by Dada J.P. Vaswani

7 Commandments of the Bhagavad Gita

10 Commandments of a Successful Marriage

100 Stories You Will Never Forget

108 Pearls of Practical Wisdom

108 Simple Prayers of a Simple Man

108 Thoughts on Success

114 Thoughts on Love

A Little Book of Life

A Little Book of Wisdom

A Simple and Easy Way To God

A Treasure of Quotes

Around The Camp Fire

Begin the Day with God

Bhagavad Gita in a Nutshell

Burn Anger Before Anger Burns You

Comrades of God - Lives of Saints from East & West

Daily Appointment with God

Daily Inspiration (A Thought For Every Day Of The Year)

Daily Inspiration

Destination Happiness

Dewdrops of Love

Does God Have Favorites?

Finding Peace of Mind

Formula for Prosperity

Gateways to Heaven

God In Quest of Man

Good Parenting

How to Overcome Depression

I am a Sindhi

I Luv U, God!

In 2012 All Will Be Well!

Joy Peace Pills

Kill Fear Before Fear Kills You

Ladder of Abhyasa

Lessons Life Has Taught Me

Life after Death

Life and Teachings of Sadhu Vaswani

Life and Teachings of the Sikh Gurus

Living in the Now

Management Moment by Moment

Mantras For Peace Of Mind

Many Paths: One Goal

Nearer, My God, To Thee!

New Education Can Make the World New

Peace or Perish: There Is No Other Choice

Positive Power of Thanksgiving

Questions Answered

Saints For You and Me

Saints With A Difference

Say No to Negatives

Secrets of Health And Happiness

Shake Hands With Life

Short Sketches of Saints Known & Unknown

Sketches of Saints Known & Unknown

Stop Complaining: Start Thanking!

Swallow Irritation Before Irritation Swallows You

Teachers are Sculptors

The Goal Of Life and How To Attain It

The Little Book of Freedom from Stress

The Little Book of Prayer

The Little Book of Service

The Little Book of Success

The Little Book of Yoga

The Magic of Forgiveness

The Miracle of Forgiving

The New Age Diet: Vegetarianism for You and Me

The Perfect Relationship: Guru and Disciple

The Terror Within

The Way of Abhyasa (How To Meditate)

Thus Have I Been Taught

Tips For Teenagers

What You Would Like To know About Karma

What You Would Like To know About Hinduism

What To Do When Difficulties Strike

Why Do Good People Suffer?

You Are Not Alone: God Is With You!

You Can Change Your Life

Why Be Sad?

CONTENTS

Author's Preface

This book is inspired by the teaching which I think is the very first call of the Gita to us all: You are not the body that you wear; you are the *atman*, the immortal spirit within!

Is this not a clarion call to awaken the dormant spirit within all of us?

It is my firm belief that spirituality is not an abstract, complex pursuit that it is often made out to be. It is born out of an inner aspiration, an awakening to the realisation that there is more to life than materialism.

Of all the aspects of human life, it is perhaps spirituality that is likely to seem rather remote and unfamiliar to many of us, especially the youth. Some of us might even consider it irrelevant to our daily lives. We are willing to spend a third of our life (or more) at work or in business, to build our financial resources. We are ready to spare time for our chosen relationships, including friends and family. We are willing to spend time and money to preserve our health and fitness. Enough time is also set aside for entertainment, leisure and relaxation. But when it comes to spiritual well-being, we are at a loss; we ask ourselves – what am I supposed to do for my soul?

I would like to tell you, that you owe it to yourself to unlock the hidden spiritual powers that are within you!

Gurudev Sadhu Vaswani taught us: "Man is essentially the soul, and spirituality is the foundation of a balanced life."

What is the soul?

Of the soul, the *atman* within, Sri Krishna says in the Bhagavad Gita:

Weapons cleave him not, nor fire burneth him. Waters wet him not, nor wind drieth him away.

…He is eternal and all-pervading. He is unchanging and immovable. He is ancient, the same forever…

[II 23-24]

This great reality is difficult for most people to grasp – for so strong, so powerful, so binding is our attachment to the body!

Ancient Indian wisdom likens the soul to a lamp shining within: it is surrounded by three separate sheathes or layers. The mind is the inner layer, the senses constitute the middle layer, and the flesh is the outermost layer.

The soul is the unchanging spirit that pervades all beings. What we call the body is but a garment that the soul has worn. In the words of the poet Shelley:

> The One remains: the many change and pass;
> Heaven's Light forever shines: earth's shadows fly;
> Life, like a dome of many-coloured glass,
> Stains the white radiance of Eternity.

As long as we remain unaware of this great truth – that the soul is eternal, and that the body is mortal – we become obsessed with the physical, material and sensual aspects of life.

The more we identify with the body, the more unhappy we become!

It is my view, therefore, that detachment from the physical, and awakening to the spiritual, is the first step to true happiness.

Therefore, our *rishis* asserted: *Tat twam asi!*

Therefore, Jesus said to the Jews, "Ye are Gods."

"Your substance is that of God Himself," said a great Sufi saint.

"Whoso knows himself, has Light," said Lao Tse.

3

In this sense, spirituality is the key to unlock true joy and peace, to discover the essential Divinity within each one of us.

If we wish to progress on the path of self-realisation, we *have to* stop identifying ourselves with the body!

Have you ever wondered why pious Hindus remove their shoes before they enter a temple or a holy place? This is merely symbolic of the idea that we move away from our habitual body-consciousness, which in turn, will help us move closer to God.

We have got to move away from the body, even as we move away from the "shoes" we wear!

Swami Vivekananda was an inspiration, an icon, a role model to the youth of this country. He believed that India's spirituality alone could save our sinking civilisation. He was, himself, a mighty spiritual genius, who carried to the modern west the message of India's ancient wisdom – that there can be no true freedom without spirituality and that no man is free until he is master of himself.

I request you to dwell upon this idea: there can be no true freedom without spirituality. Today, people are very conscious of their need for freedom, in every sense of that word. Freedom to live their own life, freedom to choose their career and their life-partners, freedom to pursue their dreams and aspirations, freedom to do as they please!

Young people today value their sense of independence and self-worth. Their way is the way of questioning everything. They do not take orders from anyone; they believe in following their own way; they live and act; they by their "own sweet will". As such, discipline is becoming conspicuous by its fast disappearance in the world today! The values we worship are aggression, self-assertion, the ability to have one's own way, the strength to impose our will on others, the power to get everybody to do what we want them to do!

May I suggest to you that we also require spiritual discipline to attain self-knowledge, to pursue the path of self-discovery, which is acknowledged to be the ultimate goal of education since times immemorial? Of what use is any form of knowledge, vocational, professional or technical, if we lack knowledge of the self?

If Indian culture and civilisation have survived the ravages of time against all odds, it is only because we have a message to give to the modern world – that there can be no true freedom without spirituality. The emphasis of Indian culture has always been on the unfolding of the inner powers, the *atma shakti*. It is precisely this *atma shakti*, this inner soul power that has enabled India to ride many a storm and quell many a tempest. When all other ancient civilisations have perished, when all other ancient religions have been wiped away without a trace, India lives on, and the Hindu faith is still vibrant and vital!

The Light of the *atman*, the Light of the self, the Light of the spirit – it was around this that our glorious culture was built in ancient India. This culture was known as *atma vidya* — the science of the spirit. For spirituality too, is a science; it concerns the discovery of the One self in all.

People are awed by the miracles of science as much as they are fascinated by the powers of spirituality. Science is the discovery of nature's laws: while spirituality is the discovery of the self. In the final analysis, both are discoveries; both are an experience of "awareness". Our *rishis* had this "awareness"; they gained spiritual knowledge through intuition.

Spirituality makes us raise the fundamental question: What is man? Or, to put it more personally, what am I? It is precisely this self-knowledge that all of us must seek, in order to find true fulfillment.

Spirituality does not mean turning your back on life; it is not renunciation or asceticism; it is not running away from the problems of life. It is the source of courage and inner strength that will enable you to take on life's challenges in the awareness that you are a spark of Divinity; that within you is a *shakti* that is of the Infinite!

True spirituality is not a matter of indoctrination. It cannot be inspired by compulsion. You are free to enquire into its principles; you must be convinced of their truth, before you accept them. The laws of life are inviolable; they need no defenders, no patrons, no protectors. Each one of us must reach the Highest by his own free choice. This is the great truth taught to us in the ancient scriptures of India.

Several cultures and religions simply do not teach people to focus on the world within them; their emphasis is often on words, rites and rituals; on a Form or a Being or Spirit *outside*; thus the innermost spirit remains out of reach of most people.

The Indian tradition on the other hand, has always placed great value on the inner space that is within all of us: on the state of inner silence and inner stillness. In this state of inner consciousness, we will also discover our own Divinity – that we are not the bodies we wear; we are not the insignificant, pathetic, frail creatures that we take ourselves to be; we will discover that we are the immortal *atman*, the eternal, infinite spirit that is *Sat-chit-ananda* – pure, true, eternal bliss!

In our constant state of superficial existence, we continue to ignore the world within. In our persistent chase after shadow shapes and worldly wealth, we lose sight of our inner consciousness. We emphasise speech, action and outward show; we forget that there is a far more valuable aspect to life called reflection, contemplation, introspection. Men and women of speech and action, there are very many; alas, men and women of reflection and contemplation, there are very few.

We are content to live our lives on the surface. Superficiality characterises everything we do. We occupy our minds with what we would like to eat, what we would like to buy, and what we could do to impress our friends and neighbours.

We have no time to think of the world within!

What are we likely to find in there, in that world within us, I hear some of you asking me.

I'll be happy to tell you what you will find within you: *not* material treasures; *not* the wealth of this world – but untapped, undreamt of resources of wisdom, peace, joy, spiritual strength, creativity and healing power!

Within us, lies a centre of tranquillity, serenity, self-knowledge and true awareness. When we touch this still centre within, we will experience true freedom – freedom from the fears, desires, tensions, insecurities and complexes that haunt us in our worldly life.

Psychologists tell us that there are three 'states' in which human beings exist: the waking state, the sleeping state and the dreaming state.

But Western Psychology stops just a little short of what our ancient sages tell us: a *fourth* state of intense concentration beyond these three – a state of which most of us are unaware!

Therefore, does our Indian tradition place great value on meditation, reflection and contemplation – on that state of inner silence and inner stillness, of which I spoke to you.

It is within us, that we will find the peace and joy we seek so desperately!

In this state, too, we will experience true freedom – freedom from obsessive fears, constant desires and negative thoughts.

In this state, we will discover our own Divinity – that we are not the pathetic, helpless creatures we take ourselves to be, but the eternal, infinite spirit of pure, true, everlasting bliss – *Sat-chit-ananda*.

The first step on this path of discovery is the Socratic injunction: 'Know thyself'. Once we realise the truth of our being, we would be able to overcome our attachments. For, all attachments are either physical, emotional or mental. But man is neither the physical body nor the mind; the truth is, man enshrines the *atman*. And *atman* is *shakti*. Once man realises this that all that he wants and all that he needs is within him, he will not have to wander outside. He will not run after money, fame and name. Such a man is not 'bound' to the world, but is a free bird in the firmament of the spirit.

Join me as we set out to explore this firmament of the spirit!

– J. P. Vaswani

SECTION I

What Is Spirituality?

What is spirituality? In simple words, it is knowledge of God, not an intellectual knowledge but an illumined personal experience of the Supreme.

Spirituality teaches us to look within. Even as there is an expanding universe outside of us, there is a larger and more wonderful universe within us of which we are not aware. One day, when our bodies drop down dead, the outer universe will vanish. Our inner Self will remain: it is timeless and eternal.

Carl Jung said: "Your vision will become clear only when you look into your heart. Who looks outside, dreams. Who looks inside, awakens." Gurudev Sadhu Vaswani said: "I have but one tongue. If I had a million tongues, with everyone of those tongues I would still utter the one word, 'Awake'!"

Our spiritual hearts are stained with many stains. They are not pure. We need to purify them. Jesus said: "Blessed are the pure in heart, for they shall see God." We can purify the heart through prayer, meditation, contemplation, repetition of the Holy Name, study of the scriptures and selfless service of the poor and lowly, the unwanted and unloved.

God is the goal of life. And God is to be realised, not merely 'understood' or talked about. Long have we chanted hymns and recited from the scriptures and rung temple-bells and offered unending prayers, while our minds have strayed afar. Long have we kept God out of our lives, 'Tis time to call Him in.

To move Godward, we need to get up and open the door and let God in. This happens only when man realises the need for God. Out of the very depths of his heart, there awakes the cry: "I have need of You, Lord! I cannot live without You!"

This is known as 'spiritual awakening'. Something happens deep within you and your life becomes new. You are filled with light and warmth, joy and peace. You realise that the life you have lived until then, a life of creature -comforts and of pride, pelf, power – was no life at all. You exclaim with Tolstoy: "To know God is to live!"

In this connection the following suggestions may be found helpful:

1)   The secret of the new life is love of God. This love grows from more to more. Love is a gift of God to man. Therefore, pray as often as you can: "I love You God! I want to love You, more and more! I want to love You more than anything in the world."

2)   There comes a stage when we realise that we cannot serve two masters at the same time. A decision has to be taken — either God or the world. We can't have both. There must be no compromise. The seeker after God, stands up for Truth — in thought, in speech, and in all his dealings with others. Truth — though she take me to the gallows! Truth — though she lead me through the flames!

A lawyer said to a businessman, who had incurred debts amounting to ₹ 40,00,000/- : "Give me ₹ 50,000/- and I shall clear you of all your debts."

"You insult me," answered the businessman. "I have incurred those debts and must pay back every single rupee!"

3) If you have wronged a person, do not waste time in making amends. Have you hurt someone? Have you cheated him? Have you spread scandals against him? Have you exploited him for selfish purposes? Then waste no time in setting right what has gone wrong.

4) Has someone wronged you? Forgive him even before forgiveness is asked. And your mind will be at peace and the world around you will smile.

5) Whatever you do — it may be a lowly act such as sweeping a room or a noble deed such as saving a life — do it wholly for the love of God. "Whatever you eat, whatever austerity you practise, whatever you give in charity, whatever you do, do it, O Arjuna, as an offering unto Me," says the Lord in the Gita. Can there be a simpler way of communing with God than this, that we offer unto Him every little thing we do, every thought we think, every word we utter, every aspiration we breathe?

6) Establish more and more points of contact with God. This will give you soul-rest, and out of you the joy of God will flow out to many. Be gentle with all who come to you: they have been sent by God to your door, not without a purpose.

There was a time when if, in the midst of work, someone came and disturbed me, I felt upset. Now I try to accept every interruption as His appointment. And I know how light and happy feels the heart that rejoices in the Will of God.

7) Help as many as you can to lift the load on the rough road of life. Sadhu Vaswani said:

Did you meet him on the road?
Did you leave him with the load?

On the road of life are many who go about carrying heavy loads. The loads are not merely physical. There are many who carry on their hearts the loads of worry, anxiety, fear. Lighten their loads! Be a burden-bearer! The day on which we have not helped a brother here or a sister there, a bird here or an animal there – for birds and animals, too, are God's children and man's younger brothers and sisters in the one family of creation – that day on which we have not helped someone in need is a lost day, indeed.

Life fulfills itself in service. There is no joy greater than the joy of those who spend themselves in serving those in suffering and pain. William Gladstone was, one day, preparing a speech to be delivered in Parliament, the next day. In the midst of his work, he was disturbed by an urgent call from the parents of a dying boy, who wanted to see the British Premier. When he returned to the writing of his speech, he said: "That speech may fail or not: the empire may fall or not: but in helping that boy I have tasted exquisite joy!"

The religion of man is the religion of service. So let us do as much good as we can, to as many as we can, in as many ways as we can, on as many occasions as we can and as long as we.

How Can We Be Like God?

In his serene and quiet ashram on the banks of the River Yamuna, a Guru was addressing a group of his disciples.

"The spark of the Divine is within you," he said to the young seekers. "You are an aspect of the Divine. You must constantly aspire for perfection; to be perfect is to be God-like."

One of the disciples was puzzled by the remark. He stood up and said to the Guru, "But sire, God is great. He is Omnipotent, Omnipresent and Omniscient. Infinite worlds exist within Him. How can we ever hope to be like God?"

The Guru said to him, "Here is my water bowl. Take it to the Yamuna River and fill it with water."

The disciple left and in a few minutes he was back with a filled bowl. The Guru looked at the bowl and said, "This is not the water from the Yamuna. I told you to get water from the Yamuna River."

"I beg your pardon, Guruji," said the disciple. "This is indeed water from the Yamuna River. I did exactly what you told me to do."

"I tell you, this cannot be water from the Yamuna," insisted the Guru. "There are fish and turtles in the Yamuna; there are cows standing in the river; there are people bathing in its waters. Where are the fish in this bowl? Where are the turtles and cows? Why, there isn't a single person bathing here! And you tell me this is the water of the Yamuna River? Go and get me the water of the Yamuna River."

The disciple was taken aback. "But Guruji," he stammered. "I brought just a bowl full of water from the Yamuna for you. How can a bowl contain all those things you mention?"

"True, a little bowl can't contain all those things," agreed the Guru. "Now go and pour this water back into the Yamuna."

The disciple went and poured the water into the river, and returned.

"Tell me, don't all those things exist in the water now?" the Guru asked him. "See for yourself, the fish, the turtles, the cows and the people; they are all in the river, aren't they? The individual soul is like the water in the bowl. It is one with God, but it exists in a limited form, and therefore it seems to be very different from God. When *you poured the water from the bowl back into the river, that water once again contained fish, turtles, cows and everything else that the river contains. In the same way, when you see your own inner Self through meditation and knowledge, you will realise that you are 'That' and that your spirit pervades everywhere, just like God. Once you are aware of this, you will know that you are an aspect of God!"*

Chapter One

You Are Not The Body You Wear

The Gita Mahatmya tells us: "In this world, taking refuge in the Gita, many Kings like Janaka and others reached the highest state or goal, and have been purified of all sins."

In the Third Chapter of the Bhagavad Gita, Sri Krishna cites King Janaka as the perfect example of *dhriti* or steadfastness. He attained perfection through detached action.

Many of us know of King Janaka as Sita's father. But we realise, with surprise, that he was a great *Mahatma* in his own right. Sri Krishna refers to this great sage-king of India, who continued to rule his kingdom even after attaining God-realisation.

What is it about King Janaka that makes him so relevant to us in this search for spirituality?

A beautiful story is given to us in our ancient legends. A great *rishi*, Yagnavalkya, comes to the palace of King Janaka, one of the greatest kings this land has known. King Janaka sat on a throne but his heart was the heart of a *fakir*, a saint, a holy man of God. This saintly ruler rejoices to see Rishi Yagnavalkya at his palace. He receives the sage, offers his *pranams*, and begs for a teaching at his holy feet.

Rishi Yagnavalkya begins to question the King. "Tell me, O King," says the *rishi*, "What is the light whereby a man lives and moves and works and walks and finally to his home returns?"

King Janaka replies readily, "O Gurudeva, the light by which all men live and move, the light by which they work and walk and then to their homes return is the light of the Sun!"

Rishi Yagnavalkya smiles. "When the Sun has set, when its light has disappeared what is the light whereby men live and move and work and walk and then to their homes return?"

The King replies, "When the Sun has set, men must live and move, work and walk and then to their homes return by the light of the Moon."

"And what if the Sun and the Moon have both disappeared?" queries the *rishi*.

"Then, men must live and move and work and walk by the light of the Fire," says the King.

"When the light of the Sun, the Moon and the Fire have all gone out," continues the *rishi*, "What is the light by which men can live and move and work and walk and to their homes return?"

The King is puzzled. He has no ready answer. He begs the *rishi* to enlighten him.

Then it is that Rishi Yagnavalkya gives him the teaching – which I believe is the message of Hinduism to modern civilisation. The *rishi* tells the King: "When all external light has gone out – when the sun does not shine, when the moon is not radiant and the fire is put out – there is still one Light that shines. It is the Light of the *Atman,* the Light of the Spirit. It is this, which is the light of all Lights. It is by this Light that the sun shines, the moon is radiant and the fire is aglow. It is this Light by which man must live and move and work and walk and to his eternal home return."

The Light of the *Atman*, the Light of the Self, and the Light of the Spirit – it was around this that our glorious culture was built in ancient India. This culture was known as *Atma vidya* – the science of the spirit. For, as I said to you, spirituality too, is a science, it concerns the discovery of the one self in all.

> ||*Idam brahma, idam kshatram, ime lokah, ime devah, imani bhutani, idam sarvamya dayamatma*||
> This Source of knowledge; this Source of power; all these worlds; all these gods; all these beings –
> All this is just the Self.
> – Sage Yagnavalkya *(Brihadaranyaka Upanishad)*

King Janaka was blessed to have Yagnavalkya as one of his teachers. It is said that Yagnavalkya was in Janaka's court until he retired to the *tapobana* (forest of meditation) to take up *sanyasa*.

King Janaka once decided to perform a special *yagna* for the welfare of his subjects. Word went round that the *rishis* and sages who participated in the *yagna* would be given rich gifts, including one thousand cows.

Now, there was a sage by the name of Udalaka, who was a great scholar and teacher of Vedanta. He had a disciple named Kagola, who was virtuous and devoted but not really astute or learned. Sage Udalaka set greater store by virtue and good conduct, rather than learning; so he gave his daughter Sujata in marriage to Kagola.

Sujata became pregnant and the child who was conceived in her womb, grew up listening to the *vedic* recitals in his grandfather's *ashram*. He absorbed the wisdom of the holy scriptures even before birth. But his father, Kagola, often made mistakes in the recital and pronunciation of the scriptures. When the child in the womb heard these, he would twist his body in pain and anguish. Thus it came to pass that he was born with eight crooked bends in his body. This gave him the name of Ashtavakra, which means "Eight crooked bends".

When Sujata heard about the *yagna* that was to be performed at King Janaka's court, she urged her husband Kagola to go to Mithila and participate in the *yagna*, so that he might earn some wealth for the benefit of their son, Ashtavakra. But unfortunately, Kagola was defeated in a debate by Bandi, a reputed scholar at the King's court, and drowned to death as a penalty.

Ashtavakra grew up, taking his grandfather to be his father. He became a great scholar even in his boyhood, and at the young age of twelve he had already completed his study of the Vedas and the Vedanta.

When Ashtavakra learnt that Udalaka was not his father and that his own father Kagola, had lost his life at a debate in King Janaka's court, he decided to confront the King, and seek an explanation from the scholars and sages in his court about the fate of his father.

In the meanwhile, King Janaka had a dream. He dreamt that he was a beggar, destitute and starving. He was in the throes of extreme hunger, indeed acute starvation. He woke up with a start and was profoundly moved by his dream. He asked himself: "What is the Truth? Who am I, am I the king who dreamt that he was a beggar, or the beggar who is dreaming that he is a king?"

Determined to get to the truth, he summoned all the sages and scholars as was his wont and requested them to give the answer to his question – offering half his kingdom for a satisfactory reply. Many scholars came, for many were tempted by the consideration of the hefty reward offered: no less than half the kingdom. But not a single one of them could provide a suitable answer to the King's question.

Ashtavakra by now arrived in Mithila, accompanied by his uncle Svetaketu. On their way to the palace, they were stopped by the approach of the King and his retinue. The King's soldiers and guards marched ahead of the procession, shouting: "Move away. Make way for the King."

Ashtavakra stood before them and said to them, "O royal attendants, our *shastras* say that even the King, if he is righteous, has to move and make way for the blind, the deformed, the fair sex and *brahmanas* learned in the Vedas. This is the rule enjoined by the scriptures and King Janaka surely knows this."

The King, surprised at these wise words of the young *brahmin* boy, stopped his retinue, and allowed the youngster to move ahead. He said to his attendants: "This boy may be no more than a stripling. But he speaks the truth. Fire is fire whether it is a tiny flame or a huge conflagration."

Ashtavakra and Svetaketu moved on and entered the venue of the King's assembly. Here too, the gatekeeper stopped them and said: "Where do you think you are going? This is a *yagnashala,* and there is no place for boys. The right of entry is reserved for venerable scholars learned in the Vedas."

Ashtavakra replied: "Don't judge us by appearances. We are not mere boys. We have observed the necessary vows and have learnt the Vedas. Those who have mastered the truths of the Vedanta will not judge another on mere considerations of age or appearance."

"Don't give me any more of your cheek," said the gatekeeper. "Just get out of this place."

Ashtavakra replied: "Gatekeeper, grey hair does not prove anything! The ripeness of the soul is not visible only in wrinkles. Kindly inform the King that I am here to meet the court Pandit Bandi."

At that moment the King himself came there and easily recognised Ashtavakra, the precociously wise boy he had met a few minutes earlier. He ordered the gatekeepers to allow the two youngsters to enter the assembly hall.

Many eminent *rishis* and scholars were seated in their grand and honourable places when Ashtavakra entered the hall. As he hobbled into the hall, moving his crooked figure towards the conclave, the sages who were already seated burst out in derisive laughter.

Ashtavakra paused, and then addressed the King. "I thought I was going to attend a meeting of philosophers," he said to Janaka. "But it would appear that I have walked into a gathering of cobblers!"

"How dare you…" protested one of the scholars, rising to his feet in anger.

King Janaka said to the young sage in all humility, "Please explain yourself, wise one."

"The men whom you have gathered here are looking at my flesh, my skin. What can they be but cobblers? This physical body that I wear is but a shoe. These men are judging me by the shoes I wear. They do not realise that I am not this body. How can these men be philosophers?"

The sages and scholars could only bow down their heads in shame!

Ashtavakra then turned to the King. "They tell me that you are going to give away half your kingdom in return for an answer that you seek to your question. But you must tell me how you can do this – does this kingdom belong to you?"

> **Ego poisons you to believe: "I am the doer."**
> Believe "I am not the doer." Drink this nectar and be happy.
>
> *– Ashtavakra Gita*

Taken aback, the King replied, "But of course it belongs to me; I have inherited it by due rights by my royal lineage."

"May I ask who owned the kingdom before you came to the throne?"

"My father."

"And before that?"

"My father's father."

"And, after you?"

"My sons will inherit this kingdom, even as I did."

"So you see, mighty King, this kingdom did not belong to you earlier, and it will not be yours in the future. Yet you claim ownership in between, and even assume the right to give a part of it away…"

The King realised that there was a serious flaw in his assumptions, and that he was actually only the caretaker of the kingdom and that it did not belong to him. Ashtavakra had made it clear to him that he could not give away what he did not own.

"Now tell me, what will you give me if I answer your question?"

The King replied in a small voice, "I offer you my body, which is my own."

"Oh King, you are making the same mistake again," laughed Ashtavakra. "Are you sure you are the owner of this body?"

"Yes, of course, I am the dweller in this body, therefore I own it, and everything is under my control."

"May I ask you, where was this body of yours 100 years ago and where will it be 100 years from now?"

Again the King had to concede that the body did not really belong to him either and that it was just given to him on loan by Mother Nature for the duration of a lifetime, after which it would have to be returned to Nature.

"Alright, said the King, "I'll give you my mind."

"You think you own your mind; you cannot even control your mind. How can you give something over which you have no control? You tell your mind to do this and it does not even listen to you?"

Eventually King Janaka realised that he was in the presence of a great Master, and asked to be accepted as Ashtavakra's disciple to be taught the mysteries of the Self.

> **If you detach yourself from the body and rest in consciousness, you will become content, peaceful and free from bondage immediately.**
> *– Ashtavakra Gita*

The essence of the dialogue between King Janaka and Ashtavakra is beautifully rendered in the *Ashtavakra Gita.*

Ashtavakra now said to the King, "I have an old account to settle in this assembly. I would like to have a debate with your Pandit Bandi."

The King said to him, "Young sire, are you aware that Bandi has overthrown in argument many great scholars in the past and caused them to be drowned as a penalty for losing the debate? Does that not deter you from this dangerous adventure?"

Ashtavakra replied: "Your eminent scholar has not hitherto encountered someone like me. Perhaps he has become complacent, arrogant and vain with easy victories over good men who were not real scholars. I have come here to repay an old debt due on account of my father, who was defeated by this man and made to drown himself, as my mother informs me. I am sure that I will vanquish Bandi. Kindly summon him."

Ashtavakra met Bandi. They took up a scholarly debate, each employing his utmost learning and wits to confound the other. And in the end the assembly unanimously declared the victory of Ashtavakra and the defeat of Bandi.

The court *pandit* of Mithila bowed his head and paid the forfeit by drowning himself in the ocean and going to the abode of Varuna. Then the spirit of Kagola, the father of Ashtavakra, gained peace and joy in the glory of his son.

Bhagwan Sri Ramana Maharishi tells us that these stories refer to more than one King, and that they were all called by the honorific title of Janaka. But I do not wish to enter into historicity. My focus is on the knowledge of the *atman*, the path of spirituality. And so we move on to another sage with whom Janaka was associated.

The story is told to us of Shuka Muni, son of the great Rishi Ved Vyasa, who was born a *gnani*. It is said that even while he was a foetus in the mother's womb, he decided not to be born upon this earth, which was infested with *maya*. But Rishi Vyasa wanted a son desperately, and so the Lord suspended *maya* temporarily, so that Shuka could take birth. Such was this great *gnani*, who was a brilliant *yogi* with astounding powers and deep knowledge.

One day, Shuka felt the desire to ascend to Vaikuntha and behold Sri Vishnu. His *yogic* powers took him to the doors of the Lord's abode immediately. But here, he was stopped from entering inside. The reason? One who had not sat at the feet of the Guru could not obtain entrance to the Lord's abode.

Bitterly disappointed, Shuka returned to Rishi Ved Vyasa and begged him for Guru *bodhana* (teaching). Although Sage Vyasa was a great Guru, he in his wisdom, knew that he could not help his son in his predicament. So he said to Shuka, "Seek initiation at the feet of King Janaka who is an enlightened being. He is the one who can illumine your soul."

31

Shuka was flabbergasted. How could a King, living in the lap of luxury and ruling the country with all the transactions it entailed, offer him initiation? With great reluctance he went to King Janaka's palace and to his horror, saw the King seated on a golden throne studded with diamonds. Beautiful maids were fanning him and pressing his hands and feet. Seven hundred queens surrounded him.

Shuka was repulsed by the sight. He himself was a great ascetic. What could the sensualist King teach him? He returned from the palace disgusted.

"Did you see the King?" his father enquired on his return. "I did," replied Shuka. "But I don't think he is going to be of any use to me. He is a worldly man, trapped in his worldly wealth. How can such a one enlighten *me*?"

"You are mistaken," Sage Vyasa said to him. "Do not be taken in by appearances. There is no greater preceptor than Janaka whom I can recommend to you."

Shuka went back to Janaka's court, but returned empty-handed, shocked by the royal splendour he saw everywhere.

"What happened?" asked his father. "Did you receive what you wanted from the King?"

"There is *nothing* I can receive from him," was the disgruntled response from Shuka.

"Dear son, go back to him and try again," insisted Vyasa.

Again Shuka went to Janaka's court – and returned without the enlightenment he sought. This happened twelve times.

Desires alone are the bondage for Self. Extinguishing desires is called liberation. Non-attachment to worldly things can only lead to continuous bliss.

– Ashtavakra Gita

On the thirteenth trip, he encountered an old man, who was throwing fistfuls of mud into the fast flowing river. The mud dissolved and disappeared without trace in the flooded river, and the old man still kept on at his task.

"Foolish old man," called Shuka, "what do you hope to achieve with your futile effort?"

"Foolish? I'm not half as foolish as Shuka, son of the great Sage Ved Vyasa, who could not recognise truth when he saw it. He is the real fool, for he allowed himself to be taken in by surface appearances. He thinks he is superior to King Janaka. He knows not that it is only Janaka who can give him the knowledge he seeks!"

Stunned, Shuka fell at the old man's feet. The old man revealed himself to be none other than Maharishi Narada, who had come down to offer the young man guidance. "Go back to Janaka," he said to Shuka. "Your father is right; Janaka is the one who can offer you the enlightenment you seek."

Chastened and subdued, Shuka returned to Janaka's palace. For the first time, on his thirteenth visit, he was stopped at the gate by guards who enquired the purpose of his visit. When he told them what he wanted, they took his message to the King. Janaka instructed them to keep him waiting outside the palace for three whole days.

For three days Shuka stood outside the palace gates. On the third day, he was led inside to the inner apartments where the Royal Ladies lived. Here, he was surrounded by every sensual pleasure that a human being could imagine. The great ascetic that he was, Shuka was unmoved, unaffected by it all. Thus, three more days passed.

Finally, the King sent for him. When Shuka entered the King's presence, he was stunned by the sight that met his eyes. The King was seated on his magnificent throne; his right leg was being luxuriously massaged with perfumed oil and sandal paste, while his left leg was placed in a blazing fire!

Progressively, Shuka's ego had been diminishing. His perception had been clouded by his pride in the self, and he had failed to see what Janaka really was. Now he saw that Janaka was much more than the wealthy, sensual King that he had beheld from the outside – he was a truly evolved, realised soul, not trapped by renunciation or materialism, not defined by sensuality or extreme self-denial.

Shuka prostrated before the King and begged for enlightenment.

"Now you are indeed ready to become my disciple," Janaka said to him. "You have realised that perception can be clouded by ego, and that pride is useless; and, above all, that only Consciousness is real."

Janaka touched Shuka, and gave him a *mantra* and instantly, Shuka felt himself transformed. He had discovered the Self within. It had always been within him, but he had been unconscious of it due to his rampant ego. When a man loses his ego, he discovers the power of his *atman*!

> **Immutable and unchanging, consciousness is the only reality that exists; one becomes bound by one's own false thought and one is freed when the false thought becomes extinct.**
> — **King Janaka to Shuka Muni**
> *(from the Yoga Vashishta)*

It is the true Guru who can destroy your false ego and lead you on to the God within you.

The Guru spells death to the ego. The Guru does not have to *implant* God within you, because He already exists there. All that the Guru does is clean away the accumulated dirt and dross that has soiled the mirror of your heart – and when the ugly stains of the ego are removed, you behold the Beloved reflected therein.

There are many modern Shuka Munis among us even today. They go forth from one Guru to another, rejecting each for one reason or another. They are haunted by their own ego, their pride of knowledge and arrogance over their *sadhana*. They imagine they are perfectly apt in meditation and renunciation, and need the Guru only for namesake. The Guru must perforce perform 'surgery' on their ego, before they can receive anything from him!

"I know this," "I can do this," "I am so and so, such and such is my designation," "I am such a one," "I am the doer," "I am the giver," – how vain and futile are such assertions!

Here is how a great poet saint puts it:

> When my ego was struck by the sword that is the Guru's love,
> That love began to kill my ego.
> Even when I was alive, I experienced death.
> My death died; and I became immortal.

How may the ego be annihilated?

The ego is subtle; its workings are not obvious. As the seeker is making progress on the path, he may pride himself on his efforts. Sometimes he thinks he is close to success. Sometimes he feels he has attained his goal. Sometimes he realises with despair, that it is very difficult to be spiritual.

Then comes to him the realisation that his efforts and endeavours are not pure but tainted, spotted. The darkest spot of them all, he realises, is the ego – the lower self – the 'I'. And then he begins to realise that he must transcend the ego to enter into the Limitless. He begins to realise that of his own accord, he can do nothing, achieve nothing. He learns to accept all that comes to him – abasement, criticism, disappointments – as the Will of God. As the love of God and Guru fills him, egoism dies. When this happens, he is reborn – born again in the life of the spirit.

This, I humbly submit, is the essence of *dwija* – one who is twice born. He is born once in the flesh; he is reborn when he realises that he is not the body he wears!

This is what happened to King Janaka. He learnt this great truth from one sage; he passed it on to another!

King Janaka also serves to illustrate the point that spiritual awareness is not the exclusive prerogative of a certain 'type' of people – people who are unworldly, committed to self-enforced poverty, prone to asceticism, self-denial or given to renunciation. People in power, people wielding authority, wealthy and influential people can take to spirituality if they so desire. Equally, householders, businessmen, scholars, office workers and students too, can take to spirituality.

Each one of us has the indwelling *atman*; so each of us is eligible to practice spirituality in our daily life. Our awareness is all that it takes to set out on the path!

Exercise in Awareness

Taught by Sri Ramana Maharishi, this is a meditative exercise which helps you realise what you are and more importantly, what is not you.

Sit down in a comfortable posture.

For the first few minutes, focus on your breathing. Be aware of the breath as it comes and goes.

Now, begin by asking yourself, "Who am I?"

Let the question resound in your mind. Do not look for answers immediately.

Be aware of the thoughts arising in your mind.

Proceed with the following questions.

"Am I this body that I wear?"

"Am I these thoughts that I am thinking?"

"Am I these feelings?"

"Am I this ego that dominates my thinking?"

"Am I one or more of the roles I am playing in my life?"

By a gradual process of elimination, discover what is NOT you. Discard those aspects as what you are not.

Perhaps at first, you will be left with the negative answer: "I really don't know who I am."

Realising that you don't know is the first step to self-knowledge.

Know Thyself

A farmer found an eagle's egg atop a hill; he brought it to his farm and put it with the rest of the eggs in the nest of a barnyard hen. The eaglet hatched along with the brood of chicks and grew up with them in the barnyard.

All his life the eagle did whatever the barnyard chicks did, for he thought that he too, was a barnyard chicken. He scratched the earth for worms and insects. He clucked and cackled like his 'siblings'. And occasionally, he would thrash his wings and fly a few feet up into the air, and be very pleased with his efforts.

Years passed and the eagle was now very old. One day, as he was shuffling about in the farmyard, he saw a shadow fall over him; he looked up and saw a magnificent bird hovering above him in the blue sky. It was gliding gracefully, effortlessly, in the powerful wind currents, borne aloft on its strong golden wings.

The old eagle was awestruck. "What's that?" he asked.

"That's the eagle, the king of the birds, the lord of the skies", said his neighbour. "He belongs to the sky. We belong to the earth – we're chickens."

The eagle lived and died a chicken, for he never really knew what he was.

Chapter Two
Discover Your True Identity

We once asked Gurudev Sadhu Vaswani, "What is the beginning of the spiritual life?"

Gurudev's answer was clear and precise. "When I lose myself, I find the Soul."

Finding your soul – that is the essence of spirituality.

There is something in each one of us beyond the reach of words. It breaks out at times in a simple gaze of the eye, in an understanding smile, in an invisible ray of the heart which travels out to a fellow pilgrim on the path, a kindred soul. If only we could learn to work the inner wireless, there would be no need to speak, perhaps no need to read or write books like this one!

Don't mistake my words. I love books. We must all continue to read books. But we must not allow books to become a barrier on the way we choose to walk. This book is not about the vanity of learning or the display of acquired wisdom. It is just a record of the reflections that a pilgrim on the path wishes to share with his fellow seekers. Read this for further reflection: but practise more! Let your reading be reflected in deeds of daily life. When you choose to walk the way of the spirit, you must become a ladder unto yourself to reach beyond yourself!

In the simplest terms, spirituality is the aspiration, the genuine effort to know our true self. As I said earlier, it begins with the realisation that we are not the bodies we wear; that this materialistic world we live in, cannot satisfy our deepest aspirations; that our unquenchable desire for wealth and power cannot really give us the joy and peace that we truly crave…

The problem with many of us is that we have completely identified ourselves with the body – the physical, material aspects of our existence. If I were to ask, "Who are you?" you would immediately point to your physical form. If I were to ask you, "Who is J.P.Vaswani?" you would point to my form, my physical body.

But we are not the bodies we wear! This is the first teaching that the Lord gives us in the Gita. The body is only a garment we have worn during this present earth incarnation.

> As the soul experienceth, in the body, childhood, youth and age, so passeth on to another body.
> The *dheera*, the sage, is not perplexed by this.
>
> [II:13]

When I urge you not to identify yourself with the body, I am asking you to move away from the allures of the materialistic world. The more we identify with the body, the more we want, the more we crave, the more we desire to possess, the more we get entangled in *maya*.

Once upon a time, there lived a wise and holy sage who had attained spiritual illumination. Many were the people who knocked at his door, eager to see him, speak to him and be blessed by him.

Whenever there was a knock at his door, he would ask, "Who are you?" The visitor would invariably say, "I am so-and-so, son of so-and-so, from such-and-such-village."

"Why have you come?" the sage would ask next.

"O holy one, give me your blessings so that…" and the visitors would place their desires before the holy one. "So that I can have a rich harvest…", "So that I may have a son…" and so on.

Receiving such answers, the sage would lapse into silence. He would not open the door. Thus many people came to him and went away disappointed.

One day, a seeker came to knock at the holy man's door.

"Who are you?" called out the sage.

"I wish I knew," came the answer. "Oh holy one, I beg you to enlighten me, for I don't know who I am, and why I came into this world. Please show me the way, so that I may attain the true goal of this, my human life."

The holy man was well pleased with this reply and opened his door to admit the seeker. He realised that the man was a genuine aspirant, thirsting for the Truth. He took him as his disciple, and initiated him on the path of self-realisation.

Ask yourself, "Who am I?" Look for the answer in the heart within. "Where do I come from? Why am I here? What is the purpose of this existence of mine?" You will be led to the truth that you are not the body you wear!

Identification with the body leads to the illusion that power, pleasures and possessions of this world can make us happy. But this is not true; instead, these material possessions only keep us in bondage – the bondage of ignorance, *avidya*. Once you are freed from this illusion, you will realise the truth of the Self, and move towards God-realisation. This is the process by which we may all move from illusion to reality; from darkness to light; from death to immortality.

The soul, the *atman*, the indwelling one, passes from body to body. It is unaffected by outer things. The Self abides: the bodies are transient.

You may well ask: why does the soul pass from body to body? My answer is: to gather experiences, and to evolve towards its abode in the Eternal. Just as the diverse bodies of our childhood, youth and age do not cause a doubt in our minds about the continuity of the self, so too, the diverse bodies of different incarnations, especially the new body after death, should not cause us to doubt the continuity of the *atman*.

The Lord tells Arjuna: "You have always been; you will always be." This is the awareness that we must try to attain – that we are immortal, that we abide in Eternity.

You are not the body! You are the immortal soul within! Therefore, do not become a slave of the body. Do not keep running after the shadow shapes that come and go!

> Know *atman* to be one, ever the same, changeless.
> How canst Thou say: "I am the meditator, and this
> is the object of meditation?"
> How can perfection be divided?
>
> *– Avadhuta Gita*

St. Francis of Assisi once observed that the
root of all evil, the root of all sin, is this sense of
identification with the body. You are not this body
that you wear – this body is only your present,
temporary address. You inhabit the body now. In
your earlier incarnation, you lived elsewhere – you
were in a different body. Now you live in another –
but not for long. Sooner or later, your address will
change. You will move on.

The body is the dress you have worn. It is a boat
which you are rowing, to cross the *sansar sagar* – the
ocean of transmigration. It is meant to take you to
the other shore.

There are some people who go one step further.
They identify themselves with the body-mind
complex.

It is the body-mind complex that is affected by
the impressions of sense-life. These impressions are
impermanent, transient. Therefore, the Roman thinker

Marcus Aurelius said, "Things themselves do not touch the soul. Let that part of thy soul which leads and governs, be untouched by the movements of the flesh, whether of pleasure or of pain."

The mind receives its impressions from the outside world, conveyed to it through the five senses. And the mind swings between joy and sorrow, happiness and dejection, excitement and inertia, elation and defeat.

Have I won the lottery? I am excited. Have I won an award? I am delighted. Have I received a substantial increment in my salary? I am pleased. Has someone praised me? Are good things happening to me? I'm content. I think life is just fine.

But life is not always so pleasant. Sometimes I lose money in business. I am depressed. Someone criticises me. I am downcast. My work is not recognised or appreciated. I lose all interest in work. I withdraw. I cut myself off from others. I grow in despondency and despair…

We are not the body, or the mind. What are we then? *Tat twam asi* – That art Thou! What That is, we have yet to discover. We have to enter upon a voyage of discovery – not like the voyages taken up by Drake and Magellan who circumnavigated the world – but the voyage of self-discovery.

My friends, I urge you to become aware of the value of this human birth. It is priceless! It has been bestowed upon each one of us for a specific purpose – that we may realise what we are, whence we came, and whither we are to return.

We are not the bodies that we wear. We are immortal spirits. We are not this; we are That!

Every day, as you wake up in the morning, I urge you to repeat this *mahavakya* given to us by the *rishis* of our ancient land – *Tat twam asi*! That art Thou! Thou art not this, the body, that thou take thyself to be. Thou art the immortal soul! This is the very first commandment of the Bhagavad Gita – Thou shalt never, ever identify thyself with the body!

The body is *asat*: it is material; it is destructible. But the *atman* is imperishable; of this imperishable soul, the Lord says:

> He never is born, nor does he, at any time, die.
> Nor, having once come to be, does he cease to be.
> He is unborn, perpetual, eternal, ancient. He is not
> slain when the body is slain.
>
> [II:20.]

Does not this assert the truth – *Tat twam asi!*

Swami Vivekananda tells us:

The essence of Vedanta is: *Aham Brahmasmi*. I am Brahman. *Tat twam asi*. That art Thou! You are essentially

Divine. Vedanta recognises no sin; it recognises only error. And the greatest error, it says, is to think that you are weak, that you are a sinner, a miserable creature...

There is no room in the Hindu way of life for such defeatism or negative thinking!

Tat twam asi! That art Thou! In the *Mundaka Upanishad*, we are told of two birds perched on the branches of the selfsame tree. One of them is always looking up at the sky; it is ecstatic, energetic and sings a song of divine beauty. The other bird, perched on a lower branch, glances downwards, and is overwhelmed by anguish and misery.

The two birds symbolise the Self – the first, which looks upward, has discovered the essential glory of the Divine Self within. The second is attached to the body, to the earth, and is weighed down by attachment and grief.

Have you read that beautiful part of the *Ramayana*, where Jambavan awakens Hanuman's spiritual power and reminds him that he is not what he seems – a mere *vanara*? Hanuman is diffident and doubtful at first – he feels that he will never be able to cross the sea and travel to Lanka. But the wise Jambavan helps him unleash his Divine potential.

Each one of us has a Hanuman asleep inside us – a tremendous soul-force that will help us cross the ocean of *maya*. This hidden *shakti* can be awakened by a Guru's guidance.

The Guru will unfold to our consciousness the truth that inside each one of us is *Sat-chit-ananda* – true, eternal, blissful knowledge. Alas, so busy are we in living the life of the body, that we have forgotten this, our essential nature. The *Guru* can awaken us anew to this realisation.

> **If you are not the body and do not have the idea 'I am the doer', the consequences of your good or bad actions will not affect you. Why do you say about the actions the body performs 'I do this' or 'I did that'? As long as you identify yourself with the body like that you are affected by the consequences of the actions, that is to say, while you identify with the body you accumulate good and bad karma.**
>
> **– Sri Ramana Maharishi**

There is a story I read somewhere, according to which Sri Rama once asked Hanuman to explain to Him how the two of them were related to each other. Hanuman is said to have replied, "O Lord, from a physical point of view, when I regard myself as the body, I am Your slave. From the mental perspective, I am a ray, an emanation, while You are the Sun, the

Light everlasting. But from the perspective of the spirit, I am none other than Your Self!"

What a wonderful story this is! Insofar as we do have a body, let this body be an instrument, a slave of the Lord. Let us seek union with the Lord through all that we are – in body, in mind and spirit. Let us use the body to perform God's Will. Let us use the mind to radiate God's love and wisdom. In the spirit within, let us seek identity with God.

The question that every spiritual aspirant has to ask himself again and again is this: "Who am I? Who am I?"

For many of us, our life on earth is nothing more than parade of ego-desires. As the ego changes, our desires too change. The little child craves for toys; the young boy wants computer games and gadgets; the young man chases after fast cars and girls; the grown-up man chases wealth and power. And so we hanker after shadow shapes, fondly imagining that fulfilling the ego desires will make us happy.

From birth to birth, from one life to another, the ego changes its shape and form like a cloud – the cloud that hides the sun, the source of light, the sense of our real identity.

Identification with the body, egoism and ignorance of the true nature of the self – these three are identified by sages as the cause of all human suffering.

Egoism can only be removed by the purification of the mind and the senses – and this is best achieved through selfless, desireless action – *nishkama karma*, as recommended by the Lord in the Gita.

Therefore, have the *rishis* of ancient India taught us: Assert your essential nature – and be free! Realise the Divine within you – and be free! Expand your consciousness, purify the mind, discover the true self – and you will recollect your essential nature – *soham* – I am That!

Do not be a miser – do not cling to the body, unable to spend your infinite spiritual wealth. Let go of ignorance – let go of the ego – and the humiliating notion that you are limited, restricted by the body and the mind. Realise that you belong to infinity, that your soul is immortal, that God's power and grace sustain you – and that you are essentially Divine!

When you grow in this awareness, you identify yourself with the Everlasting. You begin to say to yourself, "I am not this body. I am the *atman*, the deathless spirit. My spirit is the Universe. My essence is of God."

This realisation releases a tremendous energy of the spirit within you, that it can transform your life and your personality completely! Aware of the Divine within you, you begin to recognise and respect the

Divinity in others, and your consciousness expands; you become more understanding, more tolerant, more loving and forgiving, more magnanimous – in short, more Divine than human!

Identification with the *atman* is not merely of abstract value. In practical terms, it can make life joyous, peaceful and secure. I often narrate to my friends, the story of the Persian king who had his ring inscribed with the words: *This too shall pass away*. As he read these words, he gained equanimity and wisdom. He was no longer unduly elated by good news – nor did defeat and bad news depress his spirits. He had learnt the secret that the world is transient, changing – and therefore, it is futile to cling to changing objects and changing events.

May I share with you a five-fold teaching that I received in my youth from an unknown saint? These valuable lessons taught me to move away, gradually, from identifying myself with the body:

- Remember, that you are a pilgrim here, a wayfarer in quest of your lost homeland. Your Home is in Eternity.

- Be patient in the midst of the difficulties and dangers of life. Remind yourself again and again, "This too shall pass away!"

- Each day meditate on death, for death approaches us with each passing moment.

- Give the service of love to all.

- Seek fellowship with saints and holy men so that the tiny drop that you are may become a mighty ocean, wide enough to hold within it a thousand oceans.

For Your Reflection

If you would progress on the path of self-realisation, you must stop identifying yourself with the body. You must move away from the "shoes" you wear. This is indeed the significance of the custom practised by Hindus – removing one's shoes before one enters a temple or a holy place. This is symbolic of the idea that we move away from body-consciousness to walk upon the sanctified ground, which will help us move towards God-realisation.

We cannot cast off the body, literally. But we can change our perspective by dwelling on the idea that we are not the bodies we wear – we are the immortal spirits within. This makes a tremendous change in our outlook!

The human birth has invested us with a body-mind complex; but the body-mind are just instruments to aid our existence here; the truth is the indwelling spirit.

How far are you swayed by external appearances?

Whom would you respect and revere and welcome to your house – a man who arrives in a Benz? A man who arrives on a two-wheeler, or a man who walks in simply?

How much importance do you attach to people's appearance, the clothes they wear and the accessories/jewels they wear on their person?

If you give truthful answers to these questions, you will know how far you have progressed on the path of self-knowledge.

Knowing And Saying

The disciples were absorbed in a discussion of Lao-Tzu's dictum:

Those who know do not say;

Those who say do not know.

When the Master entered, they asked him what the words meant.

Said the Master, "Which of you knows the fragrance of a rose?"

All of them knew.

Then he said, "Put it into words."

All of them were silent.

Chapter Three

Defining Spirituality

The word spirit was first used to mean the animating principle of life; derived from the Latin word *spiritus* meaning "soul, courage, vigour, breath", and related to *spirare*, meaning "to breathe", it came into English usage from the Latin translation of the Bible. The word 'soul' became associated with this term much later. Today, we use the word 'spirit' with very many differing connotations, most of them relating to a non-corporeal substance as contrasted with the material body.

The word *atman*, originating from Sanskrit and having Indo Germanic links, is translated also as "essence, breath or soul". In Hindu philosophy, it is regarded as the first principle of being, the true self. Older Upanishads such as the *Brihadaranyaka,* mention several times that the Self is described as *Neti, Neti* or "not this – not this".

Profound and philosophically sophisticated, the Vedanta philosophy of *Advaita* (non-dualism) sees the "spirit" within each living entity as being fully identical with *Brahman* – the Principle; *Dvaita* (dualism) in contrast, differentiates between the individual *atma* in living beings and the Supreme *atma* (*Paramatma*) as being distinct and separate from each other. Thus *atman* refers to the individual spirit or the observer being referred to as the *jivatma*.

The Srimad Bhagavata Purana tells us:

"*Atma*" refers to the Supreme Lord or the living entities. Both of them are spiritual, free from birth and death, free from deterioration and free from material contamination. They are individual, they are the knowers of the external body, and they are the foundation or shelter of everything. They are free from material change, they are self-illuminated, they are the cause of all causes, and they are all-pervading. They have nothing to do with the material body, and therefore they are always uncovered. With these transcendental qualities, one who is actually learned must give up the illusory conception of life, in which one thinks, "I am this material body, and everything in relationship with this body is mine."

The Vedas tell us:

nityo nityanam chetanas chetananam: The Lord is the chief individual living entity, the leader of the subordinate living entities. Thus the presence of the

Divine spark in all creation is suggested; qualitatively the supreme being and the individual soul are the same; quantitatively, God is infinite power and knowledge; we are limited beings; the analogy used is that of the ocean and a drop of water from it. Because the living entities are parts or samples of God, their qualities are not different from those of the Supreme Lord.

> By such *vakyas* as "That art Thou", our own Self is affirmed. Of that which is untrue and composed of the five elements – the Sruti (scripture) says, *Neti, Neti* – "Not this, not this."
>
> *– Avadhuta Gita*

Since the nineteenth century, scholars have been concerned with a "theory of knowledge" – in academic terms, a discipline known as Epistemology, which tries to define the scope and nature of knowledge itself. Definitions are very much a part of this approach.

As someone who was basically trained in the sciences, I do value definitions. They are important for cognition, for understanding certain fundamental concepts. But the more I have seen of life and people, the more I have been fascinated by all that eludes definition. In fact, classic philosophy chooses to leave certain crucial terms undefined: for example, terms like *being, individual, ultimate, absolute,* etc. Infinity is one such concept.

Our own *Isho Upanishad* states, "If you remove a part from infinity or add a part to infinity, what remains is still infinity."

> That is whole, this is whole,
> From the whole the whole arises
> When the whole is taken from the whole,
> The whole will still remain.

Spirituality is like infinity: it encompasses so many aspects, so many approaches that each of us must choose that which suits us best.

(At this juncture, let me emphasise the difference between spirituality and *spiritualism:* modern spiritualism, as I understand it, is a new religious movement with rituals, doctrinal components, a belief in a transcendent realm, and its own experiential dimensions. Adherents of this system are united in believing that communication with spirits is possible; but beyond this central idea modern spiritualism can include a very wide range of beliefs and world-views.)

Spirituality begins with the quest to know the self; and this quest is endless in itself.

The meaning of life has been one of the fundamental issues in philosophy, theology and religion. Since the dawn of civilisation, men of thought have grappled with such questions as: Who am I? Where do I come from? Where am I going? What is the purpose for which I was made? How may I fulfill that purpose?

Spirituality is in many ways a quest to find answers to these questions.

The Sufi Masters tell us that there are three journeys on the road to self-realisation:

1. During the first journey man wanders endlessly and moves away from Truth. The restless mind pushes man to seek all the pleasures of the world and he gets caught in worldly affairs, forgetting the purpose of his journey. We may easily recognise that this is the journey that most of us are currently pursuing! We are so wrapped up in worldly pursuits that we are quite, quite unconscious of any goal that is beyond material concerns.

2. The second journey begins with the awakening of the soul. It begins with the

awareness that we have to return home.
For long have we floundered. For long have
we wandered. It is time to go back. A voice
within us urges us, "Awake. Awake. Return
to your original home." The wheel of time
has hit us hard. Now, we realise, it is time to
return. When this awareness hits us – I use
the word hit deliberately, because it is a sharp
and painful awakening – we are disturbed
and unsettled, even slightly disoriented. We
begin to question the worth and value of all
that we have achieved in worldly terms. We
are seized by a sudden feeling of restlessness,
a feeling of discontent which in turn leads to
self-interrogation, introspection and a review
and re-evaluation of our chosen goals and
objects. "There must be more to life than this!"
is the one thought that impels us at this stage.

3. The third journey follows as a logical
    consequence to the second. We realise that
    we have wandered from our path; we feel
    that we have lost our way somewhere in
    the course of our wandering. We make the
    crucial U-Turn that will take us back to God.
    God is our source and origin: He is also the
    destination of our earthly journey. He is the
    Ultimate goal of our life. When we make

the U-turn, we have begun our most crucial journey.

It is then that we begin the serious, persistent search for God. This is the quest that has taken *yogis, rishis, munis* and *jignasus* to river banks, to *tapobanas*, to mountain tops, to temples and shrines. Realised souls find Him whom they seek, without too much trouble. But the rest of us are not so fortunate. We wander hither and thither; many places beckon us and we are lost in these wanderings.

The first journey may be the result of an unheeding, unaware attitude; the second journey is the dawn of true awareness; and the third and final journey must always be a conscious, deliberate exercise, undertaken of our own free will and the effort to translate that will into reality. In other words, it is a journey towards self-awareness!

But it is not the end! For I believe that there is a fourth and final journey which represents the ultimate: it is the journey within the self, within God.

By its nature, this quest, this journey, is indefinable, infinite.

Most important of all, it is highly personal and therefore, exclusive to each one of us.

At this stage, I wish to state something clearly: spirituality is not a problem to be solved or a puzzle to be unraveled; it is cultivating an awareness, an attitude to life, as the following anecdote from the Buddhist scriptures tells us.

An elderly grandmother once approached the Buddha and told him that she longed to live a spiritual life; but she was too old and frail to withstand the rigours of monastic living; and her household chores were so tedious and time consuming that she could not set aside enough time to meditate. "What can I do?" she wailed.

"Respected grandmother," replied the Buddha, "every time you draw water from the well for your family, remain aware of every movement and motion of your hands and wrists. As you carry the water jug on your head, be aware of every step that your feet take; as you attend to the chores in your kitchen, maintain continuous mindfulness moment after moment. You too, will discover the art of Meditation."

To be what we are, and to become what we are capable of becoming, is the only end of life.
    – Robert Louis Stevenson,
    Familiar Studies of Men and Books

To know the true self, to capture the essence of human existence, to define the goal of life – this has been the quest of our greatest *gnanis,* mystics and men of wisdom. While everyone agrees that 'ego identity' is narrow and limited, the deeper sense of self eludes many of us. This is to be expected: we are told, for example, that our thumb and finger impressions, the image of our pupils are different and unique for each and every one of us.

A friend demonstrated to me the security settings on his laptop, which operates on a face recognition software. Until and unless his own face appeared before the camera built into the computer, the machine could not be 'opened' nor its data accessed by another.

If this is the unique feature of the human visage, then imagine for yourself the unique nature of the human spirit!

"The *atman* is subtler than the subtlest and not to be known through argument," so the *Katha Upanishad* tells us.

How is the *atman* unique to each one of us, if it is, as we said, a spark of the Divine? When a soul assumes a human body in a specific birth or *janma*, it takes up its new birth at that stage of spiritual evolution which it reached in its previous human birth and continues to evolve towards *atma-saakshatkara* or self-realisation in its current birth. In other words, spirituality is unique and different for each one of us, because our souls are at different stages of evolution towards ultimate Self-knowledge and Liberation.

Liberation or *moksha* is the ultimate goal of life, according to Hinduism. The easiest way to attain this goal, step by step, is to do good *karma* and avoid bad *karma*; that is, to live a good life, to do good deeds, to speak good words and to think good thoughts. In a fundamental sense, this is spirituality at its simplest and most basic form.

Most spiritual traditions teach us that knowing the true Self is the equivalent of actually knowing God. For God is immanent in all creation; He is the Indweller in every soul; so knowledge of the Self is knowledge of the Indweller, the *antaryami* who resides within all of us. In other words, spirituality, or the quest to discover the nature of one's own highest consciousness, is in essence, the quest to discover God.

But there is a practical aspect to spirituality that I wish to emphasise. It is said that God 'pierced' our five senses so that they are constantly tuned to the outer reality, and therefore, cannot grapple with what is within us. But the senses can be controlled, so that the mind and consciousness can be focussed within. In this sense, spirituality too is a discipline – essentially, self-discipline.

There is such a thing as definition by negation: you can grasp certain concepts by understanding clearly what they are *not*. This works especially with abstract and complex concepts. Thus poverty is absence of wealth. Sadness or depression is the absence of joy. In this sense, negation becomes what we call a logical complement, defining a thing by what it is not.

We can safely assume that spirituality is not the same as the following:

1. Spirituality is not the same as religion

2. Spirituality is not a rite or ritual

3. It is not a set of practices

4. It is not dogma or doctrine

5. It is not the prerogative of the evolved seeker

6. It is not abstract or esoteric to practice

7. It is not all mysticism and esoteric rites

8. It has nothing to do with what we call "the supernatural"

9. It is not about theology or philosophy

10. It is not meant exclusively for (a) the old, (b) the wise, (c) the religiously devout, (d) the super- intelligent, or (e) the *gnani* or the realised ones

11. It is not a set of specific actions or way of doing things

12. It is not asceticism or renunciation, though some people have chosen them as preferred modes to attain self-knowledge.

Through this process of negation we arrive at what spirituality is all about. Here again, I must emphasise, it is different for each one of us:

1. It is essentially a quest for self-discovery

2. It is choosing what you would want your true self to be and become

3. It is an attempt to go beyond the external world of materialism

4. It is a desire to transcend the ego, its limitations, its fears and insecurities

5. It is an effort to discover or understand the unity of all creation

6. It is the knowledge that I and my fellow human beings and my fellow creatures are part of the One Whole

7. It is uniquely personal and yet emphasises the interconnectedness of all creation

8. It is an aspiration to discover and fulfill the purpose of human existence

9. It is discovering the power of love, compassion and respect – nay, reverence for all forms of life.

10. It is the awareness that there is more to your life than worldly success and achievements

11. It is discovering the Divine within you – and within all creation

12. It is discovering true joy, peace and contentment

13. Spirituality means something different to each seeker

14. At its best, it is *yoga* – union with God.

As you can see, for me as an individual, it is easy to detach spirituality from religion, but not from God! I do believe that atheists and agnostics can also be deeply spiritual in their own way. But for me, spirituality is man's quest for God.

For Your Reflection

In Chapter XII of the Bhagavad Gita, the Lord outlines for us the attributes and qualities which make a devotee dear to Him. These are listed in the last eight verses of this Chapter, which are described as the *Gita Amritashtam* – i.e. the nectar of the Gita in eight *slokas.* Before the evening *satsang* in the Sadhu Vaswani Mission, we hear these eight *slokas* in the divine, melodious, mellifluous voice of Gurudev Sadhu Vaswani.

What are the qualities of the true *bhakta* who is dear to the Lord?

- He is free from ill-will and egoism. He bears no ill-will to any creature; he is forgiving, and is poised in pain and pleasure.
- He is content and ever in harmony, his mind and understanding dedicated to the Lord.
- He does not disturb the world, nor is he disturbed by the world.
- He is without ambition, and free from passion and fear.
- He does not rejoice, grieve or crave for anything.
- He is the same to foe and friend. He is the same in honour and dishonour; he is free from attachment.
- He takes praise and blame alike. He is satisfied with whatever the Lord is pleased to grant him.

I invite you to read and reflect on these verses in Sadhu Vaswani's lucid translation.

As you read each verse, ask yourself, "Am I such a one? Is the Lord likely to include me among His Beloved devotees?"

If you are one of those inclined to be quantitative in your analysis, let me suggest that you allot 5 marks to yourself for each *sloka* that applies to you as a devotee.

> He who beareth no ill-will to any being, is friendly and compassionate, free from egoism and self-sense, in pain and pleasure has poised mind, is forgiving.
>
> The *yogi* who is ever content, ever in harmony and master of himself, resolute, with mind and understanding dedicated to Me, he, My devotee, is My beloved.
>
> He by whom the world is not disturbed and who is not disturbed by the world, who is freed from the agitations of joy and anger and fear, he is My beloved.
>
> He who is ambition-less, is pure, skillful in action, is passionless and free from fear, he who renounces the fruit of every undertaking to Me, he, My *bhakta* (devotee), is My beloved.
>
> He who neither rejoiceth nor hateth nor giveth nor craveth, he who renounceth good and ill, he, My devout worshipper, is My beloved.

Alike to foe and friend, alike in fame and ignominy, alike in cold and heat, in pleasure and pain, freed from attachment.

Taking equally praise and blame, silent, content with what cometh, homeless, of steady mind, he, My devout worshipper, is My beloved.

They, verily, who worship this *dharma* (law) of immortality, as taught herein, and, endowed with faith, believe in Me as the Supreme, they, My *bhaktas*, are My beloved.

[Ch.XII, 13-20]

As you can see, there are eight *slokas* in all. Calculate the total you get out of 40. I think it will be a fairly accurate measure of your spiritual quotient!

The Golden Buddha

The Temple of the Golden Buddha is one of the most sacred places – and also one of the topmost tourist spots in Thailand. Inside this temple we can see the huge ten-and-a-half foot Solid Gold Buddha. It weighs over two-and-a half tons and is valued at approximately $196 million. People who visit the temple are awestruck by the gentle, compassionate glance of the Solid Gold Buddha smiling down on the visitors.

However, right next to the Golden Buddha is the incongruous sight of a large lump of clay. A plaque describes the history of the Solid Gold statue and its adjacent lump of clay. The story dates back to the year 1957, when a community of monks was assigned the task of relocating a large clay statue of the Buddha from its dilapidated temple to a new location. The statue was carefully lifted and loaded on to a crane; and the crane began to lift the statue to load it on to a truck, when it broke down half way. As it was about to rain, they covered the statue with a piece of tarpaulin, and left it for the night. One of the monks stayed close to the statue to keep watch on it during the night.

All of a sudden, a mysterious gleam began to shine forth from the statue. Amazed by the sight, the monk uncovered the tarpaulin and saw the gleam shining ever brighter. Determined to get to the bottom of the mystery, the monk began to chip away at the clay with a chisel; now the gleam became bigger and brighter. Hours later, the clay had been chipped off completely and the monk stood face to face with a huge Solid Gold statue of the Buddha, the likes of which had never ever been heard of, let alone seen by anyone!

Historians who came to see the statue had their own theory to offer; centuries earlier, when Thailand was still the kingdom of Siam, it had been invaded by a neighboring country. To prevent looting and destruction of the beautiful statue, monks attached to the temple had covered it in clay and allowed the clay mask to solidify. Thus the statue remained, until that historic day in 1957.

Many of us are like this priceless golden statue – a shell of hardness and negativity conceals the real self within us, which is a spark of Divinity akin to the golden Buddha! As we grow older, the hard clay crust begins to build up over the golden self inside us. We need the Guru, who can work like the monk with the chisel, and uncover the golden self inside the clay covering.

Chapter Four

Why Do We Need To Be Spiritual?

"All that is, is physical and material," an atheist writes. "There is no Soul. Your mind is the subjective experience of what the molecules in your brain cells are doing. Galileo kicked us out of the Center of the Universe. Darwin kicked us off the Pinnacle of Creation. Freud kicked the Soul out of our Brains. There is nothing more to life than materialism."

The distinguished psychologist, Watson, tells us, "No one has ever touched a soul or has seen one in a test tube or has in any way come into relationship with it as he has with the other objects of his daily experience. Nevertheless to doubt its existence is to become a heretic and once might possibly even have led to the loss of one's head. Even today a man holding a public position dare not question it."

"The 'miracle of life' is no miracle – it is a big chemical reaction," says an atheist thinker. "When those reactions stop, the cell is dead." He adds for good measure: "When the bacterium dies, does it get an afterlife?"

After debating or denying the afterlife of the mosquito, a dog, a mouse and a chimp, he concludes: "The whole notion of your 'soul' is completely imaginary. The concept of a 'soul' has been invented by religion because many people have trouble facing their own mortality. It makes people feel better, but the concept is a complete fabrication."

"Can someone tell me where exactly in the human body the soul is located?" asks another young man in doubt. "Is there an area of the brain, a structure that corresponds to the soul?"

All I can say in response to the above is this: until recently, scientists believed that the atom was indivisible and indestructible...now we know differently.

You might remember the definition by negation I referred to earlier – the *Neti, Neti* of the Upanishads:

The *Mandukya Upanishad* describes the *atman* in the following way:

> Not inwardly cognitive, not outwardly cognitive, not both-wise cognitive, not a cognition-mass, not cognitive, not non-cognitive, unseen, with which

there can be no dealing, ungraspable, having no distinctive mark, non-thinkable, that cannot be designated, the essence of the assurance of which is the state of being one with the Self, the cessation of development, tranquil, benign, without a second (*advaita*) — [such] they think is the fourth. That is the Self. That should be discerned.

Words and concepts and definitions will not get us very far on the path of the spirit. Debates and discussions can go on *ad infinitum*, without either party managing to convince the other.

Nowadays, Human Resource experts do not stop with IQ or EQ; they talk of an essential SQ or Spiritual Quotient which makes a leader great.

> **When I let go of what I am, I become what I might be.**
> – Lao Tzu

Even the US army conducts periodic exercises to assess the 'spiritual fitness' of its soldiers along with the more conventional physical fitness tests.

Good schools promise to cater to the spiritual growth of the young students entrusted to their care. Our own Mira Schools were started by Gurudev Sadhu Vaswani with the clearly spelt out objective of cultivating the soul of the students.

Spirituality is a value; it is an attitude to life; an approach to the purpose of existence. If some of you are content to live life at the material level, and have no needs beyond the sensual, the material and the emotional – well, that's the end of the matter!

All of us subsist on a physical plane; we cannot do without those basic needs – *roti, kapda aur makaan* as they are called – food, clothing and shelter. However, all of us have desires that go beyond these needs; we crave for more wealth, more possessions, more acquisitions; but the intelligent ones among us know that wealth and possessions cannot really make us happy. We live by our passions; beyond what we crave passionately, we live by our own sets of morals and values; we look to higher ideals; we are fascinated by the rare moments in our life when we are filled with awe, wonder and a sense of mystery…feelings, moods, aspirations that send our spirits soaring…

We know that none of these finer feelings can be captured by a materialistic way of life!

In the past, the distinction between spirituality and the workaday world was so sharp that people turned their back on one to face the other squarely. They renounced the world and worldly activities to contemplate on the higher things of life. But today, the boundaries have blurred.

> Every human soul has seen, perhaps before their birth, pure forms such as justice, temperance, beauty and all the great moral qualities which we hold in honour. We are moved towards what is good by the faint memory of these forms, simple and calm and blessed, which we saw once in a pure, clear light, being pure ourselves.
> – Iris Murdoch

Let me make this clear: attending a weekly *yoga* class or doing a couple of meditation sessions does not automatically make one spiritual. Oh no, there is more to spirituality than part-time efforts.

What I mean about the blurring of boundaries is that all of us, laymen and women, students and working professionals, businessmen and managers, young and old are deeply concerned about our holistic growth as human beings. Everybody is concerned about their inner life; everyone craves for a sense of peace and harmony that is central to their being. We may not want to renounce the world to find that elusive peace; but we are ready and willing to spend some time focussing our attention on the rich interior world that is within us.

Friends tell me that there is talk of something which the scientists call the "God gene"; the God gene hypothesis proposes that human beings inherit a set of genes that predisposes them to believe in a higher power. The idea, I am told, has been postulated by geneticist Dean Hamer, the director of one of the leading genetics research institutes in the U.S. who has also written a book on the subject titled, *The God Gene: How Faith is Hardwired into our Genes.*

My readers must decide, depending on their preference, whether spirituality is 'hardwired' or programmed as 'software' into their being!

Spirituality, like faith, is a very personal concept. Atheists deny it; agnostics speculate about it in a detached manner; I do believe that there are thousands of people who practice some form of spirituality in their daily lives – through inner reflection, contemplation or even through silence and service – without actually codifying their behaviour.

I say spirituality is personal to each one of us: we choose our own modes and practices in tune with our beliefs and higher needs. In this sense, spirituality is a means to an end; and this 'end' or 'goal' may also vary from person to person. In our Hindu way of thinking, the highest goal is the goal of Liberation – freedom from worldly bonds, freedom from ignorance and illusion, freedom from the eternal cycle of birth-death-rebirth. The purpose of this human birth is to free ourselves from this vicious cycle. We may imagine that freedom is doing as we please; we may labour under the illusion that freedom is the ability to fulfill all our desires and satisfy all our sensual cravings: let us understand that all this is only going to shackle us deeper and deeper in bondage. True freedom is the capacity to do what we ought to do, to follow the path of goodness, truth and *dharma*, to be able to live with a pure heart, a clear conscience and an untainted mind. Freedom is breaking away from bad habits, addictions and wrong attitudes; freedom is conquering the lower self; freedom is the ability to rise to the highest level of consciousness and the purest level of thought that we, as human beings, are capable of! It is this level, this height of awareness that we reach when we follow Sri Krishna's profoundly simple, yet powerful advice in the Gita: "Whatever you do, whatever you eat or pray, do it as an offering unto Me!"

Spirituality is as simple as this: let all our thoughts and words and deeds be an offering unto the Lord!

> **Knock, And He'll open the door**
> **Vanish, And He'll make you shine like the sun**
> **Fall, And He'll raise you to the heavens**
> **Become nothing, And He'll turn you into everything.**
>
> – Rumi

Sister Shanti, Gurudev Sadhu Vaswani's spiritual daughter, once said to him, "Beloved Dada! I feel I cannot measure up to difficult spiritual practices. Is there any simple *sadhana* which I can perform easily and on which I can build my spiritual life?"

The Master said to her, "Even as the daisy turns to the sun, so must you turn to the Beloved! You must turn to God all the time!"

By sheer coincidence, a beautiful sunflower lay on the table. Pointing to it, the Master said to Shanti, "The sunflower is so named because it always faces the sun. It blooms with the rising sun, it turns its face towards the sun, following its path across the sky from east to west, and with the setting sun, it closes its many eyes! Be like the sunflower; it is the simplest *sadhana* that we can all undertake."

Is it not sad that we human beings are so fascinated by the glitter and glamour of the material world, that we live in forgetfulness of God and never really face Him? We forget to pray; we forget to thank Him for the countless blessings He has bestowed upon us; we forget to seek His blessings; we are swept away by the flood of worldly concerns and material desires.

Is this not ironic too, that the sun is millions of miles away from the earth, and yet the sunflower faces the sun persistently. As for God, He is here; He is everywhere; He is nearer than you believe; if truth were to be told, you don't have to go out to look for Him – for He is to the Indweller within each one of us! All we have to do to 'find' Him, is to look inward!

This, then, is spirituality at its simplest: it is to remember God – not once a day, not occasionally, not when you have a little free time – but to live and move in His presence, and feel His Divine Energy flowing through you!

Exercises in Spiritual Wisdom

1. Practice Integrity of Speech:

   Always speak that which is true, useful and pleasant. Let your words reflect your thoughts and let your actions bear testimony to your speech. Do not gossip about others or criticise them harshly. Speak kindly, gently, sweetly to all – especially to those who are older and those below you.

2. Learn to be Objective about People and Life:

   Do not imagine that the whole world is hostile to you and that others are only looking to spoil things for you. Let others live their own lives, while you live yours. Respect others' opinions, by all means; but do not become a slave of others' views; don't look for constant approval and praise from others.

3. Develop the Spirit of Understanding:

   Try to understand others; enter into their feelings and empathise with them. At the same time, express your feelings clearly so that others may understand you better! When you communicate with others clearly and precisely, misunderstandings and needless strife can be avoided. This will also make for harmony in relationships.

4. Live in the Present:

   The past is over and done with; the future is yet to come; therefore, make the most of the here-and-now! Live life in the awareness that the present moment is precious, and that it is already slipping out of your hands! You too, will change from moment to moment; you will be different when you are healthy, as opposed to when you are unwell. Under all circumstances, just do your best. Remember, life is too short to be small, too precious to be trivial.

Is That So?

A holy man lived in a hut on the outskirts of a village. He lived a life of prayer and meditation, and only went out to beg for alms once a day. The villagers loved him and respected him, as one who lived a pure and simple life. No one had ever seen him angry or annoyed.

There was a beautiful girl whose parents owned a food store in the village. The family lived near the holy man's kutiya. *Suddenly, without any warning, her parents discovered that she was with child.*

This made her parents very angry. She would not confess who the man was, but after much harassment at last, she pointed an accusing finger at the holy man.

In great anger the parents went to the saint and accused him of misconduct and immorality. They called him vile names and abused him. "You are a wolf in sheep's clothing!" they screamed at him. "Is that so?" was all he would say.

He was now an outcast, shunned by the whole village. Nobody knew how he survived and what he ate, for no one would give him alms.

When the child was born, the parents brought it to the holy man's kutiya. *"You are responsible for this child, and you should take care of it," they said to him. "Is that so?" was all he said, calmly, as he accepted the child.*

A year later the girl-mother could stand it no longer. Her conscience smote her. She told her parents the truth – that the real father of the child was a young man who worked in the fishmarket.

The mother and father of the girl were horrified. They told the rest of the villagers. Everyone rushed to the holy man's kutiya *to beg for forgiveness. The parents fell at his feet and apologised profusely to him. "We wronged you," they cried in distress. "We have come to plead for your forgiveness and to take the child away."*

The holy man gave them the child. All he said was: "Is that so?"

Chapter Five

Connecting With Spirituality In Daily Life

The Founder of the Society of Jesuits, St. Ignatius Loyola, firmly believed that every human experience is, among other things, an experience of God. In other words, every human experience has a spiritual dimension. His position can be explained thus: God is Omnipresent in every situation of our life; He is watching us, watching over everything we do; God desires a personal relationship with each of us. Thus, at every moment of our life, we are in contact with God. Everyone encounters God; there is no escaping this encounter! And this is what essential spirituality in daily life is all about: the awareness that God is watching me, God is watching over me!

There is a beautiful story by Tolstoy entitled, "He Who Sees His Neighbour Has Seen God". It tells us of an old and devout shoemaker, who dreams that Jesus Christ is going to visit him the following day.

He gets up early next morning, gets the house spick and span, bakes a fresh loaf of bread and prepares some hot soup to serve God when He comes visiting. His 'preparations' for the Divine Guest completed, he sits at the window of his basement dwelling and watches passers-by eagerly, looking for Christ. Being a shoemaker, and seated at his basement window, he keeps looking at people's shoes and wonders which of them could be God.

However, no passer-by comes knocking at his door. He is hungry, but does not feel like eating, lest he should miss God. He sees a desperate woman with a crying child coming down the street; she is distraught, and the child is obviously hungry. He invites her to come in, comforts her, and gives a bowl of milk for the hungry child; he also offers the mother some soup and bread and helps her as much as he possibly can.

Back at the window, he sees a man at work, shoveling the accumulated snow, even as he shivers in the bitter winter cold. The shoemaker invites him to come and get himself warm and shares his simple meal with him.

Time passes. Day melts into twilight. The shoemaker waits patiently till midnight. He has not seen Jesus, and disappointed as well as exhausted, he prepares to go to bed. As is his custom, he opens the Bible to read a passage from it before retiring for the night, and finds these words: "Whatever you did unto one of these, the least of My brethren, you did it unto Me."

The old shoemaker's heart lifts up with joy and love, for he realises that Christ did visit him — not once, but several times in the day — in the person of His needy brothers and sisters!

The old shoemaker was only sitting at his basement window all day; he only helped two or three people whom he happened to see from his window; but who would disagree with me if I say that he had spent a spiritually uplifting day?

One of the reasons why we do not connect with God is because God has not become real to us. To many of us, God is a distant being. He is a far off, shadowy presence, dwelling on a distant star. I ask so many people, "Where dwelleth God?" With an uplifted finger, they point to the heavens above, as though God dwelt way beyond our reach. True, God dwells in the heavens above, but there is not a nook, not a corner on the earth, where He does not dwell.

Alas, many of us do not feel His presence. He is not yet real to us.

What we need, above all else today is the rediscovery of the great truth that God *is* — that He is real; that we need to renew our faith in Him.

It was Tennyson who said: "Closer is He to us than breathing, nearer than hands and feet." What a tremendous blessing this is, that God is so close to us and that He is always available to us! We can go to Him at any time of the day or night, without previously having to fix an appointment with Him. And we can share with Him the deepest, innermost secrets of our hearts, without any hesitation or reservation. Others may laugh at us, belittle our fears and worries, call us childish or foolish. But we can be sure that God will understand us. For He loves us much more than we can ever imagine. His love is understanding; it is patient; it is forgiving. We can go to Him anytime we like – but we go everywhere else except to Him!

We need to know God. We need to move close to Him. We need to make God real in our daily lives!

Who are you? Other people have told you many things about yourself — some complimentary, some otherwise. But all that is not really you. You must now try to find who you are. This is the biggest challenge of life. You must discover yourself. It is not easy to do so — but it can be done!

Mullah Nasruddin was out in the street searching for something.

"What are you looking for?" they asked him.

"I have lost my keys," he answered.

"Where did you lose them?" he was asked.

And he said, "I lost them in the house."

"Then how is it that you are looking for them here?"

And the Mullah said, "Because in the house it is dark, out here it is so bright!"

We have looked for ourselves out here, but we will not be able to find ourselves until we look within, until we turn inside where it is dark.

Let us take out a little Personal Quiet Time (PQT) for ourselves every day. Let us make this our daily appointment with our own selves, our True Self, the Real Self, the Self Supreme that, for want of a better word, we call God. Begin with fifteen minutes, then gradually increase the period to at least one hour. At first, the practice may appear to be meaningless, a sheer waste of time. But if you persist in it, silence will become alive and the Word of God will speak to you. And you will realise that practising silence is, perhaps, the most worthwhile activity of the day.

In silence, let us pray, meditate, repeat the Name Divine, do our spiritual thinking, engage ourselves in a loving and intimate conversation with God.

Let me say to you, spirituality in daily life is all about practising what you have learnt and understood in your efforts to know your true self and grasp the purpose of your life. Once your insights are clear, you need to translate them into deeds of daily life: into good thoughts, good words and good deeds.

> **Spirituality can refer to many different things, but in the following I will focus on this very basic aspect: disengaging from the identification with a limited ego in favour of a more open-ended identity. Three aspects of this initial phase of spiritual development seem to be important from a social point of view:**
>
> 1. **Letting go of the desire for permanence and control.**
> 2. **Decentering, i.e. commitment to values based on a universalistic perspective (what is good for all rather than what is good for me and my group).**
> 3. **Mindfulness, i.e. being present and choosing in all situations, rather than acting out of habit, conventions or impulses.**
>
> **– Thomas Jordan**

Over the years, there is one way I have discovered to connect with the Divine, and I believe it has really drawn me closer to the Lord. I would like to share it with you. It is to sit in silence, in the calm and quiet stillness of the night, before you retire to bed, and go over all the events of the last twelve hours. Start anti-clockwise: at 10 pm or 9 pm (which is just past) and recall your actions during the day that is just over.

Ask yourself: What have I done during the day that is just over?

For some of you, the day might involve questions such as the following:

What was the action I did before I retired to my bed? Was I just watching TV? Or was I spending precious free time with the members of my family?

How and where did I eat my meal – seated with the family around the dinner table, or taking my plate to sit in front of the TV?

How did I spend my evening? Slouched over a newspaper, or reading a good book?

In what frame of mind did I leave work? Irritable and exhausted, or with the sense of having accomplished a day's useful activity?

How did I behave with my colleagues at work? Was I annoyed and suspicious about them, or did I appreciate what they did?

How did I treat my subordinates? Was I kind and courteous at all times, or did I use harsh words to criticise them?

In what frame of mind did I enter the office this morning – with the feeling that work is worship, or feeling lousy about my job and my colleagues?

The routine I have given above is only an indication. You must fill in details of your own daily schedule. Was I kind and loving to the children? Did I attend all my lectures and pay attention to what was being taught? Was I helpful and polite to my customers? How often did I lose my temper? How often did I speak or think harshly? How many people did I refuse to meet?

Think in the reverse direction. You will realise the mistakes you have made, knowingly or unknowingly. Call God, seek His guidance. Ask Him to forgive you; ask Him to help you to forgive yourself. Ask Him to help you become a better person tomorrow; ask Him for the gift of a more worthwhile life tomorrow.

Pray to God, "O Lord! Forgive me my faults; forgive my mistakes which I have committed in the last 24 hours. Give me the strength to correct them. Dear God, bestow on me the awareness of the true purpose of my life, and the wisdom to improve my *karma* and to do good deeds!"

May I say to you, as you grow in spiritual awareness, right actions and right thinking will come to you spontaneously!

One way to ensure that you always do the right things – and do everything right – is to do everything in the spirit of offering to the Lord. It does not matter how lowly your station may be; it does not matter how humble the task you perform. It was Martin Luther King who said:

> If a man is called to be a street sweeper, he should sweep streets even as Michelangelo painted, or Beethoven played music, or Shakespeare wrote poetry. He should sweep streets so well that all the hosts of heaven and earth will pause to say, "Here lived a great sweeper who did his job well."

Unfortunately, many of us are prone to equate "greatness" with fame, fortune and power. However, true perfection consists in the way we attend to life's little details. Therefore, we must learn to live in the present; to concentrate on the task before us, the task at hand.

A man came to the Buddha and asked him, "Are you the Messiah?"

"No," answered the Buddha. "Are you a saint, then?" the man wanted to know.

"No," was the reply.

"Then surely, you must be a teacher," the man proclaimed.

The same answer came. "No."

"What are you then?" demanded the man impatiently.

"I am awake," the Buddha answered.

He was expressing a great spiritual truth in those simple words. For the goal of all spiritual practice is simply to awaken. The great ones of this earth – wise, loving, evolved souls – are no different from the rest of us. They simply recognise and remember who they are. This is why the most enlightened teachers tell you that they are your fellow pilgrims, fellow-seekers on the path.

There was a spiritual seeker – *jignasu* – who was told about a holy man, a sage who lived on a lonely, remote mountain-top. It was believed that this wise man had an answer for every question – the solution to every problem. Merely by spending a few minutes in his presence, one's life would be charged forever.

Naturally, the seeker was athirst to meet such an evolved soul. "If only I could just see him," he said to himself, "I would count myself blessed! If only I could share a few seconds with him, I would feel truly enlightened!"

He decided to set out in search of the sage's abode. For days together, he walked across hills, rivers, valleys and streams to locate the mountain where the great Guru lived. After a tough and exhausting climb he finally arrived at the sage's front door.

Trembling with intense emotional excitement, he knocked at the door. It was opened by a lowly man in poor clothes, whom he took to be a servant. The servant greeted him and led him through the house. They passed through several corridors and rooms, and the servant kept on talking as they walked. However, the seeker's mind was so fixed on the experience ahead of him, that he hardly paid any attention to what the man was saying. The servant glanced at him as he talked and finally, they both arrived at a locked door. He opened the door which led on to the backyard. Wordlessly, he indicated that the visitor should leave the house.

"But I've come all the way to meet the Guru," the seeker protested. "I must have at least a few minutes with him!" "You just did," answered the sage as he let the man out and shut the door firmly.

We are so pre-occupied with 'big' issues, we have no time to spare for the here and the now. Our answers, the solutions to our problems are not always to be found on a mountain-top; they may be staring you in the face right where you are!

Some people alas, became permanent, professional 'seekers'. They are reading books pondering deep questions, attending seminars and conferences on philosophy and spirituality and engaging in a lifelong quest. They forget that God can speak to them through the ordinary people they meet, through the grass, the flowers, the sun, the moon and the stars. They fail to realise that His ways are indeed mysterious, and that He can express Himself through the touch of a friend or the smile of a loved one or the shining eyes of a child.

Why Life Purpose and Spirituality Are Important?

There is a growing body of evidence indicating that spiritual practices, such as prayer or meditation, are associated with better health. Harvard professor Anne Harrington also argues that spirituality is important to health because:

1. **It promotes a healthy lifestyle and provides good community**
2. **Contemplative practices reduce stress**
3. **Belief is a healing power**
4. **Because the search for life purpose often involves connection with others and contemplative practices, much of this research also applies there.**

Your *mukti*, your liberation, your salvation does not necessarily come from the hands of a powerful, impressive, authoritative figure. It can come to you through humble people whom you meet on the by-ways of life.

– Barb Leonard and Mary Jo Kreitzer,
Centre for Spirituality and Healing

Many of us are apt to imagine God as a sort of Old Testament figure – with long, flowing robes and a white beard, seated on a cloud, hurling lightning and thunderbolts at the sinful world. God lives within you, in the temple of your heart; He speaks to you in silence; He speaks to you through your intuitions, visions and dreams! Every person you meet is a manifestation of God! Every creature that breathes the breath of life is an aspect of the Maker. Each and every one of them can teach you valuable lessons in a new, unexpected and unique way! Therefore, is the Lord described as *Deenabandhu* and *Deenanath* – He is the friend, the brother of the humble and the lowly. When we take them seriously, we will surely find the answers we are seeking.

Here are a few simple practical suggestions to bring spirituality into your daily life:

1. **Begin the day with God.**

    The first thing we do on getting up in the morning shapes the entire day. Does it not stand to reason that we should begin the day right?

    Every morning, when you awake, there is a choice before you: you can choose optimism, faith, positive thinking and right attitude; or you can choose pessimism, defeat, negative thinking and despair. What would you choose?

Begin the day well – and God will take care of the rest of the day!

Every day, as you wake up in the morning, let there be a prayer on your lips, a simple prayer. Let me share with you the prayer that I offer to God:

O Lord! This new day comes to me as a gift from Thy spotless hands. You have taken care of me throughout the night, and I am sure You will keep watch over me throughout the day. Praise be to Thee, O Lord. Blessed be Thy Name. Blessed be Thy Name. Blessed be Thy Name!

You can reword this prayer if you like, in your own way. But make sure you begin the day by remembering God – with a prayer on your lips.

2. **Leave off fretting and worrying about every little problem. Leave it to God to take care of you and the others.**

    Put God first. He will automatically free us from our worries, and take care of all our 'concerns' and 'problems'. There is a beautiful line in the *Sukhmani Sahib*, a Sikh Scripture which I love to meditate on:

Avar tyag tu tisay chitar…

Renounce everything; throw out everything; don't think of anything – but meditate on Him; i.e. concentrate on Him; think of Him, dedicate all your work to Him!

If you wish to think of Him, you must empty your mind of all else. So long as you hold worries and anxieties in the mind, so long as your mind is not empty you cannot think of Him — and you will not be at peace. Therefore, empty your mind of all worries and anxiety. Be like the lion, not like the dog!

Que sera, sera! *Whatever will be, will be!* So why worry?

But it is not enough to succumb to fatalism and say, "I can't change what is to happen." I would like you to go one step further and say, "Whatever happened, whatever is happening, whatever will happen is all for the best." We need to assert again and again, that there is a meaning of mercy in all that happens to us. All experiences in life come to teach us something. We must accept it as a blessing—and we will be abundantly blessed.

Instead of worrying, let us turn to God in prayer and place all our burdens at His Lotus feet. This will give us an immediate feeling of peace and relaxation, enabling us to tackle the problems and perplexities of life in a spirit of calm surrender.

Why should we carry heavy burdens on our minds and hearts, when we can easily cast our burdens at the feet of Him who is strong enough to bear all the burdens of all the worlds?

Therefore, empty your mind of all worry and anxiety. Cast your burdens at His feet and He will give you the calmness, courage and confidence to face the challenges of life!

3. **Count Your Blessings!**

A few years ago, when I was in the U.S. I gave a talk on, "How to make problems work for you". On the very next day, a brother wrote to me, "I am on a gloomy express train carrying an excess of negative baggage. What can I do to get off this grouchy track?"

Then and there I put down a few words on

paper—I wrote a small poem which I would like to pass on to you. There is not much of music or imagery in it, but I do believe that if we all follow the teaching it has to offer, it will be to our advantage:

When all is dark as a starless night
And there's not a ray of hope in sight
Then count your blessings one by one
You will be amazed at all that God has done!

Should we not feel grateful to God for the gifts He has bestowed on us; two eyes with which to see the beauty of the world around us, two ears with which to hear music, song, conversation and children's laughter; two hands with which to do a thousand things; two feet which can take us wherever we choose to walk!

And that is not all. He has given us people who love us—family, brothers and sisters, friends and well-wishers!

Count your blessings instead of your crosses
Count your gains instead of your losses
Count your joys instead of your woes
Count your friends instead of your foes
Count your smiles instead of your tears
Count your courage instead of your fears

Count your full years instead of your lean
Count your kind deeds instead of your mean
Count your health instead of your wealth
Love the world as much as you love yourself
Count your blessings!

4. **Accept God's Will.**

May I pass on to you a *mantra* which is sure to
bring you peace? It is a prayer which a saint,
a holy man of God used to offer again and
again. Inscribe it on the tablet of your heart.
Repeat it again and again, remember it by
day and night, for it is really simple:

Yes Father, Yes Father,Yes and always Yes!

Yes Father, Yes Father,Yes and always Yes!

There are people who are upset with
me because I advocate the philosophy of
acceptance. They say to me, that this will
make people lazy and lethargic; they will give
up all their drive and ambition and simply
sink into passive resignation.

I beg to differ! People who believe in the
supremacy of the Almighty, people who
learn to accept His Divine Will, never ever
give in to lethargy and pessimism. They
do as the Lord bids them in the Gita —

they put in their best efforts; they do not slacken; they do their best to achieve what they want. But if they do not achieve the desired results, they do not give in to despair and frustration; they do not give in to disappointment.

"Would you know who is the greatest saint in the world?" asks William Law. "It is not he who prays most or fasts most; it is not he who gives most alms or is most eminent for temperance, charity or justice; but it is he who is always thankful to God; who wills everything God Wills, who receives everything as an instance of God's goodness and has a heart always ready to praise God for it."

Wisdom consists in accepting God's Will — not with despair or resignation, but in peace and faith, knowing that our journey through life has been perfectly planned by Infinite love and Infinite wisdom. There can be no mistake in God's plan for us!

Again and again, we try to run away from difficult situations; again and again we rebel, react with anger and bitterness. How can we ever be at peace?

The answer is simple: Grow in the spirit of surrender to God; develop the spirit of acceptance. "Not my will, but Thy Will be done, O Lord!" This must be the constant utterance on your lips.

To seek refuge is to trust the Lord — fully, completely, entirely. It is to know that He is the one Light that we need in the darkest hours of our life. He is the all-loving One whose ears are ever attentive to the prayers of His wayward children. He is the all-knowing One who does the very best for us. With Him, all things are possible: and if He chooses *not* to do certain things for us which we want Him to do, it is not because He cannot do them, but because He knows better — He knows we require something else for our own good.

So it is that he who has taken refuge in the Lord is ever at peace. "Not my will, but Thy Will be done, O Lord," he prays. Whatever happens, "I accept! I accept! I accept!" is his *mantra*. "Yes Father, Yes and always Yes!" is his response to all incidents and all accidents of life. Nothing, no accident, no loss, no tragedy can disturb his equanimity.

5. **Do your best – and leave the rest to God.**

Work is worship—and *karma*, or action, is unavoidable for those who are born on this earth. But the secret of inner peace is to work without attachment to the results.

The laws of nature drive all of us to activity, for we cannot survive without action. But the wise ones act without attachment—with detachment—without looking for results. Success and failure do not influence their attitude to their duty.

Of course, some of you are bound to ask, "Is it really possible for us to act without desiring any kind of results?"

In the Bhagavad Gita, Sri Krishna has given us not one, not two, but three strong motives which should guide all our actions:

1.   Duty—for the sake of duty

2.   Work—for the sake of inner purification

3.   Action—as offering to the Lord

In fact, the Lord even goes on to tell Arjuna that desireless action is actually better than renunciation of action.

There are people who are constantly chasing

'goals' and 'targets'—more money, a better job, higher pay, and greater satisfaction.

Yet others grumble and complain all the time, because they feel their work is unrecognised, unrewarded, unappreciated.

How may we avoid such disappointment, frustration and this restless drive?

Simply by surrendering the fruits of action to the Lord! Let us stop chasing after 'personal satisfaction' and 'individual happiness'. Let us make our work, all our work, an offering to the Lord.

Do your best, but leave the rest to God! When you allow yourself to become an instrument of God, you will find that you can actually work better, and achieve greater success—for you will be freed from your own personal limitations.

When you rid yourself of the desire to 'achieve' results, when you are free from anxiety and stress that arises from expectations, you escape the twin perils of egoistic arrogance on one hand, and dejection/depression on the other. If your efforts are crowned with success, it is His doing; if you should face failure, it is His Will!

In this way you are really putting into practice the maxim — work is worship. Your work becomes an act of devotion — and when it is performed in this spirit, work will always be a wonderful, pleasant experience for you!

It is not the *amount* of work we do that matters, but the *way* we do it; it is not *what* we do, but *how* we do it. There are many people who toil and drudge and slave, day after day, month after month, year after year — and their work is but a shadow on the wall. It vanishes the moment it is born. True work, abiding work, the work that transforms lives, flows out of the centre within the heart; the centre of harmony and happiness, peace and joy.

Convert your work into *yagna* — an offering and you are linked with the Lord. But remember, you must offer Him nothing but the best that you are capable of! The light shines in your life when you connect yourself with the Great Light: a new power, a new *shakti* will course through your veins, and you will find that God never fails you!

6. **Seek not power! Seek service!**

Let us do as much good as we can, to as many as we can, in as many ways as we can, whenever we can and as long as we can!

The way of spirituality is the way of love, compassion, the spirit of caring and sharing and service. It is also the shortest and quickest route to God. The way of service is closely allied to the way of brotherhood — for we need to assert, again and again, "I am my brother's keeper!"

And who are our brothers? Our brothers and sisters are all those who suffer and are in need of help — men, women, birds and animals. We must become channels of God's mercy, help and healing, so that His love may flow out to them through us and our actions. When we become instruments of God's love, there is no limit to what we can accomplish. In God's Divine Plan, we can become the sanctuary of the weary and heavy-laden; we can, with our efforts, become a source of sweet, refreshing waters in the wilderness that is this world.

There is a simple question that all seekers must ask themselves: I give it to you in the words of Gurudev Sadhu Vaswani. *How can we claim our love to God if we do not love our fellow human beings? How can we call ourselves human beings if we watch our brothers and sisters suffering and struggling?*

God is Absolute Love—and if we love God, we must be imbued with the longing to serve our fellow men. I believe that true service is a spiritual activity, which at its best, is born out of the Love of God. It was a true saint of God who said: Spirituality without work is as bad as work without spirituality!

We all have something to give! Let us give with love and compassion, and we will make the world a better place!

How can I refrain from quoting those beautiful lines that have never failed to inspire me!

> I shall pass through this life but once.
> Any good, therefore, that I can do
> Or any kindness that I can show to any fellow creature,
> Let me do it now.
> Let me not defer or neglect it,
> For I shall not pass this way again.

For Your Reflection

Simple Assertions for Spirituality in Daily Life

1. In every situation, every routine task that you face, there are two responses for you to choose from: one is to take it up as a dead weight, a boring, demanding, dull thing to do; the other is to take it on as if it were God's work, rising to the challenge with dedication, honesty, sincerity and integrity. Today, as you start the day, assert to yourself: Whatever I do today, I shall do it in a spirit of offering to God.

2. Every day, we face obstacles, delays, little or big problems in carrying out our work. We can react to these with bad temper and irritation, or we can take them on with patience, understanding and a smile. Today, as you start work, assert to yourself: I shall treat every obstacle as an opportunity to strengthen my spirituality.

3. Very often, people forget their ideals, their Guru's precepts and the tenets of their inner faith in the workaday world. While it is not possible to spend hours reflecting on one's ideals, it is nevertheless a healthy practice to remember these values and precepts constantly. Today, in the midst of your busy routine, take time out to remember the teachings of your

Guru or a spiritual elder or saint. Assert to yourself: These are the ideals I value; these are the ideals I would like to live by; may God grant that I may not lose sight of them in my daily activities.

4. Throughout the day, regard everyone you come across in the course of your transactions as a soul, rather than a mere physical being – a client, customer, co-worker, superior or subordinate. Assert to yourself: I am dealing with the Divine in this being; I am transacting with the God in him or her.

You will find that these simple assertions transform your life with love and beauty. You will find yourself operating from a higher level of consciousness.

Where Is Your Furniture?

Gurudev Sadhu Vaswani was simple in his dress and diet and daily living and, as the truly great are, he was in his simplicity, sublime.

At one time, he lived in the Hari Mandir – a big hall in which a mattress was spread on one side. He slept on the mattress at night, and during the day, sat on it and did his work. There was a small desk on which he did his writing, as he sat on the floor. And there were many books spread all over.

One day, a Frenchman visited him. He had learnt of the Master through the writings of Mon. Paul Richard, who had said , "I have been blessed, for amidst the deserts of Sind, I have found a true prophet, a messenger of the new Spirit, a saint, a sage, and a seer, a rishi of new India, a leader to the great future – Sadhu Vaswani."

The Frenchman had expected to see the saint living in a beautifully furnished house. He was astonished to see that Sadhu Vaswani's dwelling was a simple hall with a mattress, a desk and books.

He asked Gurudev, "Where is your furniture?"

The Master asked him, "Where is yours?"

The Frenchman said, "I have no furniture. My furniture is in my home in France. I am only a traveler here."

Softly, Gurudev answered, "So am I!"

Chapter Six

Getting In Touch With Our Higher Consciousness

Let me open this chapter with one of the best loved *mantras* in our sacred scriptures:

Om Asato Maa Sad Gamaya
Tamaso Maa Jyotir Gamaya
Mrityor Maa Amritam Gamaya
Om Shaantih, Shaantih, Shaantih!

From the nonexistent, from the unreal, from the apparent, lead me to the other side, to the Existent, the Real. From the darkness of ignorance, lead me to the Light of wisdom; from the unreality that is death, lead me to the eternal life of the *atman*.

These words which are familiar to most of us first occur in the *Brihadaranyaka Upanishad*, and constitute what is known as the *abyaroha mantra* — that is, the *mantra* which can elevate, heighten our consciousness. *Aaroha* literally means 'ascent'; this invocation too, can take us onward, upward, Godward. This *mantra* is at once a prayer, a chant, an invocation to the Divine. In the original text, it is repeated continuously, to produce the required effect — that is, freedom from falsehood and the darkness of ignorance. The three lines of this verse are also known as the *Pavamana-Mantras*, or purifying chants. It is thought that they can help the true seeker rise from the mortal to the immortal level where his *atman* truly belongs.

Like so many of our great *mantras*, this is not a request for worldly gains: the *jignasu* or seeker realises the limitations within which the human life binds his *atman*, and asks the Supreme Being for transcendence – to rise above the mortal coils through the purificatory power of the chant: thus the significance of its name, the *Pavamana Abyaroha Mantra* – it cleanses and purifies us from within; it helps us ascend to the highest level of consciousness.

> **You must override your ego in order to access the natural flow of Divine Energy. Your ego is an imposter, pretending to be you. Unmask it and set your spirit free...**
>
> **– Michael Nitti**

One of the vital requirements for this process of thought-control, is the conquest over the ego. When the ego – the lower self-asserts itself, it drags the mind down with it. It restricts our consciousness and erects barriers on the path of our spiritual progress. But these barriers must become stepping-stones, not stopping stones on our path. The way to overcome these barriers is to adopt a way of life, a code of conduct for the seeker, as recommended by our ancient scriptures.

Today, we often hear of senior executives in multinational firms being dismissed from their posts and replaced by others who are more observant, more respectful of the rules – the corporate code of conduct, as it is called. We go to banks and insurance firms, and we see that people who deal with us are normally polite and courteous. If they were not, they too would soon be replaced by others. As responsible employees, they follow a code of conduct while on duty.

Is there not a code of conduct for us if we wish to live a higher life, a more evolved life in moral and spiritual terms? The Hindu scriptures give us such ethical guidelines, through *yamas* and *niyamas* (restrictions and observances). They are the essence of our duty to ourselves and others – the dos and don'ts that are fundamental to a life of *dharma*.

Here are the *yamas* – the don'ts:

1. Practise *ahimsa* (non-injury). Do not harm others by thought, word or deed.

2. Practise *satya* (truth). Refrain from lying and breaking promises.

3. Practise *asteya* (non-stealing). Do not steal or covet what belongs to another.

4. Practise *brahmacharya* (celibacy). Do not be promiscuous in thought, word or deed.

5. Exercise *kshama* (patience). Do not be intolerant and insensitive to others.

6. Practise *dhriti* (steadfastness). Overcome inertia, indecision and changeability.

7. Practise *daya* (compassion). Conquer cruelty and callousness towards all beings.

8. Practise *arjava* (honesty). Renounce all forms of deception and wrong doing.

9. Practise *mitahara* (moderation in appetite). Don't eat too much, don't consume food of violence.

10. Practise *saucha* (purity). Avoid impurity in mind, body and speech.

The ten practises recommended by the *niyamas* — the dos:

1. *Hri* (remorse). Recognise your errors, confess and make amends. Apologise to those whom you have hurt. Accept correction.

2. *Santosha* (contentment). Nurture contentment, seeking happiness in what you are and what you love. Cultivate the attitude of gratitude.

3. *Dana* (giving). "Give, give, give!" was the *mantra* emphasised by my Beloved Master, Gurudev Sadhu Vaswani. He said: "If I had a million tongues, with every one of them, I would still utter the one word, 'Give, Give, Give'!" Give liberally and generously, without any thought of reward or recognition.

4. *Astikya* (faith). Cultivate firm, unshakable faith in God and your Guru. Trust in the scriptures and in the wisdom of the saints.

5. *Ishvara-pujana* (worship). Cultivate devotion through daily prayer and meditation.

6. *Siddhanta-shravana* (spiritual listening). Be eager to listen to the scriptures. Study their teachings. Choose a Guru and obey his teachings implicitly.

7. *Mati* (cognition). Develop spiritual will and firm intellect under the guidance of your Guru. Strive constantly for knowledge of God.

8. *Vrata* (sacred vows). Embrace religious observances and never waive in fulfilling

them. Honour your vows as spiritual contracts with God.

9. *Japa* (recitation). Choose your sacred *mantras* and chant them daily. Recite the sacred sound, word or phrase given to you by your Guru.

10. *Tapas* (austerity). Practise discipline in your daily life. Practise self-denial, so that you may light the spark of transformation within you.

The *yamas* and *niyamas* have come down to us through the ages. They form the very foundation on which we should build our lives. They are fundamental to all living beings, who seek to attain life's highest aim – freedom from the bonds of *karma*, and attainment of the higher consciousness.

There is a universal intelligence that we call God or Soul or Spirit or Consciousness, and it is everywhere and in all things.

– **Wayne Dyer**

God has given us this rare and precious gift of the human life that we may grow in perfection, awareness and consciousness. Let us set aside our lower passions and desires and make an effort to progress on this path, for this is the true goal of life. Let us make the persistent effort to achieve this goal. This will give rise to *sattvic* virtues in us. As we grow in *sattvic* nature our spirits will be cleansed and we will attain the state of the *stithaapragnya* that the Gita extols.

Maharishi Patanjali tells us in his *Yoga Sutra*:

Maitrīkaruṇāmudito-pekṣāṇāṁ-sukha-duḥkhapuṇya-apuṇya-viṣayāṇāṁbhāvanātaḥcitta-prasādanam ||33||

All that is mutable in human beings (*chitta*) is harmonised through the cultivation of love (*maitri*), helpfulness (*karuna*), conviviality (*mudita*) and imperturbability (*upeksha*) in situations that are happy, painful, successful or unfortunate.

These are in fact, four positive attitudes that will help us retain our sense of balance and equanimity. They are *maitri* (friendship to our fellow human beings); *mudita* (joyous respect to spiritual superiors); *karuna* (compassion to those who are less evolved than we are); and *upeksha* (indifference to those who are crude), in all kinds of life-situations.

Is this not what the Lord describes as equanimity – *samattvam* – in the Gita? This is the highest level of consciousness we can aspire to. Therefore Sri Krishna tells us: "*Samattvam yoga uchyate* – Equanimity is called yoga."

Maitri and *karuna* lead us on to the path of selfless service. When we start living and working for others, hen our lives become richer, more rewarding, more meaningful. We are able to tap our inner *shakti* to its highest potential; we become more energetic; we become more creative; we solve problems easily. Above all, we grow in the consciousness that all life is One, all life is reverent, all men are brothers – and that birds and animals too, are our brothers and sisters in the One family of Creation. Is not this the highest form of consciousness – this awareness of the Unity of all life?

Psychiatrists as well as spiritual teachers now agree that there are three states of consciousness in all of us: the conscious mind with which all of us are familiar; the subconscious, which is the hidden but powerful part of our psyche, with which we connect only during sleep; the super-conscious which represents the highest degree of awareness that we are capable of. It is the source of the brightest light, the highest power of which we are capable. (Walking the path of spirituality means that we seek to establish contact with our super-consciousness.)

This is not always easy!

I recall a memorable evening, when my Gurudev Sadhu Vaswani, was pacing up and down the terrace of Krishta Kunj — his residence in Karachi. As he looked down at the street below, he exclaimed, "Prisoners! Prisoners!"

I looked down too — but I saw no prisoners. I saw the traffic, and I saw a number of people who were going about their business. But there was no sign of prisoners!

Actually, Krishta Kunj was situated quite close to the Karachi District Jail, and prisoners would pass by the house from time to time, as they were led out by their wardens for labour routines, or accompanied by policemen to appear in court. But on this occasion, there were no prisoners to be seen. Surprised, I said to him, "But Dada, I see no prisoners here!"

Sadhu Vaswani's reply still echoes in my ears. For long have I meditated on the profound wisdom of his words to me that evening: "Prisoners, prisoners of desire are the people," he said. "Alas, they know not of their bondage!"

Prisoners of desire are we all! We are bound by our own joys and sorrows. We are happy with what the world gives us; we take great joy in our pleasures and possessions. We celebrate the birth of a child — and we mourn over his loss when he passes away. We weep for a while — and then we beget more children. We are not aware of the fetters that bind us!

We live in a world of allurements and entanglements. The sharp arrows of desire, of craving, of animal appetite, of passion and pride, of ignorance and anger, of hatred and greed, wound our souls, again and again. Our souls bear the scars of many wounds: they need to be healed.

Those of us, who become aware of our bonds, make the effort to seek liberation. This state of awareness is known as *mumukshatwa* — the desire to attain liberation. In this condition, our deep consciousness is awakened and urges us to take to the road less travelled – the way of spirituality.

To realise our true Self, to access our highest level of consciousness, we need to go within ourselves and, in the words of Gurudev Sadhu Vaswani, "sink deeper and deeper". No one else can do that for us; we need to do it ourselves. We need to strip ourselves of all pride and passion, selfishness, sensuality, and sluggishness of soul. We need to remove veil after veil until we reach the inmost depths and touch the Pure White Flame.

Exercise for Aspirants

Do not try to measure your progress by your experiences. Your real progress can only be measured by the change in your consciousness and the change that this brings about in your behaviour, attitude, reactions and responses.

What are the marks of a pilgrim who seeks to be in contact with his higher self?

1. Such a seeker loves one and all.

    His love is universal and unconditional. It is love without any attachments. This is the best kind of love that a human being is capable of; it is the true art of living. From a practical point of view, you should love your near and dear ones, your children, your parents and other family members. But let this love be your duty, and not lead to an attachment! A pilgrim's heart is filled with an abundance of love. But he is not attached to anyone, he is not attached to any object or any being. Fulfil your obligations, do your duty, but be detached.

2. The seeker's thoughts are clear.

    His speech is pure. His actions are pure. The Lord tells us in the Bhagavad Gita, that actions and words that cause harm and pain to others must be avoided. Therefore, the pilgrim must say and do what is true, what is good for everyone, and what is not injurious to any living being.

3. He walks the path of truth.

We often speak lies and that is the root of all sin and suffering. *Satyam vada, krodam makuru* is the very first lesson of spiritual life. The seeker always speaks the truth; he is always true to his higher self.

4. He keeps himself away from all gossip and controversies.

He does not criticise anyone nor does he hear any complaints and criticism from others. Once a devotee came to Gurudev and said, "My mind wanders when I sit to meditate." Gurudev asked him, "Do you criticise anyone?" The devotee replied, "No. I do not criticise anyone nor do I degrade anyone." Gurudev then asked him, "Do you hear the gossip criticising others?" The devotee replied, "Yes. I do listen to the criticism of others." Gurudev said, "Even if you do not criticise anyone, but hear others' criticism, you become a passive participant in gossip."

A true seeker keeps himself away from all unpleasant, unproductive talk.

5. He realises the Oneness of all creation.

Once a saint gave his disciples the teaching: "Do not become a pair of scissors, but be like a needle." The disciples were puzzled; they asked the saint to explain this. The saint said, "The needle sews clothes, stitches up tears and cuts in the fabric. But the scissor cuts the cloth asunder. Hence, wherever you go, be like the needle and patch up differences; sew up tears and cuts; bring people together. Bind them in the silken thread of your love, because in reality we all are one!"

On the spiritual plane we all are one. There is no difference between you and me. In the physical world we find everyone different and hence we behave selfishly. We all are one. Hence we have a moral responsibility towards everyone of our fellow human beings, every being that breathes the breath of life. Our conduct should be ethical. There are people who think of their profits only, they do not care about others' welfare. The only motive of their life is to earn higher profits. These men are like scissors.

6. He is an epitome of compassion.

    His compassion moves out not only to men but birds and animals. He does not eat flesh-food, because to him the animals are as dear as human beings.

7. He always speaks gently.

    He speaks sweetly. Every one of us has a choice, either to speak harshly or to speak gently. We should always speak gently and sweetly.

Sant Gyaneshwar once said to his disciples, "When you get up from the sleep in the morning, regard it as the last day of your life."

Once we realise that we have only 24 hours left we would try to do as much good as possible. We would try to be sweet and gentle and helpful.

8. He constantly chants the Name Divine.

The Name of God is a great purifier and the purification is the very first step on the mystic path.

9. He meditates on God every day.
    He does not miss his daily appointment with God.

Fix a time for your meditation. Resolve that you will meditate for 15 minutes or half an hour or an hour in meditation. During this period you can chant the Name Divine, you can commune with God, meditate on some inspirational teachings or pick up a sentence from a spiritual literature on compassion, oneness, etc. and reflect on it.

10. He prays for the Universe.

His prayer is, "All men, all birds and all animals, all living and non-living things, may they all, without exception be happy."

Pick up at least a few of these attributes; put them into practise in deeds of daily life for your own evolution on the spiritual path.

The Dawn Of Realisation

A devoted spiritual seeker came to meet the Jewish holy man, Baal Shem Tov. He appeared to be in deep despair, and said to the holy man, "It's no use! I have laboured hard and long in the service of the Lord, and yet I feel I have received no improvement. I am sad to tell you that I am still an ordinary and ignorant person."

The holy one answered: "You have indeed made remarkable progress! You have gained the realisation that you are ordinary and ignorant, and this in itself is a worthy accomplishment."

Chapter Seven

Spirituality And Religion –
Multi-faith Spiritual Traditions

The Concept of the Soul

In terms of religion and philosophy, the soul is defined as the immaterial essence of a human being. Many philosophers agree that it is this essence that makes every human being unique. Most religions also see the soul as an aspect of Divinity in man, with an afterlife that follows the death of the physical body.

The world's ancient cultures attributed souls to all living things. However, despite such widespread belief in an essential and animating principle of life, we find a variety of theories and concepts about the relationship of the soul to the body.

> ...the words "spiritual" and "religious" are really
> synonyms. Both connote belief in a Higher Power
> of some kind. Both also imply a desire to connect,
> or enter into a more intense relationship, with
> this Higher Power. And, finally, both connote
> interest in practices, and daily moral behaviours
> that foster such a connection or relationship.
> – Robert C. Fuller

As we saw earlier, in **Hindu thought**, the *atman* is
an aspect of the Universal, Eternal Self (*paramatman*),
of which each individual soul (*jiva or jivaatman*)
partakes. The *jivaatman* is also eternal and undying;
but is confined in a physical body during its human
incarnation. At the death of the physical body, the
jivaatman passes on into a new existence, which is
determined by its cumulative *karma*, the result of
its actions in that and previous births. Accordingly,
it goes through a state of bliss or pain as reward or
punishment of its *karma*, to be subsequently reborn
in another form (human or non-human). This birth-
death-rebirth cycle persists until the soul evolves
towards *karmic* perfection, when it finally merges
with the *paramatman* – a state described simply as
Liberation or *moksha*.

Judaism regards each soul as the expression of
God's intent and vision in creating that particular

being. But it is the human soul that is both the most complex and the most lofty of souls. According to ancient Jewish scholars: "She is called by five names: *Nefesh* (soul), *Ruach* (spirit), *Neshamah* (breath), *Chayah* (life) and *Yechidah* (singularity)."

Buddhism denies both the concept of the individual self and the *atman*; it asserts that any sense of having an individual eternal soul or of partaking in a persistent universal self is illusory. This is referred to as *anatta* in Pali, and *anatman* in Sanskrit. This is in tune with the larger Buddhist belief that nothing has a real essence, including the notion of the individual soul or self as the essence of a person. According to Buddhist philosophy, belief in such "essences", especially the belief in individual souls is the root cause of our imprisonment in *samsara* (i.e. our fundamental ignorance and suffering); the abandonment of such ignorance would lead one to *nirvana* (enlightenment and buddhahood).

Jainism propounds the doctrine of two eternal, coexisting, independent categories known as *jiva* (animate, living soul: the enjoyer) and *ajiva* (inanimate, non-living object: the enjoyed). Jains believe, moreover, that the actions of mind, speech and body produce subtle *karma* which becomes the cause of bondage. One can attain salvation (*moksha*) only by freeing the soul of *karma* through the practice of the three "jewels" of right faith, right knowledge and right conduct. The *Tirthankaras* are liberated souls who were once in bondage but became free, perfect, and blissful through their own efforts; they offer salvation from the ocean of phenomenal existence and the cycle of rebirths.

Christian concepts of the soul, as known today, were introduced into Christian theology by St. Gregory of Nyssa and by St. Augustine. In the Middle Ages, St. Thomas Aquinas reasserted the Greek philosophers' concept of the soul as a motivating principle of the body, independent but requiring the substance of the body to make an individual. After each individual's death, the soul enters an interim state – into a realm of bliss or that of perdition. At the Last Judgement the resurrected souls of all Christians will be assigned either to eternal life or eternal damnation.

> St. Anthony, famous among the blessed souls as the First of the Desert Fathers, was asked by a philosopher: "Father, how can you be really happy when you are deprived of the pleasure of books?"
> St. Anthony replied: "My book, O, Philosopher, is the nature of created things, and any time I want to read the words of God, the book is before me."

The **Islamic** concept, like the Christian, holds that the soul comes into existence at the same time as the body; thereafter, it has a life of its own, its union with the body being a temporary condition. Pious Muslims believe that their earthly life is a trial in preparation for the next realm of existence. The Holy Qur'an asserts that on the Day of Judgement God will decide the fate of each soul according to his or her record of deeds.

Zoroastrianism believes that all living creatures have a soul, *urvan* or *ravan*, as it is called. There are two aspects to all forms of existence: *Mainyu*, the spiritual existence, is the co-existent as well as the dual opposite of the physical existence, *gaetha*. Human beings are constituted from both the material and spiritual existences. Our spirit shapes and determines the nature of our attitude, our mentality and every thought, word and deed. With human beings, a person's character and that of their soul is built on the spirit a person chooses and is within that person's control through free will. The fate of the human soul depends on store of thoughts, words and deeds. The human soul receives in the afterlife what it has given out in this life. The soul creates its heaven or hell, both of which are a state of spiritual existence and not places. All souls come from God. At the end of time, all souls will be cleansed and will return to God.

Sikhism regards the Soul (*atma*) as a part of God (*Waheguru*). Various hymns from the sacred scripture, the Guru Granth Sahib proclaim this belief: "God is in the Soul and the Soul is in the God." And, again: "The soul is Divine; Divine is the soul. Worship Him with love." and "The soul is the Lord, and the Lord is the soul; contemplating the *Shabad,* the Lord is found." The *Atma* according to Sikhism is the "spiritual spark" or "light" in our body because of which the body can sustain life.

Western philosophy too, has continued to discuss the nature and the existence of the soul. René Descartes regarded man as a union of the body and the soul, each one being a distinct substance acting on the other; he saw the soul as equivalent to the mind. Benedict de Spinoza felt that body and soul formed two aspects of a single reality. Immanuel Kant concluded that the soul could not be proved or comprehended by reason; but he added that the mind must inevitably conclude that the soul exists because such a conclusion was necessary for the development of ethics and religion. To William James at the beginning of the 20th century, the soul was merely a collection of psychic phenomena.

> Spirituality exists wherever we struggle with the issue of how our lives fit into the greater cosmic scheme of things. This is true even when our questions never give way to specific answers or give rise to specific practices such as prayer or meditation. We encounter spiritual issues every time we wonder where the universe comes from, why we are here, or what happens when we die. We also become spiritual when we become moved by values such as beauty, love, or creativity that seem to reveal a meaning or power beyond our visible world. An idea or practice is "spiritual" when it reveals our personal desire to establish a felt-relationship with the deepest meanings or powers governing life.
>
> – Robert C. Fuller

Spirituality and Associated Practices

What is it to walk the path of spirituality, according to these different faiths?

Spiritual practice or spiritual discipline refers to those activities, practices of daily life that contribute to our spiritual development. Therefore, a spiritual practice moves a person along a path towards a goal. The goal is variously referred to as salvation, liberation or union (with God). A person who walks such a path is sometimes referred to as a seeker or a pilgrim on the path. Readers familiar with my writings will know that I refer to the path, the way of the spirit repeatedly. It is a universal metaphor used in many spiritual traditions of the world; walking the path is variously referred to as the *Sharia* in Islam, the *Marga* in Hindu thought and *The Way* in Tao and Christianity.

Once again, my account of these various spiritual practices must begin with the Hindu way of life, for that is the tradition which I have tried to practice and which I am most familiar with.

Hinduism allows for three approaches to the nature of existence: 1) Materialism, or the concept that the world of matter, that which we perceive with the senses is real, and has its own place in the scheme of things; we must note that this approach does NOT deny consciousness – for it is only our consciousness that makes us apprehend this material world. 2) Dualism, which asserts that both matter and consciousness are real. According to this view thought follows life; one does not preempt the other. If these are two contradictory features of our life-experience, then both are equally valuable. 3) Spiritualism emphasises the ultimate reality of consciousness. It would be right to say that pride of place is accorded to spirituality among the three approaches. To put it in the form of a popular expression, "We are not human beings undergoing a spiritual experience; we are spiritual beings undergoing a human experience."

Vedanta (which literally means "end of the *Vedas*," or the final teaching of the *Vedas*) represents the essence of Hindu spiritual thought. It represents the very sublime heights of Eastern spiritual traditions and its echoes are found in Buddhism, Jainism and Sikhism. It is a spiritual way that leads the individual soul to its ultimate goal — union with Brahman, the Supreme Soul.

How can we describe Hindu spiritual practices? To quote the words of my friend and fellow pilgrim from Pune, Yogacharya Shri. B.K.S. Iyengar, "*Sadhana* is a discipline undertaken in the pursuit of a goal. *Abhyasa* is repeated practice performed with observation and reflection. *Kriya* or action, also implies perfect execution with study and investigation. Therefore, *sadhana, abhyasa* and *kriya* all mean one and the same thing. A *sadhaka* or practitioner, is one who skillfully applies...mind and intelligence in practice towards a spiritual goal."

Judaism does not have an official or systematic creed or set of beliefs. Some Jews adhere to a complex set of beliefs and rituals; but others hold on only to certain ritual practices; all of them are considered to be "Jewish". The Ten Commandments are at the core of Jewish belief. We will all agree that following them is a tremendous spiritual discipline in itself. Jews believe that the Commandments or *mitzvot*, which God has given and which relate to all areas of life — food, clothing, prayer, relationships, business dealings, morality and so on — must be obeyed in letter and spirit.

Moving away from matters of belief, many historians and scholars insist that emphasised practices/observances of Jewish Law are equally important for Jews as religious beliefs. They maintain that the requirements of Judaism as a faith includes adherence to traditional customs and required observances such as *Shema*, which is an affirmation of Judaism and a declaration of faith in one God; praying three times a day; recitation of certain prayers and benedictions while performing certain acts throughout the day; and observing Jewish dietary laws.

Mention must be made of **Kabbalah** (meaning: receiving) which is a discipline and school of thought concerned with the mystical aspect of Judaism. It is a set of esoteric teachings that is meant to explain the relationship between an infinite, eternal and essentially unknowable Creator with the finite and mortal universe of His Creation. In solving this paradox, *Kabbalah* seeks to define the nature of the universe and the human being, the nature and purpose of existence, and various other ontological questions. It also presents methods to aid understanding of these concepts and to thereby attain spiritual realisation.

With reference to **Christianity,** we may begin with Jesus's words to Peter, "Stay awake and pray, so that you won't enter into temptation. The spirit is willing, but the flesh is weak." (Matthew 26:41). We also have St. Paul's exhortation in his Epistle to the Collossians: "And whatever you do, in word or in deed, do everything in the name of the Lord Jesus, giving thanks to God, the Father through Him." Solitude, silence, reading from the Bible and meditating on the same, prayer, contemplation and simplicity in life are some of the practices recommended by the Church.

In the present context it must be mentioned that the Christianity of the 20th century is changing. In place of beliefs and dogmas, Christians are seeking experiences and wider connections. Practitioners of this new tradition envision a new Christianity — one based on progressive understandings of the faith in a multi-faith world and one arising from the great ocean of spirituality that unites all traditions in an essential Oneness. Learning spiritual practices from other communities is part of the new landscape of Progressive Christian Spirituality. So is gathering in groups to do practices together, one of the hallmarks of the growing inter-spirituality movement.

In **Jainism,** the devout are urged to carry out certain acts that aid spiritual development every day. These include:

- prayer
- honouring the *Tirthankaras*
- paying respect to monks
- repenting for sins
- self-control through meditation
- going without something pleasurable

Somadeva, a great Jain teacher of the 10th Century, also included Charity and reading the Scriptures to this list.

In **Buddhism,** the Pali word "*yoga*", found in several early Buddhist texts, has been often translated as "Spiritual Practice". In Zen Buddhism, it is not just meditation (called *zazen*), but also the writing of poetry (especially *haiku*), painting, calligraphy, flower arranging and the maintenance of Zen gardens which are regarded as spiritual practices. The elaborate Japanese Tea Ceremony is also considered spiritual.

Islam believes that the real place for the growth of the spirit is in the midst of life and this workaday world – and not in solitary places or spiritual isolation. The first necessity for progression along the path of spiritual development is *faith*. The second stage is that of *obedience*, meaning that man gives up his independence and accepts subservience to Allah. The third stage is that of *desisting from everything which Allah has forbidden* or has disapproved of; to undertake all that Allah has commanded and to observe the distinctions between lawful and unlawful, right and wrong, and good and bad in life. The last and the highest stage is that of *godliness*. It signifies that man has attained highest excellence in words, deeds and thoughts, identifying his will with the Will of Allah and harmonising it, to the best of his knowledge and ability, with the Divine Will. Islam lays down 'five pillars' to facilitate spiritual development: Statement of Faith (*Shahadah*); Prayer (*Salat*); Fasting (*Sawm*); Almsgiving (*Zakat*) and Pilgrimage (*Hajj*).

In **Zoroastrianism,** there are three basic moral principles that guide human life: 1) *Humata,* or "Good Thoughts", the intention or moral resolution to abide by *Asha*, the right order of things. 2) *Hukhata*, "Good Words", the communication of that intention. 3) *Havarashta*, "Good Deeds", the realisation in action of that intention.

Living these three principles in deeds of daily life is to follow the law of *Asha*. These three principles are included in many Zoroastrian prayers, and children commit themselves to abide by them at their initiation ceremony, marking their responsible entry into the faith as practicing Zoroastrians. They are the moral/ spiritual code by which a Zoroastrian lives.

In **Sikhism,** simple, precise and practical guidelines are laid out by the Gurus for the practice of the "Sikh way of life". The Gurus emphasise that a Sikh should lead a disciplined life engaged in *Naam Simran,* meditation on God's Name, *Kirat Karni,* living a honest life of a house-holder and *Wand Chako,* sharing what one has with the community. This translates into hard work, honest living, love of fellow humans and through them service of the God, the Universal power. This way of life is stripped of all complications, esoteric rituals and exploitation of others in the name of religion. No benefits are gained by birth or station of life or social status; everyone has to undertake the rigours of *Simran* (meditation) and *Sewa* (selfless service) to progress spiritually. The Sri Guru Adi Granth asks the Sikh to "Practice truth, contentment and kindness; this is the most excellent way of life. One who is so blessed by the Formless Lord God renounces selfishness, and becomes the dust of all."

Today, we live in a world characterised by **Multi-faith** – that is, many faiths existing alongside each other. **Religious pluralism**, is another approach which asserts that all religions are equally valid as a way to God, and are to be respected as such. It is an approach to living in a religiously and spiritually diverse world that respects the integrity of different faith traditions and promotes greater understanding and mutual respect between the various belief systems of the world.

We have so much to learn from one another!

Let me end this chapter on a lighter vein with this amusing story.

A distinguished Professor of Comparative Religion was being ferried across a river by an illiterate boatman. The professor began to chat with the boatman as he was leafing through the pages of the encyclopedia that he was carrying.

"Tell me, my good man, have you read the Bible?"

The boatman had to answer in the negative.

"Ah! One-fourth of your life has been wasted!" sighed the professor. "Have you at least heard of the Gita?"

"No sir," replied the boatman regretfully.

"One half of your life thrown away!" exclaimed the professor. "Surely, you have heard of The Book of Common Prayer?"

"What's that?" said the boatman and received the retort: "You have wasted three-fourths of your life!"

As this discussion was going on, the boat sprang a leak and water began to enter the boat rapidly through the crevices. Now it was the turn of the boatman to ask the scholar, "Sir, can you swim?" The professor replied, "I have read several books on swimming and gathered a lot of information on it, but I cannot swim." The boatman then commented, "Then your entire life has gone to waste. The boat is about to sink!"

The professor's bookish knowledge was of no use to him. So too, if we wish to cross this vast ocean of worldly life and experience happiness through it, we should actually practise Spirituality and not just acquire theoretical knowledge.

Exercise in Awareness: Life Is A Great Teacher

I have always held the view that this world is a school, and the various life experiences we undergo here are meant to be valuable lessons in spiritual growth for us. As the Buddhist proverb tells us, "We must make each person we meet our ultimate object of reverence."

Each person we meet on the rough road of life, each fellow traveler on the path has something to teach us. Some of these people may be virtuous, noble and blessed with such noble qualities that they can inspire us to greater virtue. Equally, we may come across others with negative traits and unpleasant attributes, who may act as permanent reminders of how we ought not to be!

I urge you to observe carefully, the people you meet in the course of the day.

Has someone been kind and courteous? Let them inspire you to become kind and generous.

Has someone been harsh and unkind to you? Let them teach you to realise that others are as sensitive as you, and to avoid harsh criticism and hostility.

Have you heard sweet words of praise and appreciation from someone? Make sure you pass them on to others.

At least one day during the week, look upon each person you meet as a teacher. Look carefully at what this person has to teach you in terms of good and bad, in terms of what to imbibe and what to avoid.

Learn as much as you can from every encounter. At the end of the day, review your learning experiences, and evaluate what each of them has taught you.

The more you are open to learning from life, the more you will evolve spiritually! And let me add, you yourself will become a wonderful source of inspiration and learning for others!

Let me close with the words I love to repeat to myself: The day on which I have not learnt something new from someone is a wasted day indeed!

Right and Wrong

When the renowned Zen teacher Bankei held his seclusion-weeks of meditation, pupils from many parts of Japan came to attend. During one of these gatherings a pupil was caught stealing. The matter was reported to Bankei with the request that the culprit be expelled. Bankei ignored the case.

Later the pupil was caught in a similar act, and again Bankei disregarded the matter. This angered the other pupils, who drew up a petition asking for the dismissal of the thief, stating that otherwise they would all leave in a body.

When Bankei had read the petition he called everyone before him. "You are wise brothers," he told them. "You know what is right and what is not right. You may go somewhere else to study if you wish, but this poor brother does not even know right from wrong. Who will teach him if I do not? I am going to keep him here even if all the rest of you leave."

A torrent of tears cleansed the face of the brother who had stolen. All desire to steal had vanished.

Chapter Eight

Sadhanas For Spirituality

In its basic form, the Sanskrit word *sadhana* is "the means of accomplishing something". To be more specific, it refers to a spiritual practice prescribed by ancient Indian religions, especially Hinduism and Buddhism. In short, *sadhana* is a spiritual discipline which is essential for all seekers of truth. But, as we may appreciate, every seeker after truth is different in temperament, in personality, in mental and in spiritual strength. Therefore, there are several *sadhanas* or techniques available to the seeker on the path of spiritual growth.

There are literally hundreds of *sadhanas* or means that one can undertake in pursuit of spiritual growth: we can take to prayer, which is one of the simplest and easiest; we can take to *puja* or organised ritual worship; we can choose *dhyana* or meditation, which is nothing but a journey inward in pursuit of truth; we can choose *japa yoga*, which is intensely focused chanting of a sacred *mantra; naam smaran* (*naam simran* as it is known in Sikhism) is one of the simplest and most effective; there are tougher austerities too, like fasting, penance, *tapasya* and so on.

Why should we practice *sadhana?* What will it achieve for us? What will we get out of it? These are questions that many people ask themselves when they hear about *sadhana* and its necessity for the seeker.

If these questions arise in your mind too, I can offer you a simple answer: there is a simple input-output ratio that operates in *sadhana*; you will get as much out of it as yo u put into it! Put in sincerity, dedication, commitment, faith and perseverance: and you will achieve your goal – indeed, you will achieve much more than you expect, with the grace of God.

Always do some *sadhana* no matter how short, because every effort of the individual mind to meet the Universal Self is reciprocated a thousand-fold.

– Yogi Bhajan

At this point, you may come up with yet another question: if the grace of God is all that it is described to be, why should we fritter away our effort in *sadhanas*? Isn't it better to leave our spiritual growth in His safe hands, and just live our daily life? Moreover, our saints and sages tell us that spiritual progress can only happen with the grace of God. Isn't it better for that Divine grace to drop from heaven on us like the gentle rain?

To this question too, I have a simple answer: why wait for God's grace when you are not sure whether you have deserved it by your actions in this birth and in all the countless births that have gone before this one? His grace is sure to come to you when you work for it sincerely; *God helps those who help themselves,* is not just a commonplace statement; it is the proven truth. The great saints and sages of this land undertook the greatest austerities and penances to grow in the life of the spirit; then can we show reluctance to undertake a few disciplines for such a great goal?

Let us look at a few of the simple *sadhanas* I mentioned:

Prayer

At its simplest, prayer is turning to God. At its most mystic, prayer is stopping the current of your worldly life to give a few moments to God exclusively!

Prayer is reposing all your faith in God; not helplessly, in passive submission, but with active, dynamic faith that your life is safe in His hands.

We know what it is to pray. We know the efficacy of prayer. We know how powerful prayer is. We know, in the words of the poet Tennyson, "More things are wrought by prayer than this world dreams of." And yet we do not pray.

Why don't we pray? That is the question. Why don't we pray? Whenever we are in trouble, whenever we are hard pressed, when we are surrounded by adverse circumstances, when we are passing through a dark night when not a single star doth shine, when we suffer from a disease that the doctors declare as incurable, when we face a financial crisis and are on the verge of bankruptcy, when we are involved in problems of personal relationships – what do we do? We call upon friends; we run to our relatives; we turn to our lawyers, doctors, to government and police officers – but we don't go to God. Ah, the question is, why don't we pray?

On my travels as a pilgrim, I have often put this question before people I meet. One of the reasons they give me is, "We live in a world of stress and strain. Ours is an excited, agitated age. We carry so many worries, so many anxieties, so many fears in our hearts. We do not even have the time to pause for breath – how do we find the time to pray?"

My friends, you find time for everything else. You attend to your business or profession. You make time for family and friends. You set aside time for parties, picnics and movies. How is it that you cannot set aside 15 minutes out of your busy schedule, to sit quietly and commune with God?

We need to know God. We need to move close to Him. We need to make God real in our daily lives. And prayer is the one *sadhana* that can help us achieve this.

Let us pray again and again. Let us pray without ceasing. Prayer is the health of the soul, the strength of Life. It had been truly said that if we do not pray for a day, we miss something. If we do not pray for a week, we become weak!

Pray, pray! But remember that your prayer must be backed by your life, by your daily actions. If you pray in the morning, as you take up your position on the battlefield of life, and your actions do not bear witness to the prayer that you have offered, you are no better than a hypocrite. Therefore, let your actions bear witness! It is actions that God asks of us. It is life that he wants, not words. Therefore, let me close with the words of the great English poet: "He prayeth best who loveth best both bird and man and beast."

Meditation

The word "meditation" is derived from the Latin root which means "to heal". The healing, calming, de-stressing technique of meditation is essential to the seeker on the path of *sadhana*.

Some scholars say that the root of the word 'meditation' is similar to the root of medicine and medicate — which means "paying attention to" something. When we meditate, we pay attention to those depths in our being which are not known to the people outside – which are, perhaps not familiar even to ourselves! Thus meditation has been described as a process of inner attention.

While many regard meditation as a difficult art, it is actually quite simple. Meditation is directing our attention to the Eternal and keeping it there for a while. Within every one of us is a realm of peace, power, perfection. Through practice, we can, at will, enter this realm and contact God. When we do so, we become conscious of infinite power, a wondrous peace, and realise that everything is perfect and in its own place.

Like all spiritual experiences, meditation is something that cannot come to us from without. It is true, in the early stages of our spiritual unfolding, the "exterior" life, in a large measure, does shape the "interior" life. What we think and feel, what we read and hear, what we do and speak during the day, is echoed within us in the hours of silence. So it is that we must take the greatest care of our outer life. We must keep watch over our thoughts and feelings, our aspirations and desires, and our words and deeds.

Meditation is gazing inward by opening another aperture of the mind. It is turning away from all outer objects to seek Him whom the *rishis* call *Ekam evadvityam* — the One without a second, the One and only Reality. Meditation is entering upon the interior pilgrimage in which layer after layer of unreality is to be torn. The pilgrim, therefore, proceeds by negation: *neti, neti,* not this, not this! These are not God: I seek Him alone!

Let me also warn you, meditation is not mere escapism. If we wish to run away from our responsibilities, duties, commitments and obligations, as well as our problems and sufferings, meditation is not the answer. Our frustrations and failures and disappointments will not equip us to take on the spiritual discipline that meditation requires.

Meditation is a process of self-awakening through which we connect ourselves to God. *Dhyana Yoga*, as it is called is nothing but establishing our rightful union with God, as God's children. It enables us to be receptive to God's voice, which can only be heard in inner stillness. In His voice is true wisdom; in His message to us is true Peace. Meditation leads us on to this Divine Peace.

Meditation is not the same as reflection, contemplation or introspection — though all of these may be useful aids in preparing for meditation. Some people even spend hours with closed eyes, fantasising; or stare vacantly with open eyes, daydreaming. These are certainly not to be confused with meditation.

Some people describe meditation as an art; others call it a science. It would be truer to say that it is a process or technique by which we link ourselves with the highest state of "awareness" or "consciousness" that we can reach.

To grow in the inner life, the life of the Spirit, we need to withdraw from the outer world of noise and excitement. Therefore, we stress on the practice of silence everyday. Each day, we must spend some time—at least an hour—in silence. At the very start, perhaps, it will be difficult to sit in silence for an hour at a stretch. Then it would be well if we practise silence for about a quarter of an hour, four times a day.

In due course, the mind will become calm and clear as the surface of a lake on a windless day. Such a mind will become a source of indescribable joy and peace. Significant are the words of the Upanishad: "The mind alone is the cause of man's bondage: the mind is, also an instrument of man's liberation."

Naam Smaran

The spiritual aspirant needs to draw closer to God day by day. How may we achieve this closeness? The answer is to keep memory; to remember the true homeland of the soul from whence we came and to which we must all return.

Think of God in any form that draws you. He is the Formless One, but for the sake of His devotees, He has worn many forms and visited the earth-plane again and again. Call Him by any name that appeals to you. He is the Nameless One, though the sages have called Him by many Names. Do not quarrel over Forms or Names. You stick to the One that draws you: let others stick to the One that draws them. All forms and names ultimately lead to the One who is beyond the form and the formlessness. "On whatever path men approach Me," says the Lord in the Gita, "on that I go to meet them – for all the paths are Mine, verily Mine!"

Sitting in silence, let us repeat the Divine Name or meditate on some aspect of the Divine Reality or on an incident in the life of a man of God. God, it s true, is Nameless: but the sages have called Him by many Names. Choose any Name that appeals to you: repeat it again and again. Repeat the Name— yes, but not merely with the tongue. Repeat it with tears in the eyes. Repeat it until you can repeat it no longer, until you disappear from yourself, your "ego" is dissolved, and you sit in the presence of the Eternal Beloved.

The Name of God is like the waters of the Ganga. The River Ganga is like a mother: Ganga Ma! It purifies those that bathe in it. As you come out of the waters of the River Ganga of the Name Divine you will feel cleansed, washed, purified. Impure thoughts and sinful impulses wake up in the mind, again and again. Never yield to them, but sing the Name of God – not in a mechanical way, but with deep feeling and emotion of the heart. Pour into the unclean mind, the purifying Ganga of the Name Divine. Purity is needed. Whenever an unclean thought comes to you, immediately, in that very instant, say to yourself, "I was made for greater, nobler, loftier things: I shall not be a bundle of unclean, impure desires," and start repeating the pure Name of God.

The Name of God is at once pure and purifying. It purifies those that sing it with deep love and longing of the heart.

> Discipline helps good thoughts and qualities
> to develop, which in turn leads to *Shraddha* or
> awareness in action. For one who has *Shraddha*,
> everything becomes *Puja* (worship). Nothing will
> be wasted, everything will be practical.
>
> – Sri Amritanandamayi Ma

I sometimes think of the Name Divine as a locked door. If only we can open it, we, too, may live in the abiding presence of the Beloved. The way to open it is the Way of Love.

We may, also, meditate on some form of God as we utter the Name Divine – on Krishna or Christ, on Buddha or Nanak, on a Saint or a Holy One. There should, however, be no attachment to the Form: all Forms, ultimately, have to be left behind. Significant are the words of Meister Eckhart: "He who seeks God under a settled Form lays hold of the Form, while missing the God concealed in it." Meditate on the Form to which you feel drawn, and then go beyond it. Enter into the Form to meet the Formless One!

Our lives need to be renewed, if possible, daily – through contact with God. The rain of God's mercy pours everyday; and those of us who receive it are washed clean, renewed and re-strengthened for the struggle of life. May I suggest to you a simple exercise? Every morning, as you sit in silence, close your eyes and imagine the Life of God coursing through every part of your body, filling it through and through. The Life of God is in us already: we have to be conscious of it. Say to yourself: *Every moment the Life of God –* call Him by what Name you will, Krishna, Buddha, Christ, Guru Nanak: they are all so many names of Him who is Nameless – *is filling every nerve and cell and fibre of my being!*

Mantra Jaap

A *mantra* is a sacred utterance; it is specially associated with India's great ancient scriptures, the *Vedas*, which are a collection of hymns and sacred utterances that have survived for millennia through oral transmission. Thus, a *mantra* is linked with oral utterance; its special powers are in the depth of its meaning as much as in the sound vibrations it produces in oral recital. Thus many people believe that there is a transformative power associated with the *mantra*, which can bring about a spiritual transformation.

In Hinduism, it is a sacred verbal formula repeated in prayer, meditation or incantation, such as an invocation of a God, a verse from the ancient scriptures, or even a syllable or portion of a scriptural utterance containing mystical potentialities.

What is the significance of a *mantra*?

Every word has power. Some words have less, some have more. A *mantra* is a word or a combination of words which have great power. If you recite a *mantra*, again and again, you release tremendous spiritual energy which, among other things, helps you to concentrate your wandering mind. The mind, as we know, has this tendency to keep on wandering all the time! As the mind wanders, we wander with the mind. This wandering is the root cause of our unhappiness. If the mind is still or focussed, we grow in peace of mind which is the secret of true happiness.

Normally, the rays of the sun do not have the power to burn. But if a number of rays are brought to a focus at a point, fire can be produced. Likewise with the mind. If it can be concentrated on one word, one idea or one set of powerful words, tremendous power is released. And the mind, in addition to what is happening outside, can know many things that are happening inside.

Naam is individual, *mantra* is universal. Usually *Naam* remains a secret and is to be repeated in a particular way. The *mantra* can be repeated by anyone in the way that he chooses.

Any *mantra* or Holy Name or Word or Syllable that draws you may be taken up. God is the Nameless One: the sages have called Him by many Names. All Names will lead you to the Nameless One. There is the ancient *mantra*, "*Om*" or "*Rama*". There is the *maha-mantra*, "*Hare Rama, Hare Rama, Rama, Rama, Hare, Hare; Hare Krishna, Hare Krishna, Krishna, Krishna, Hare, Hare*".There are other *mantras*: "*Om Namoh Bhagavate Vaasudevaaya*", "*Om Namah Shivaaya*", "*Om Sri Rama, Jaya Rama, Jaya, Jaya, Rama*", "*Rama Krishna Hari*", "*Satnaam*", "*Waheguru*", "*Om Mani Padme Hum*", "Jesus", "Lord Jesus Christ, have mercy on me", "*Jehovaah*", "*Allah*", "*Ahura Mazda*". The list is endless. Choose your favourite *mantra*; choose one that has a special appeal to you; choose one that suits your need; having chosen it, make it your own; internalise its energy, its positive vibrations and its life-giving pulse. Repeat it constantly until it becomes part of your consciousness. Believe me, it can transform your life!

Naam smaran, mantra japa, kirtan and *dhyana* are at the very foundation of *abhyasa*. Together, they quiet the agitated mind, cleanse the mind of all its impurities, leaving us calm and serene to enter into meditation.

Pranayama

The meaning of *pranayama* is explained thus: *prana* means "life force or energy" and *yama* means "control of that energy". Some scholars interpret this as *ayama*, meaning "expansion" – in this case *pranayama* is "extension or expansion" of the flow of energy.

Prana also means "primary energy" – the life that animates the universe. Thus there is the indelible link between man and the universe, for the same life-force is manifest in both. Further, it is the breath which links the body and the mind. Hence its importance to mental, physical and spiritual well-being cannot be under estimated.

Prana or breath is the primary energy of life. It is this which links the body with the mind. Hence its importance to our mental, physical and spiritual well-being.

Pranayama is a unique, systematic deep-breathing exercise, associated with *yoga* and meditation. When it is practised properly, it enables the lungs to absorb optimum levels of oxygen so as to purify the blood, and ease the strain on the heart.

Deep breathing brings immense benefits to us, including a stable mind, steady thinking, inner peace, good health and a longer life.

> Sow in the field of your heart the seeds of good
> thoughts, charged with humility; irrigate it with
> the waters of love; protect the growing crop
> with the pesticide called courage; feed the crop
> with the fertiliser of concentration; then the
> *bhakti* plants will yield the harvest of *jnana*, the
> eternal wisdom, that you are He, and when that
> revelation comes, you become He, for you were
> always He, though you did not know it so far.
> – Sri Sathya Sai Baba, Sadhana:
> *The Inward Path*

Which is the right way for me?

As we saw earlier, the Lord tells us of three
margas in the Gita: the path of knowledge or *jnana
marga*, the path of action or *karma marga*, and finally,
the path of devotion or *bhakti marga*, are all revealed
to Arjuna by the Lord. He has been allowed to raise
questions and clear his doubts. Repeatedly, he has
asked the Lord: "Which path is the best?" Sri Krishna
has assured him that all the paths can lead to the
liberation of the soul. Yet again Arjuna asks of the
Lord: Who is a better *yogi* – the one who combines
devotion with action, or the one who combines
devotion with knowledge? For Sri Krishna had
earlier said that the *yoga* of knowledge is difficult
to accomplish – whereas the one who follows the
path of action can realise the Supreme Reality

successfully. Now, Arjuna wants to know which one of these would go hand in hand with the path of devotion.

Sri Krishna in His considered reply arranges the different disciplines both in the order of their intrinsic excellence, and also in the order of their ease of performance for the aspirant. What He emphasises is that though one of the paths may be intrinsically superior to the other, it is of no use if aspirants cannot practise them well. Thus the focus shifts to the receptivity, the response, the ability of the *sadhaka* or the seeker. The preference and the aptitude of the aspirant thus becomes the criterion for the path that is to be selected. Sri Krishna relates the various techniques to achieve self-realisation:

- On Me alone fix your mind; let your understanding dwell in Me.

- If you are not able to fix your thoughts steadily on Me, try to reach Me through the practice of concentration and meditation.

- If you are unable to do this, you can attain to Me even by performing actions for My sake.

- If you are unable to do even this, then taking refuge in Me, renounce attachment with the fruits of all actions.

Thus, we may see that the different paths to attain the Supreme Reality are placed in order:

1. Comprehension of the Supreme Reality through Rational Understanding.

2. Concentration on the Supreme Reality through Meditation.

3. Performing actions that are dedicated to God.

4. Performing actions desirelessly and selflessly – without expectation of results.

5. Single-minded devotion to God.

The *jnana marga* is the most difficult and the final one, the way of surrender, is perhaps the simplest, easiest – and the one that is accessible to us all! Those of us who are at a higher stage of spiritual evolution, may proceed from knowledge to devotion. But for the rest of us, devotion must be the starting point to attain Divine Knowledge, and the first step of spiritual discipline.

The marvellous thing about the Gita is that it tells us to choose the path that appeals to us, the one that suits us best. This is in tune with the liberalism, pragmatism and freedom from dogma that characterises *sanatana dharma* at its best. What matters is the spiritual discipline that enables one to reach the goal – not its technique or methodology. In fact, Sri Krishna assures us that none of us can go astray if we follow any one of the paths: *In whatever way people approach Me, on that way I meet them.*

In the final chapter of the Gita, the Lord integrates the paths to utter the final secret to Arjuna:

> Fix thy mind on Me; be devoted to Me; sacrifice to Me; prostrate thyself before Me. So shalt thou come to Me. I pledge thee My troth; thou art dear to Me.
> [XVIII-65]

And, even more emphatically:

> Abandoning all rites and writ duties, come unto Me alone for refuge. Grieve not! I shall liberate thee from all sins.
>
> [XVIII-66]

This is the final and most inspiring message of the Gita. It is also the quintessence of spiritual discipline. This is not escapism; this is not shifting our responsibility on to God; in fact the Lord has insisted that we should never shirk our duties – rather, we must free our mind from egoism and desire. Divine grace is obtained through unconditional surrender to the Lord. The Lord should be made the single goal of our life, the sole object of our worldly endeavours.

To me this is what spirituality is all about.

For Your Reflection

A Simple *Sadhana* for All: *Kirtan Yoga*

Singing the Name Divine is the surest, easiest way to become completely harmonised in the Lord! It achieves the impossible, by keeping all our senses under control! We are singing or chanting; we are listening to others chanting around us; our hands are folded together in tribute, or we are clapping gently in rhythm with the chanting; we keep our eyes closed in the involvement of the *kirtan*; or we are gazing at the radiant face of the Guru or focusing on the image of our *ishta devata*; the tongue is tasting the nectar of the Name Divine; the smell of incense and *agarbattis* fills the air; it is a feast divine for all the senses!

A western scholar of Hindu beliefs and practices actually describes this as *kirtan yoga*! It is easy, simple and practical; all of us can practice it effortlessly!

Singing the Name Divine in groups is particularly beneficial. It cleanses and heals body, mind and soul. It clears your aura. It paves the way for the Life Beautiful! Therefore, dear brothers and sisters, let us all chant and sing the Name Divine— not mechanically, but with love and devotion!

There are two types of '*kirtan*'. One, in which you simply chant the Name Divine; the other in describing and singing His glories. The first type of *kirtan* is what you do for a few minutes in *satsang*. *Kirtan* should not be limited to time. It should not be bound by the minutes and hours. *Kirtan* should be continuous; it should bring joy and ecstasy to the group chanting. *Kirtan* is spiritually elevating! When continued for a long time, it spreads its beautiful, peaceful vibrations and uplifts the soul!

The second type of *kirtan* is singing the glories of the Lord, such as describing the *'Leela'* of Krishna in Brindaban! His miraculous birth, His *raas leela* with the *gopis*; His games with cowherds; His tantalising ways! Singing those glories of the Lord or even thinking about Him is also a form of *kirtan!*

For *kirtan* only one thing is absolutely essential: devotion for the Lord and yearning for His Lotus Feet. Devotion comes with faith. Devotion or *bhakti* is an emotional upsurge. It powers us from within. It comes with a certain conviction. The chant by itself or singing by itself does not purify you. It is your *bhava* — your emotion which will release the subtle forces of cleansing that will purify your inner instrument and elevate your soul to sublime heights of *bhakti*. Ultimately it is your intense devotion which will kindle the yearning for the Lord. This is the beginning of true transformation. This is when you see the spark of Divine Light which dispels the darkness of the *kaliyuga* that is enveloping you on the outside.

Kirtan is 'Sahaj Marg' – it is an easy path. You can do *kirtan* anywhere, anytime of the day. You can think of the life of great ones, anywhere and anytime of the day. The beautiful thoughts about the Radiant Ones will purify your interior and a day will come when you will behold the golden light within!

Milarepa's Ordeal

It is not an easy task to prepare the disciple for the spiritual journey! Most true disciples will tell you how they passed through their own ordeal of fire – their personal agni pariksha – before they were accepted, initiated by the Guru.

What an ordeal Milarepa had to pass through before he attained the grace of the Guru! His determination and perseverance are truly heroic, and serve as an inspiration to millions of seekers even today – a whole millennium after his life.

Milarepa was a great Tibetan yogi, whose name is synonymous with Guru bhakti. His story is truly inspiring. One day, Milarepa goes to his Guru, Marpa, and begs to be accepted as a disciple. Marpa asks him, "Do you have sufficient faith?"

Milarepa answers with humility, "Master, my faith in you is beyond words."

The Guru wants to put his disciple to a test. "Here are some rocks," he tells Milarepa. "Build a meditation tower at this spot."

Milarepa sets to work immediately. He builds a sturdy and aesthetically pleasing tower with steady and strenuous labour. He is certain that it will please his Guru. When the Guru arrives to see it, he exclaims, "What a fool you are, Milarepa! You have wasted your time and energy. I did not want a tower here, at this corner, but there, at that corner!"

A few more days of strenuous labour – and the second tower is ready. Once again, the Guru expresses his dissatisfaction. "You are an idiot! I did not want the tower here!"

Milarepa controls his frustration and disappointment. He builds a third tower – it meets the same fate, the same rejection from the Guru.

The process is repeated several times. And Milarepa, as we say, has reached the end of his tether. He loses his optimism, his patience and all hope of advancement. His faith is completely shaken. He only wants to run away from the Guru – never to return.

The Guru's wife learns of his despair. She comes to his rescue. "The Guru is only testing you!" she says to him. "It was you who told him that your faith in him was beyond words – limitless as the sky. Where has your faith gone?"

Milarepa's faith is renewed. He builds yet another tower. When it is ready, the Guru embraces him, saying,

"You are truly my child. Let me share with you the secret which I have shared with none else!"

Milarepa sits at the feet of the Guru and receives from him what only a Guru can pass on to his disciple. He is enlightened. He is emancipated from the seemingly endless cycle of birth-death-rebirth.

Chapter Nine
The Dark Night Of The Soul

As the seeker moves on the path of the Spirit, there are periods when he feels utterly depressed and despondent. He feels that he belongs neither here nor there. It is as though he is passing through a parched, dry desert. Nothing appeals to him: Everything appears dull, dark, profoundly pessimistic...

Some of the early mystics have called this phase the dark night of the soul.

Do you know, there is one of our most loved scriptures that actually opens on this very note. The first *adhyaya* of the Gita, as Sadhu Vaswani points out, is a section on Arjuna's profound feeling of despair and depression — *Arjuna Vishada Yoga*. Indeed, the first step in spiritual life is *vishada* — darkness of the soul.

Anyone who has ever set out in quest of the life spiritual will tell you this: they pass through this

period characterised as "the dark night of the soul
At the very first step we take on the spiritual path
we cry out in sorrow, "What is the meaning of life
What does it all mean? Why are we here? Whither d
we go from here?"

> There is no coming to consciousness without
> pain. People will do anything, no matter how
> absurd, to avoid facing their own soul. One does
> not become enlightened by imagining figures
> of light, but by making the darkness conscious.
> – Carl Gustav Jung

Even Jesus cried out, "My God! My God! Why
hast Thou forsaken me?"

Did not Draupadi too, experience this darkness
of the soul when she cried out, "All have left me,
my kinsmen, my brothers, my father – even You, O
Krishna!"

All of us must pass through a period of loneliness
and internal conflict before we can enter into self-
knowledge, true awareness of the self. It is in this
loneliness that we can shed our ego, and realise that
we are not alone.

And so, Arjuna the great hero, Arjuna, the
brave warrior, stands confounded on the field of

Kurukshetra.

> My limbs fail, my mouth is parched, my body
> quivers, my hair stands on end. My Gandiva bow
> slips from my hand and my skin burns all over; I
> am not able to stand steady; my brain is reeling.
> [I: 29 – 30]

Arjuna is sad and lonely. His mind is agitated;
his consciousness is clouded. This hero of a hundred
fights, suddenly begins to suffer from nervous fright.

It is not the possibility of defeat or victory that
agitates Arjuna. His mind is torn by doubts and fears
and anxieties.

Let us note here that Duryodhana is not in the
least bothered by such worries. Never, ever does
he reflect upon the injustice or *adharma* of his cause.
He simply does not differentiate between good
and evil.

But then, the Gita is not addressed to Duryodhana.
It is addressed to Arjuna, who in this great war
between good and evil, stands firmly on the side
of *dharma*. He has made the choice between good
and evil long ago—but now, he is torn asunder by a
seemingly irresolvable conflict.

Arjuna, like so many of us, is bewildered by the
choice he has to make. He is in the grip of uncertainty.

He faces the classic dilemma —to act or not to act.

It is only the honest, conscientious people who are forced to confront such perplexing situations. As for selfish, unscrupulous men, they are guided and motivated only by their own desires and narrow interests.

Truly has it been said by innumerable commentators that the 'battle' here is not a fight between armies, but a war within a soul. They tell us that the chariot symbolises the body, in which the mind (Arjuna) is seated, along with Sri Krishna, the *Atman,* the Self. The horses symbolise the five senses. And Kurukshetra is the plane of action, the plane of friction, the world of strife and contradictions that we inhabit. Therefore, have the wise ones taught us that life on earth is a battle, and all of us must fight the good fight, for the just cause.

True – when we fight others, we hurt them, we harm them, we inflict violence on them. And even when we conquer our near and dear ones, we lose! But when we chose to fight all that is base and weak and selfish and petty within us – we cannot help but win! This is what happens when we tread the path of spirituality with courage and conviction.

> **Facing the darkness, admitting the pain, allowing the pain to be pain, is never easy. This is why courage – big-heartedness – is the most essential virtue on the spiritual journey. But if we fail to let pain be pain – and our entire patriarchal culture refuses to let this happen – then pain will haunt us in nightmarish ways. We will become pain's victims instead of the healers we might become.**
> **– Mathew Fox,**
> ***Original Blessing***

It was Swami Ramdas who said, "There is no greater victory in the life of a human being than victory over the mind...The true soldier is he who fights not the external, but the internal foes."

Fortunately for Arjuna, Sri Krishna holds the reins of the chariot – for God is always on man's side in the fight against evil. So when Arjuna says, "I will not fight," and sinks into silence and despair, Sri Krishna is at hand to guide him with words of wisdom. "Weep not," the Master tells His dear, devoted disciple, "but be a man, a master-man! Abandon weakness! Stand up in courage! Stand up and fight!"

Sadhu Vaswani emphasised the heroic note in the Gita. He called the Gita, the "Song of strength", the "Song of *shakti*".

Uttishta! Paramtapa! Stand up, Arjuna!

Each one of us is called upon to fulfill our tasks in life. To fight the good fight, as I have said repeatedly. Evil is within us, evil is outside us. Everywhere, there are wrongs to be righted, weaknesses to be fought and conquered. We cannot say, "I will not fight!"

The Lord tells us, even as He tells Arjuna: "Stand up and fight! For life is a battlefield."

Stand up and fight evil! Stand up and fight injustice! Conquer the ego! Vanquish your weaknesses!

The message of the Gita is the message of courage, heroism and *atma shakti*. It is this *shakti* that we need to overcome despair, doubt and pessimism on the spiritual path. The Gita teaches us that weakness is a sin, while *shakti* is a spiritual virtue.

There is yet another significant fact that we may note. It is often thought that the divine religious teachings of Hinduism, the *Vedas* and the *Upanishads*, originated in the *tapobana* or the forests of meditation. The Gita, which contains the essence of the *Upanishads*, was on the contrary, delivered on the battleground. The symbolical inference we must draw is this: the great Hindu teachings are not just meant for renunciates who have withdrawn from the world: they are dynamic, vital; they represent the science of Action, no less than the science of Reflection and Contemplation. The Gita's message is not for meditation alone; it is for deeds of daily life; it is for action; it is for you and me.

Why does Arjuna fall a prey to such confusion, despair and dejection? He has been the hero of many battles, and until this point, has not felt any doubts or reservations about this war, which he has resolved to face as a sacred duty and obligation, as a fight against evil and unrighteousness.

Until the crucial moment Arjuna asks his Divine charioteer to drive him to the middle space between the two armies, Arjuna was firm in his resolve, steadfast in his determination, unshakeable in his faith.

Arjuna is no coward; nor is he foolish, unwise. From social, ethical as well as the narrow worldly point of view, he marshals his arguments to prove that the battle he is about to fight is not really worthwhile.

Arjuna is not suffering from momentary weakness or fear. He is in fact passing through a deep spiritual crisis caused by the realisation that the social, moral, religious and ethical values that he had always cherished as precious and dear to his heart, are suddenly crumbling down all around him. The fundamental principles of his life are challenged by the disturbing reality of the situation he finds himself in.

Such a crisis can come to only noble souls. The unthinking, insensitive, average person does not face such despair or indecision. It only happens to a person whose faith in his values is threatened.

Do we really have to be in a state of such utter despair and dejection before we attain wisdom? Arjuna's despair is no ordinary despair – it is not for nothing that it is called *Vishada Yoga* – or the *yoga* of despair. To feel such acute despair is also a step in the process of *yogic* achievement. It is not a state of *tamas* – slothful inaction – leading to utter frustration. It is the *yoga* of despondency which develops into a deep spiritual quest for the truth. It is an awakening of the consciousness that the mind must evolve beyond its narrow confines and expand its consciousness.

> **Place no hope in the feeling of assurance, in spiritual comfort. You may well have to get along without this. Place no hope in the inspirational preachers of Christian sunshine, who are able to pick you up and set you back on your feet and make you feel good for three or four days – until you fold up and collapse into despair. Self-confidence is a precious natural gift, a sign of health. But it is not the same thing as faith. Faith is much deeper, and it must be deep enough to subsist when we are weak, when we are sick, when our self-confidence is gone, when our self-respect is gone.**
> **– Thomas Merton**

The time of spiritual awakening, which puts you on the path of self-growth, is an exhilarating experience to begin with. Walking on this path, you feel that you are making your life meaningful and worthwhile; you are happy to walk this path. But, you must know, no path is straight and smooth. It has its share of obstacles, steep gradients, unexpected curves and bends. So too with the path of life. A single trauma can shatter you, and make you feel helpless and ruined. Despair and melancholy constantly seem to wait on you. Troubles and anxieties surround you. At such times, you feel abandoned, your faith becomes vulnerable.

Sri Ramakrishna Paramahansa would often tell his disciples, that there is no magic in turning milk into *ghee*. If you want *ghee*, (as every housewife in those days would tell you) you have to go through the process of making *ghee*. First you have to boil the milk, then remove the cream, store the cream and make it into curd, then separate out its 'whey', churn the solid into butter and then melt it to get *ghee*. The same is true of an aspirant. He has to put in his own effort and go through a process. The 'bliss' is to be earned. There is no magic wand, or magic formula, which will bring it to you 'in an instant'.

The same is true of 'blessings'. The blessings of a saint or a holy one, are to be earned and earned the

hard way. By merely calling out, "Bless me, bless me,"
you will not be showered with the blessings you seek.
Let me say to you, even to get the blessings of a saint's
glance, you have to work hard – through devotion,
humility and service.

Gurudev Sadhu Vaswani urged us to study and
follow the norms and the spiritual regimen strictly.
He said,

> By merely jumping into the ocean
> You do not get oysters with pearls:
> Dive deep into the ocean,
> Dive tirelessly and you will find
> The invaluable treasure of pearls that you seek.

Ask any pearl-diver, and he will tell you that in
order to dive deep, you have to take the requisite
training. You have to learn swimming; you have to
acquire the special skill of diving underwater; and you
have to develop an eye for the oysters with pearls!
You have to go through a long and tedious learning
process, before you can even spot, leave alone lay
your hands, on a pearl!

Is this not true of all human endeavours? It is true
of our learning to walk. A toddler just learns to crawl
at first; then he takes a few steps with support, then
he steadies himself and learns to walk and finally
learns to run. During this learning process, the child

tumbles and falls, often bruising and hurting himself, before he is able to acquire the skill of walking steadily and straight.

This journey on the path of *abhyasa* is difficult. There are pebbles and stones and thorns on the way; there are hills and tunnels to cross – there is the dark night of the soul to go through.

Do not despair at the hurdles on this journey! Let me assure you, at the end of the tunnel is the light; after the strenuous climb, there is the peak of panoramic view. So do not give in to despair, if you fall and hurt yourself. Sri Krishna says, "O Arjuna, none of your efforts will be wasted. This path is the right one. It is also beneficial for all."

Nothing in this universe goes waste. Every effort brings its reward. Hence do not despair. Put in your effort and see the magic happen! Gurudev Sadhu Vaswani has outlined for us, the regimen to be followed on this path.

The first discipline to be observed is *naam simran*, chanting the Name Divine.

The second discipline is *dhyaan* or meditation.

The third discipline is *kirtan*, singing the glories of the Lord!

The fourth discipline is prayer with devotion.

The fifth discipline is service to mankind.

Chanting the Name Divine, cleanses us o all 'interior' filth and ugliness. It takes away th negativity that is deep within us. Meditation create inner spaces into which we might receive Divine vibrations. *Kirtan* helps us to bond with the Cosmi Divine Energy. It attracts Divine Light, because praising the Lord, singing His glories is a way o: acknowledging His Presence. Prayer too, is a form of connectivity. It links you with the Divine Source. Selfless service, performed in humility, is the purpose of this human birth, and it is our bounden duty to see that it is fulfilled. As Gurudev Sadhu Vaswani has said, "Service of the poor is worship of God".

It is true, there are difficulties in following these five disciplines. But, I repeat, there is no need to give in to despair. Give yourself time. For example, chanting the Name Divine is a cleansing process, but a slow one. Meditation too, is difficult, as the nature of this human mind is to wander in many directions. Hence, choose the image of a holy one, and try to meditate on that physical object. Slowly the physical object will fade away, leaving the Divine Cosmic space, and you will learn to meditate on the Abstract Invisible Infinite! Meditation, as I have stressed repeatedly, is best done at the *Brahma Mahurat* — early dawn. Just try to meditate early in

e morning, for a week, and you will be amazed at
e change within you!

Let me warn you, once again; the way of the
spiritual aspirant is not all roses; there are thorns too.
We must therefore cultivate the spirit of acceptance;
we must accept joys and sorrows, triumph and failure,
ps and downs; in the midst of these *dwandas* (binary
opposites) of this world, we must still keep our faith
intact! He who would walk the way of the *atman*
must be prepared to accept suffering and starvation,
poverty and pain, and in the midst of it all, give
gratitude to God.

The way of the *atman* is not always easy. Life is
a challenge, which must be met with the weapon of
faith. Illness may come unto you; death may stare you
in the face; your dear ones may let you down when
you need their support desperately. You may have to
face storms of misunderstanding. Disappointments
may crowd around you. Your friends may scoff at
you, laugh behind your back and call you a fool.
Occasionally, they may even taunt you, "Where is
your God?" And, in the day of your anguish and
misery, you yourself may say, in the heart within, "I
can bear it no longer! I am broken in body, mind and
spirit! In this big, wide world, there is none whom I
can call my own. I feel forsaken as a beaten, battered
boat on a stormy sea! Not this path for me!"

If you survive this period of despair and frustration — and believe me, you can do so through constant prayer and repetition of the name of God you arrive at a stage of blessedness. Your struggle will be over. With you it will no longer be a matter of hope or faith or trust — it will be a matter of knowledge. You begin to *know* that you are in God Hands and that He will provide for you at the right place, at the right time!

Is it not true that we often imagine God being deaf, dumb and blind to our miserable cries for help "Comforter, where is Thy comforting?" we call, in the words of the poet. Little do we realise that He is there *with* us, working *through* us, to perform His miracles We may not see how He works, but He is sure to help us out of our suffering. It is this profound truth that i expressed in the words of the Lord in the Gita: *Know this for certainty, Arjuna: My devotee is never lost.* All we have to do is cling to Him in faith and hope: He will not, indeed He *cannot* let us down!

Exercise in Awareness

How can we cultivate the faith that can help us cross the dark night? So let me pass on to you a few practical suggestions:

1. The first essential thing is a change of outlook. As it is, we depend too much on ourselves, our own efforts and endeavours. We keep God out of the picture. True, human effort has its place in life. But we need to understand that above all efforts is His Will. And He is the Giver of all that is! So let not our work be egotistic — but dedicated. Let us learn to work as His agents, the instruments of His Will. Our children are His children. We are here to serve them to the best of our ability and capacity. It is His responsibility to provide for them — may be through us, or others. And His coffers are ever full!

2. The second essential thing is to share what we have with others. Therefore let us set apart a portion — say one-tenth of our earnings to be utilised in the service of God and His suffering creation. This is one of the laws of life — the more we give, the more we get out of the little that remains.

3. Do not be scared of anything. Trust in the Lord and face the battle of life. There is no power on earth that can lay you low.

4. Trust in Him. Turn to Him for everything you need. Make Him your Senior Partner – and success will flow into your life as rivers flow into the sea!

5. We must contact God again and again. It is necessary for us to repeat His Name again and again, to pray without ceasing. A prayer which may prove helpful is, "Lord! Make me a channel of Thy mercy!"

6. To become a channel of His mercy, we must surrender all we are and all we have, at His Lotus-Feet. So may we become His instruments of help and healing in this world of suffering and pain.

Interior cleansing through these measures and simple spiritual disciplines – *naam simran, dhyaan,* prayer, *kirtan* and *seva* – are essential, for we cannot offer God, a dirty, polluted heart. We have to create a beautiful temple, where we can invite Him to reside! Once the cleansing and purification are accomplished, all you have to do is call upon God, with deep devotion and yearning, promising Him, that you will serve Him with dedication – by serving His myriad broken images, the poor and the forlorn of this earth. When you call upon Him, in this state of mind, He will willingly come along and enthrone Himself in the beautiful, pure throne of your heart, and you will experience the Divine Bliss, that the seekers of this ancient land have sought from time immemorial...

He who hath surrendered himself hath found the greatest security of life. And we need wander no more. All his cares and burdens are borne by the Lord Himself. How beautiful are the words of the Gita:

> They who worship Me
> Depending on Me alone,
> Thinking of no other —
> They are My sole responsibility!
> Their burdens are My burdens!
> To them I bring full security!

Good Luck? Bad Luck?

There is a Chinese story of an old farmer, who had an old, weak, ailing horse for ploughing his field. One day, the old horse ran away into the hills.

The farmer's neighbours pursed their lips and offered their sympathy to him. "Such rotten luck!" they remarked.

"Bad luck? Good luck? Who knows?" replied the farmer, philosophically.

A week later, the old horse returned, bringing with it a herd of wild horses from the hills. This time, the neighbours swarmed around the farmer to congratulate him on his good luck.

"Good luck? Bad luck? Who can tell?" was his reply.

Sometime later, while trying to tame one of the wild horses, the farmer's only son fell off its back and broke his leg.

Everyone thought that this was bad luck indeed.

"Bad luck? Good luck? I don't know," said the farmer.

A few weeks later, the king's army marched into the village and conscripted every able-bodied young man living there. The farmer's son, who was laid up with a broken leg, was let off, for he would be of no use to them.

Now what could this be – good luck or bad luck? Who can tell?

Something that seems to be bad on the surface may actually be good in disguise. And something that seems to be attractive and 'lucky' may actually be harmful to our best interests. The wise ones leave it to God to decide what is best for them. They know that all things turn out good for them. They know that all things turn out good for those who love God and accept His Will unconditionally.

Chapter Ten

Advantage Spirituality

"What's in it for me?"

They tell me that this is an age when most people are focused on the I-Me-Myself syndrome. In such a time, I can't blame you for asking me what the path of spirituality will offer you in terms of making you feel good about yourself. Let me add too, that your question is fair and right. If you have read my book this far, you know very well that the picture I have painted is not exactly what the poet called "the primrose path" of dalliance and self-indulgence. It is the path of *shreya*; it is steep and thorny, a tough climb upwards to a higher level of consciousness, a new dimension of life. I am fully aware and I am sure you are too, that you will be investing considerable resolution, will-power, time and effort to tread this path.

You may ask freely, "What's in it for me?" I am sure you are not going to be disappointed with the answer.

> For loosening *karma's* bonds and ending births,
> This path is easier than all other paths.
> Abide in stillness, without any stir
> Of tongue, mind, body. And behold
> The effulgence of the Self within;
> The experience of Eternity; absence
> Of all fear; the ocean vast of Bliss.
> – **Sri Ramana Maharishi** *on Spiritual Knowledge*

Some of you may object to this kind of selfish quid pro quo (reciprocal exchange) attitude on the grounds that it is not compatible with genuine spirituality. I beg to disagree! The Paramacharya of Kanchi once remarked that the pursuit of *atmic* evolution was definitely one of the most self-centred pursuits that one could take up! Well, not self-centred in the worldly sense, but nevertheless relentlessly focussed on one's true self, to the exclusion of others. Just as you can't eat for your dear ones or sleep or rest on their behalf, you cannot undertake spiritual discipline for others' evolution. You can certainly pray for others, work for others' benefit and serve others selflessly. But your *sadhana* cannot be transferred on to others for their development or Liberation. In this matter, it is strictly each one for himself or herself! Great saints and sages can spend their lifetime praying and striving to promote spiritual aspirations in you; but it is *you* who must respond to their call and take the matter up in your own hands. Your Guru can bless you and guide you and bestow his grace upon you; but *you* must work for that grace and deserve it when it is bestowed on you!

But to return to my original question: what are the benefits that will accrue to you when you walk the spiritual path? How will your life improve when you practice spirituality in deeds of daily life?

If you have read about the top athletes of our times, you will know that they undergo the most strenuous physical, mental and emotional discipline to qualify for world events and to even attempt to win those elusive Olympic medals. But I haven't heard any one of them complain that they have worked so hard or made such sacrifices to train themselves for the pursuit of their dreams. They know that true success is to be earned!

Let us pause for a moment and remind ourselves of the goal we have chosen for ourselves on this path; it is nothing less than Union with the Divine. Is this not a goal worth striving for?

> **Incidental causes or actions do not lead to the emergence of attainments or realisation, but rather, come by the removal of obstacles, much like the way a farmer removes a barrier (sluice gate), so as to naturally allow the irrigation of his field.**
>
> **– Maharishi Patanjali,** *Yoga Sutras*

At this point, I would like to remind you of Christ's words: "But seek ye first the Kingdom of God, and His righteousness; and all these things shall be added unto you".

Walk the path of the spiritual seeker, and you will be amazed by all the benefits you reap, here in this workaday world!

1. You will discover your higher self – the self that you were not really aware of, the noble, courageous, better self that is not cowed down by insecurities and limitations. You will find your negativities and fears and complexes dissolving like the proverbial mist before the morning sun. You will discover your Higher self, which, sages agree, is ultimately indefinable, unlimited. In the words of Gurudev Sadhu Vaswani, you will discover that you are

not a weakling, a pathetic creature, but that there is a *shakti* within you which is of infinity! You will become conscious of this magnificent self, as you connect to the Source of all positive power and energy in this Universe, and draw upon His strength to add to your own.

2. You will discover the true joy of life. You will realise that life is a joyous, blessed journey, when you have set for yourself the goal of spiritual evolution. It is a life worth living, because it is leading you onward, forward, Godward!

3. You will discover a subtle change in your perspective that makes you realise that the world is not what you had imagined it to be – an arena of strife and defeat and struggle and pain. Note, I'm not saying that the world will change, but your view of the world will most certainly change for the better. Is not perception more important than fact?

4. In a very subtle way too, you will find yourself taking charge of your own life, becoming the master rather than the slave of your circumstances. Once again, I emphasise that

circumstances may not improve dramatically, but your attitude will, and that makes all the difference!

5. With your changing attitude and new perception, you will rediscover the magic, the wonder that is life. You will take nothing for granted; nothing as given; you will learn to appreciate and be grateful for countless blessings that the Almighty has so generously bestowed on you – including the air you breathe, the wind that caresses you softly, the lovely smile on the face of the children you see in the neighbourhood, the song of the bird, the bloom of the rose, the scent of rain on the earth... and oh, a thousand other things which you will rediscover with a sense of wonder and gratitude!

6. The spirit of gratitude and thanksgiving that this leads you to, will itself transform your life; for as wise men tell us, no one can feel grateful and be unhappy at the same time. And thanksgiving, like positive thinking, generates even more to be thankful for.

7. You will find that walking the path of the seeker will give you a new sense of balance, a new sense of equanimity that enables you to

take on joy and sorrow, triumph and defeat, pain and pleasure and all those vicissitudes of life with an even hand. You will not be cowed down by sorrow; nor will you lose your head with success. You will come to appreciate that joy and sorrow are like sunshine and rain, and we can't do without either.

8. You will attain to that inner peace and harmony, that is greater than all the wealth of this world. And as this is achieved through a change in your thinking and your attitude, it will not be threatened by adverse changes in your external circumstances.

9. You will discover a new sense of purpose in living your life to the fullest, giving, sharing, caring, supporting, sympathising and offering your hand of help and healing to all who come in contact with you. Once again, in the words of Gurudev Sadhu Vaswani, you will realise that life and all its bounties have been given to you as a loan, in a sacred trust, to pour out in service and sacrifice on those less fortunate than you.

10. In connecting thus with your fellow human beings, you will find the wellspring of compassion that is within you. Compassion

is the very crown of all virtues; it ennobles and elevates the healer and the healed; the giver and the receiver. You will therefore find yourself becoming a source of blessing to all around you.

11. You will discover the tremendous joy and peace that are to be found in solitude and silence – two of the greatest gifts that life bestows on the sensitive, thinking individuals. You will find too, that in silence and solitude, you draw ever closer to God.

12. This may sound like a contradiction of what I said just now – but you will find that you never ever feel lonely or isolated! You will realise that you are not alone— that God is ever with you, guiding you, guarding you, watching over you and protecting you with His loving grace.

13. Blessed by the showers of His love and grace, you will find yourself radiating love and peace all around you. The love that envelops you will also extend over your friends and loved ones in the warm glow of its radiance.

14. Love, service, sympathy and sacrifice will so beautify your being that your life will become

a thing of beauty – inner beauty that only grows with age.

15. You will grow in inner strength and faith – the triple faith in yourself, in the universe and in God, which is the key to a truly meaningful life that is well lived in every sense of the term!

What better way to end this section than by invoking the *Shanti Mantra* on all of us, fellow pilgrims on the path:

> *Aum*, may He protect us, may He be pleased with us,
> May we work together with vigour
> May we have no contention or hostility between us.
> *Aum*, peace, peace, peace.

For Your Reflection

Practical Benefits of Everyday Spirituality

Spiritual Practices need not always be ritualistic, esoteric and metaphysical. If you do it with mindfulness, even gardening, cleaning, cooking and washing the dishes can become spiritual activities.

- A spiritual bent of mind gives you focus and clarity even when you have a tight and stressful schedule.

- It improves your concentration and gives you the energy to do routine tasks well.

- It lifts dull and monotonous tasks above their level and makes them joyous activities.

- It gives you a sense of balance, a mindful perspective on life.

- It enables you to live in the here-and-the-now.

Nothing Exists

A highly educated scientist, decided to renounce worldly life and find a Guru who would teach him the truth of the spirit scientifically. He travelled east and west, visiting one master after another, trying to gather scientific evidence for life, existence, perception and reality. He quizzed several holy men and pronounced them unlearned; he entered into loud debates with saints and told them that they were wanting in perception. In short, he found no teacher who could match him in scientific precision and method.

One day, he arrived at the ashram *of a holy man who offered him shelter for the night. As they prepared to retire to sleep, the seeker decided to show the hermit that he was no ordinary wandering ascetic, but a man of high attainment.*

Beginning to show off, as usual, he said to the hermit, "The mind, consciousness, life, death and God are all illusions. Nothing exists except in perception. Can you show me the soul? Have you ever seen the atman? *The true*

ture of phenomena is emptiness. There is no realisation,
delusion, no sage, no salvation. There is no giving and
thing to be received."

The hermit, who was listening to him with eyes closed,
id nothing. Suddenly he whacked the seeker with a small
ne that he had with him.

"Ouch!" exclaimed the scientist. "You stupid, horrid
d man, why did you do that?"

"If nothing exists," inquired the hermit, "where did
is anger come from?"

Chapter Eleven

Science And Spirituality

My friends very kindly refer to me as a "scienti
turned philosopher".

May I say to you in all humility, I do not lay clair
to either epithet! As I have said to you repeatedly,
am a pilgrim on the path, in quest of the truth of th
spirit, and in quest of fellow pilgrims from whom
can learn something new every day.

It is true that my early training has been in th
sciences, and that was before I chose to heed the cal
of the spirit to follow my Guru. All that I am, all that
say and write, I learnt at the feet of my Guru. Indeed
my life has been devoted to spreading his word, his
message in my own humble way.

Once, we put a question to Sadhu Vaswani:
What is true knowledge, the absolute knowledge,
the greatest wisdom? Gurudev Sadhu Vaswani
replied, "True knowledge is the realisation that I am

nothing, He is everything. This realisation makes man humble and gentle. And there is no wisdom greater than this."

"Wilt thou know thyself? Then be not a wanderer abroad. But go within thyself!" he said to us.

What was Gurudev Sadhu Vaswani's message?

Let me answer that question with another question that is often put before me, by scholars and aspirants alike. "Which is Gurudev Sadhu Vaswani's best book?"

My answer is always the same. "Sadhu Vaswani's best book is an unwritten book." For his greatest master piece was not written with pen on parchment, but with his life on the tablets of our hearts. Indeed, his life was his message.

He took upon himself the task of spreading the word of God, and the message of India's ancient Hindu scriptures. He contributed to the revival of the Vedic religion, moving away from rite-and-ritual bound customs and dogmas, dominated by priests. He started Gita classes and Sunday classes where men and women from all walks of life could come and participate in reading, reciting and listening to discussions on the holy scriptures. In the narrow lanes of Hirabad, in Hyderabad-Sind, he single handedly revived the New *Bhakti* Movement, with *naam sankirtan* resounding in the streets, and *prabha* *pheri* in the sacred hours of the dawn.

> **Arise! Awake!**
> **How long will you in slumber lie?**
> – Sadhu Vaswani

His life was one of unceasing service and sacrifice. He worked day after day, wanting nothing for himself, seeking only opportunities to serve the poor, the lowly and the lost. At the advanced age of seventy-nine, his body became weak, but he felt that he had the "strength of ten" because in his heart was love and every fibre of his being thrilled with faith in Man and God.

Gurudev Sadhu Vaswani's teaching, in brief, was that in the love of God and the service of His suffering children (and the birds and animals too, are His children), was the secret of true life. He believed in the unity of races and religions, in the One Spirit. His heart rose in reverence for all saints and prophets of East and West. "My religious philosophy," he said, "is theomonistic. My reverence for Krishna and the Buddha and Christ and Nanak is too deep for words. And I have learnt, not without some study and meditation, to salute Muhammad among the Prophets of God."

Sadhu Vaswani's life was a veritable beacon of hope and faith for lost and wandering souls. He took it as his mission to spread the light of love wherever life took him. At a time when man turned upon man, his message of love and harmony appealed to those who realised that humanity stood on the brink of an abyss. He resolved to spread the message of the prophets and saints of the East and West and lead countless souls out of darkness into light!

"The noblest work," he asserted, "is to cultivate the soul." He lived a life that bore witness to this ideal. He lived the life spiritual; it was, in every sense of the term, the Life Beautiful!

Such is my heritage; such is my training; such is the truth I believe in. I say this to you at the outset because I would like you to know that what you read in these pages are not the pronouncements of a scientist or a spiritualist; they are the reflections of a pilgrim on the path, who has learnt all that he knows at the feet of his Guru.

The English word 'science' traces its origin to the Latin root *scientia* which means 'knowledge'. Science, therefore is knowledge (of something) acquired by study.

The West has specialised in science and technology, even as India specialises in spirituality. Therefore, I will look at the Sanskrit origin for 'spirituality'.

The Sanskrit term for spirituality is *atma vidya*, which literally means 'the science of the spirit'. Spirituality, I feel, is also a science. It is also concerned with the quest for truth. It is also a process of experimentation leading to a great discovery – the discovery of the self.

> What is the most important thing that will happen in the 21st century? The fusion of science and spirituality. That will happen. Why? Because this world in which we live changes, develops, progresses and evolves according to a certain law: The Law of Interpenetration of Dialectic. This law, advocated by German philosopher Georg Hegel, teaches us that "things which oppose and compete with each other come to resemble each other." If this Hegelian law is correct, science and spirituality will come to resemble each other, merge with each other, and fuse into a higher and greater "something".
>
> – Hiroshi Tasaka

People are awed by the miracles of science even as they are awed by the powers of spirituality. Science is concerned with the material world, with the understanding of nature's laws. Spirituality seeks to understand the inner world by which we, as human beings are determined. Therefore, my position is clear: both science and spirituality are processes of discovery; both are concerned with a quest for the truth; both lead to 'awareness'; both are experiential.

India's ancient *rishis* gained this knowledge; but they reached it through a process of intuition.

This poses a problem for a few contemporary scholars. Spirituality, they argue, is essentially undefined; its truth is not something which may be determined by scientific means. Science insists on observation, objectivity and repeatability of experiments to prove the validity of its theories; spiritual 'discoveries' and 'truths' are by their nature, experiential – and uniquely subjective.

Swami Vivekananda saw the intrinsic link between science and spirituality. As a distinguished scholar of the Ramakrishna Math, points out to us, the essence of Swamiji's thesis is this: the search for unity in diversity in the external world is called science. The search for unity in diversity in the internal world is called spirituality.

The trouble with a few of our scientifically inclined brothers and sisters is that they have a closed mind (a very unscientific attitude to adopt) when it comes to matters of the spirit and consciousness.

I recall this amusing anecdote narrated by Swami Vivekananda. In the course of his lectures in England, Swamiji pointed out that the practical application of psychology had been taken up in India from very early times. Talking to his European audience about the *Yoga Sutras* of Patanjali, Swamiji said to them, "About fourteen hundred years before Christ, there flourished in India a great philosopher, Patanjali by name. He collected all the facts, evidences and researches in psychology and took advantage of all the experiences accumulated in the past."

Swamiji added with a smile, "It is taught here in the West that society began eighteen hundred years ago, with the New Testament. Before that there was no society. That may be true with regard to the West, but it is not true as regards the whole world."

Often, while Swamiji was lecturing in London, a very intellectual friend of his would argue heatedly with Swamiji. One day after using all his weapons against Swamiji, he suddenly exclaimed, "But why did not your *rishis* come to England to teach us?" Swamiji replied, "Because there was (at that time) no England to come to. Would they preach to the forests?"

His point was made emphatically: today, we may be a poor, overpopulated, undeveloped country; but this is only in terms of a materialistic world. But we are the inheritors of a great spiritual tradition, a formidable legacy of spiritual culture, which the world is beginning to turn to with increasing respect.

I repeat, India has specialised in *atma vidya*, even as the West has specialised in science and technology. The greatest scientists were always aware of this. So let me give you the words of Carl Sagan:

Science is not only compatible with spirituality; it is a profound source of spirituality. When we recognise our place in an immensity of light years and in the passage of ages, when we grasp the intricacy, beauty, and subtlety of life, then that soaring feeling, that sense of elation and humility combined, is surely spiritual. So are our emotions in the presence of great art or music or literature, or acts of exemplary selfless courage such as those of Mohandas Gandhi or Martin Luther King, Jr. The notion that science and spirituality are somehow mutually exclusive does a disservice to both.

The origin of the Universe; the evolution of human civilisation; and the knowledge of the true self, the nature of consciousness: these are issues about which science is still asking questions. I foresee a future in which science will join hands with spirituality, especially the great spiritual traditions of India, to further the quest for truth. Already, people in the west (with or without the scientific temperament) have come to realise that in the practical business of daily living, Indian practices and *sadhanas* can offer them much more healing and relief than modern medicine can. Psychoanalysis is gradually being rejected in favour of meditation and *yoga*…

I began with the words of Gurudev Sadhu Vaswani, who has been the greatest influence on my spiritual life. I end with the words of Albert Einstein, the greatest scientist that my generation gave to the world:

The finest emotion of which we are capable is the mystic emotion. Herein lies the germ of all art and all true science. Anyone to whom this feeling is alien, who is no longer capable of wonderment and lives in a state of fear is a dead man. To know that what is impenetrable for us really exists and manifests itself as the highest wisdom and the most radiant beauty, whose gross forms alone are intelligible to our poor faculties — this knowledge, this feeling ... that is the core of the true religious sentiment. In this sense, and in this sense alone, I rank myself among profoundly religious men.

For Your Reflection

Scientist, economist and poet, Hiroshi Tasaka proposes three strategies to bring science and spirituality into a meaningful fusion for the benefit of mankind in the 21st century:

1. Teach Modern Science in the Religious Community: A sense of wonder and mystery is shared by both.

2. Deepen Modern Psychology through the Wisdom of Traditional Religions and Spirituality: The most important question for the science of psychology in the 21st century is "Who am I"? As we saw, religion and spirituality have been grappling with this question for thousands of years. So, we can actually add profound insights to modern psychology through the vast wisdom of traditional religions and spirituality fostered throughout their long history.

3. Create a New Economic Principle by Combining the Internet Revolution and the Wisdom of Compassion in Traditional Religions and Spirituality. According to Tasaka, modern capitalism has become "greedy capitalism" because it is monetary in approach and stimulates the avarice and money-mindedness of people. But the Internet revolution that

started in 1995 has been reviving an old economic principle called "gift economy" or "voluntary economy", which refers to economic activities of people motivated by satisfying the mind, through sharing, affection, generosity and compassion for other people. So, if we combine the Internet Revolution, modern economic science, and the wisdom of compassion in traditional religions and spirituality, we will be able to create a "compassion capitalism" in the 21st century.

It May Be Too Late Tomorrow!

Dennis E. Mannering teaches adult literacy classes in the U.S. One day, he did what was considered unpardonable – he gave his students compulsory homework! The assignment was to "go to someone you love within the next week and tell them you love them. It has to be someone you have never said those words before or at least haven't shared those words with for a long time".

Now that may not sound like a very tough assignment, but the fact was that most of the men in that group were over 40 and were raised in the generation of men who were taught that expressing emotions is not "manly". Showing feelings or crying (heaven forbid!) was just not done. So this was a very threatening assignment for some.

In the next class, which was a week later, he asked the group members if someone wanted to share what happened with the 'assignment'. One of the men raised his hand. He appeared quite moved and a bit shaken.

As he unfolded out of his chair (all 6'2" of him), he began by saying that at first, he had been quite angry with

Dennis when the assignment had been given. He thought to himself, "I don't have anyone to say those words to and besides, who was Dennis to tell me to do something that personal?"

But as he began driving home his conscience started asserting itself. "You know exactly what you have to do," it whispered to his heart. "You know exactly who you must say 'I love you' to."

The fact was that five years ago, this man had had a vicious disagreement with his father and really never resolved it since then. They had simply avoided seeing each other unless they absolutely had to at Christmas or other family gatherings. But even then, they hardly spoke to each other. So, he decided on that unforgettable day that he was going to tell his father that he loved him.

"It's weird, but just making that decision seemed to lift a heavy load off my chest", the man said to the class.

The next morning he was up bright and early. At 9:00 he called his dad on the phone. When the father answered the phone, he just said, "Dad, can I come over after work tonight? I have something to tell you." The father responded with a grumpy, "Now what?" The son assured him it wouldn't take long, so he finally agreed.

At 5:30, he was at his parents' house ringing the doorbell, praying that his dad would answer the door. He was afraid if his mom answered, he would simply lose his

erve and tell her instead. But as luck would have it, dad
id answer the door.

He didn't waste any time – he took one step in the
'oor and said, "Dad, I just came over to tell you that I
ove you."

It was as if a transformation came over the father!
His face softened, the wrinkles seemed to disappear and
e began to cry. He reached out and hugged his son and
said, "I love you too, son, but I've never been able to say it."

"It was such a precious moment," the man recalled,
wiping his eyes. The rest of the group was listening to him,
quite mesmerised. "I didn't want to move. Mom walked by
with tears in her eyes. I just waved and blew her a kiss.
Dad and I hugged for a moment longer and then I left. I
hadn't felt that great in a long time.

"But that's not even my point. Two days after that
visit, my dad, who had heart problems, but didn't tell me,
had an attack and ended up in the hospital, unconscious.
I don't know if he'll make it.

"So my message to all of you in this is: Don't wait to do
the things you know need to be done. What if I had waited
to tell my dad – maybe I will never get the chance again!
Take the time to do what you need to do and do it now!"

Chapter Twelve

Let Us Begin Now!

I believe every one of us realises at one stage or another, that there is more to this life than accumulating wealth, progressing with our work, rising in our careers, enjoying material pleasures and sense indulgences. On the one hand, we realise in our heart of hearts that we must make the most of this precious life; on the other we are only too well aware that this life is transient, and that the journey of the soul must continue even after we have ceased to be here. Even those of us who refuse to acknowledge God and dismiss the concept of the soul are mystified and intrigued by what awaits us after death, "that undiscovered country" from which nobody returns to tell us what it was like. In short, everyone agrees that we must make a fresh new beginning to live the life that is purposeful and meaningful, before it is too late.

For those of us who follow the Hindu way of life, our perception is very clear: the purpose of this human

fe is to escape from the wheel of birth- death-rebirth
nd attain Union with God; this Union is therefore
alled in Hindu terminology as true Liberation, *mukti*,
vhich is above and beyond all worldly notions of
reedom.

To live a life that is pure, beautiful, selfless; and
ffered as an *ahuti* for the glory of God – is this not
adhana at its best? It is the *sadhana* of daily life, living
ife as it ought to be lived!

> **Whatever you can do or dream, begin it
> now. Every thought you have, especially with
> emotional feelings behind them, creates a force
> of energy.**
>
> **– James Van Praagh**

But when we have made up our minds to live life
thus, there remains nevertheless, a little bewilderment,
a little mystification: where and how do we begin?

Gurudev Sadhu Vaswani's message for aspirants
can be summed up in what I call the blessed eight-fold
path. The steps on the path are:

1. Man is a pilgrim, a wayfarer. His pilgrimage
    is to the eternal, where is his true home.
    Nothing here belongs to him. Everything is
    given to him for use. He must use it wisely
    and well.

2.   Man has wandered outside himself. He need to embark on the interior pilgrimage.

3.   He must practise silence everyday and sinking deeper and deeper within, behold the imprisoned splendour. Gurudev Sadhu Vaswani's emphasis was more on the unfolding of the heart than on the development of brain power. "Awaken thy heart, O man!" he said, again and again.

4.   To be able to do so he must annihilate the ego, and walk what Gurudev Sadhu Vaswani called, "the little way".

5.   The non-egoistic man is a picture of forgiveness. He does not remember the hurts that have been inflicted on him.

6.   The non-egoistic man has surrendered his will to the Will Divine. He greets every happening with the *mantra*, "I accept"!

7.   The heart of such a man is filled with Divine Love. He beholds God face to face.

8.   He feels the thrill of the presence of God in all that is around him. And he becomes a servant of those who suffer and are in pain.

It is upto man to chart the course of his own spiritual progress. Man is known by the company he keeps. Man certainly has a choice here. The company of the good and virtuous ones keeps him healthy and positive. Bad company makes him miserable and loathsome. Hence, we must choose the company of those who will lead us towards a life which is positive and beautiful. We must seek the company of saints and sages. When we absorb the holy and positive vibrations of their environment, our hearts and souls are energised, our thoughts and aspirations are uplifted and purified.

> **Your daily life is your temple and your religion. When you enter into it, take with you your all!**
> **– Khalil Gibran**

We are well aware that this gross physical body that we wear needs nourishment. Unless we eat healthy, nutritious food at timely intervals, we know we cannot live an active, healthy life. Proxy eating cannot give your body the nutrients it needs. You have to involve the 'self'. In other words, I cannot eat for you when you are hungry! You have to eat your food yourself. The same is true of spiritual sustenance: I cannot cultivate your soul! You have to work for your own spiritual growth. You may seek out a Guru for guidance and sure enough he will show you the path, but you have to move forward on your own steam. The environment surrounding such a holy Guru is pure and serene, and man tends to absorb its positive energy. His soul flourishes in this benign and blessed environment. "The Soul selects her own society," sang a woman poet. Such an association nourishes and sustains our spiritual evolution. Such is the environment offered to all of us in the *satsang*.

The external environment has profound effect on both mind and the body. There is a story told to us of two brothers. One of them had a spiritual bent of mind. He went to the *satsang* every day, listening to discourses attentively and participating enthusiastically in the *bhajan* and *kirtan* sessions, and enjoying the uplifting vibrations of the *satsang*. For, as those in the know of such things would agree, the *satsang* is not just an evening programme; it is a whole way of life which has a tremendous influence on the way we think, the way we react, the way we choose to live.

The younger brother preferred to go to the club in the evenings, and spent his time in gambling. When the young man was asked why he did not follow the example of his brother, he became angry. "Look, I am young," he retorted. "I am in the prime of my life. I should be out, making the most of my youth and enjoying myself. I am not a soft weakling like my brother to spend my precious leisure hours in singing *bhajans* and listening to discourses in the *satsang*. I need to build up my business and maintain my professional contacts, which can help me. *Satsang*? No way!"

His brother often pleaded with him, "Please brother," he would appeal, "I am asking you for a favour, just once, only once, come with me to the *satsang*!"

One fine day, the younger brother relented. He was in a good mood. "Alright, favour granted," he smiled. "Just to please you, I will come with you to the *satsang*. But on one condition: after today, you must never, ever, mention the word '*satsang*' to me." His innate apathy for *satsang* was as strong as ever. It was just to please his brother, that he had agreed to go with him to the *satsang* — just once!

Next day, at a prior appointed time, the spiritually inclined brother went to pick up his brother from his house. But the young atheist had already left for the club, leaving behind a message of regret and apology expressing his inability to join the brother for *satsang*. This was repeated several times: the spiritually inclined brother coaxing and cajoling his worldly brother to attend *satsang*, just once! But all his efforts were in vain, for the brother kept postponing his appointment for *satsang*, on one pretext or the other. Today it was a business meeting; tomorrow, a party at the club and so on and so forth: as we all know, we don't have to try very hard to find excuses; they find us faster than we can think!

> **Don't ask what the world needs. Ask what makes you come alive and go and do it. Because what the world needs is people who have come alive.**
> **– Howard Thurman**

Many of us are bound to recognise our likeness in the younger brother, who simply avoided a visit to the *satsang*. We lose golden opportunities that come our way, for we are so engrossed in our worldly affairs, in our ego self, in self-glorification and self-indulgence; we turn a blind eye to anything that is other than our 'ego centric' self.

Do Not Postpone. Do not leave for tomorrow, what you can do today. Your stay on this earth plane is only for a limited period of time. Do not miss the opportunity of making the best use of your existence here, for the human birth is like the magical philosopher's stone. It is *Paras*. It is given to you, to 'transform' your mundane self into a pure beautiful lotus which blossoms forever. It is given to you, to purify the self. Do not postpone. Begin your work today and now. As the saying goes, what you can do tomorrow, do today and what you can do today, do it now. Do not postpone, lest you miss this golden opportunity forever.

Begin your *sadhana* now, this very moment! Start right away!

Begin to be now what you will be hereafter.
                                        – William James

Here is a simple daily routine that I recommend to beginners:

1. Rise in the early hours of the dawn, when Divine vibrations are at their most positive. The *Brahma Mahurat* as it is called, is specially conducive to spiritual growth.

2. Begin the day with a few minutes of silent prayer. Let us practise silence every day, preferably at the same time and the same place — for this is our daily appointment with our own selves, our True Self, the Real Self, the Self Supreme that, for want of a better word, we call God. Begin with fifteen minutes, then gradually increase the period to at least one hour. At first, the practice may appear to be meaningless, a sheer waste of time. But if you persist in it, silence will become alive and the word of God will speak to you. And you will realise that practising silence is, perhaps, the most worthwhile activity of the day.

3. Take your first steps too, on the path of
    abhyasa. Start with a simple meditation
    exercise to still the wandering mind and give
    it focus and concentration. Very many people
    who meet me tell me that they face one major
    problem when they start to meditate — the
    wandering mind. "We close our eyes and sit
    in silence," they say, "but our mind wanders.
    And it's not just that the mind will not be still;
    we get such thoughts as would never disturb
    us otherwise, when we are at our routine
    work. However, when we try to enter into
    silence, they come to bother us. Why does
    this happen?"

    Our minds are prone to distraction. Truly
    has it been said that the mind is a monkey; it
    wanders from one object to another from one
    form to another. When we are at work we
    do not realise the restlessness, the fickleness
    of the mind. But when we sit in silence – the
    mind begins to play its tricks. It wanders,
    and we too, wander with it.

    What can you do to stop the wandering mind
    in its tracks? What can you do to train the
    mind in *ekagrita* — one-pointed focus?

One of the best ways I know, to control the wandering mind, is to develop love for God. As we all know, when we love something or someone deeply, our mind constantly gravitates towards that person. We have to apply the same principle to *abhyasa* — cultivate love for God in our hearts. I truly believe that concentration is not possible until we awaken love in our hearts — the utmost love for God.

There are experts and practitioners who insist that *abhyasa* is based on emotionless detachment; and that God need not have anything to do with meditation. But I am firmly of the belief that for the beginner, love for God can be the greatest motivating, inspiring, uplifting factor. Therefore, begin your *abhyasa* by developing love for God.

4. Set aside some time during the day for meditation. You will make excellent progress on the path of *abhyasa* by setting aside a regular time and following a regular schedule for meditation. When this becomes a fixed habit, a definite part of your daily routine, it will help you to advance further on the path.

The ancient scriptures tell us that four 'auspicious' hours of the day and night are particularly suited for meditation:

a) The sacred hour prior to the dawn — the *Brahma Mahurat* or hour of the Gods as it is called.

b) The hour of the noon — when everything is hushed and nature seems to be still. Even birds and insects are quiet - and people at home are resting.

c) Early evening — when lamps are lit, the sun sinks down in the western horizon and the earth and the sky assume a different colour, a different light, a different aura.

d) The midnight hour — when the world is asleep; and even the moon and the stars watch over us in quiet and stillness. Many people believe that midnight is the most peaceful time for meditation.

I have a personal preference for the early morning hour, and I have no hesitation in recommending it to you, too. The mind is quiet, peaceful, refreshed and rested after the night's sleep; all the negative impressions accumulated on the previous day have been erased, and you have a fresh, clean, blank page on which to begin writing. Above all, when you begin the day with God and meditate before you start your daily routine, you will not only find yourself spiritually and emotionally energised; you will also get a positive direction and power, to take you through the rest of the day.

5.   The life of meditation must be blended with the life of work. For we must not give up our worldly duties and obligations in order to meditate. We must withdraw ourselves from the world for a while and give ourselves wholly to God. Then we must return to our daily work, pouring into it the energy of the Spirit. Such work will bless the world. Through such work God Himself will descend upon the earth. Work of the true type is a bridge between God and humanity. So, with one hand let us cling to His Lotus Feet and with the other attend to our daily duties.

6.   There is a simple breathing exercise suggested by the Vietnamese Buddhist Master, Thich Nhat Hanh, which may help you to grow in concentration.

Close your eyes. Become aware of the breathing process — the going in and coming out of your breath.

As you breathe in, say to yourself, "I am aware that the breath is going in." As you breathe out, say to yourself, "I am aware that the breath is coming out." Repeat this five times saying "in" and "out".

As you inhale, say to yourself, "I am aware that the breath is becoming deep." As you exhale, say to yourself, "I am aware that my breath is becoming slow." Do this five times repeating, "D-e-e-p", as you inhale, "s-l-o-w" as you exhale.

At the next step, say to yourself as you inhale, "I am aware of the present moment as I breathe in." When you exhale, say to yourself, "I know that this moment is perfect." Do this five times repeating "P-r-e-s-e-n-t" as you breathe in; "P-e-r-f-e-c-t" as you breathe out.

Repeat the word "c-a-l-m" as you inhale; repeat the word "r-e-l-a-x" as you exhale, five times.

This exercise in breathing will help you considerably with your meditation.

Breathing is with you 24 hours a day — you are never without it, it is your best friend. Use it to harness the power of concentration.

7. Shampoo your mind at least once a day! Shampooing means cleansing. Now, we need to cleanse our minds, we need to unclutter our minds. Our minds are full of wrong thinking, wrong ideas. The minds of so many of us are full of negative thoughts. We must cleanse them of their negativity. To do this, we must get right down into our consciousness and cleanse ourselves of all those rotten thoughts that hold us captive today — thoughts of impurity, selfishness, greed, lust and hatred. Our minds should be clean and uncluttered. It is only then that we can hope to be happy. Otherwise, with all those negative thoughts in the mind within, how can we be at peace with ourselves?

8. Cultivate the subconscious mind so that its tremendous power can be harnessed for your spiritual growth.

   How may we cultivate the subconscious mind?

   a) Always entertain positive thoughts. Never harbour thoughts of jealousy, hatred or lust.

b) Do not react emotionally to things that happen.

c) Never make any negative suggestions in regard to what you want to be. Thus, for instance, never say, I have a bad memory. This will only lead to loss of memory. Rather say my memory is improving.

d) Never hate or resent people. Let love and forgiveness be the law of your life. Many types of illnesses are caused by intense hatred and resentment.

e) Read books, and if at all you must watch TV, watch programmes that inspire and uplift you rather than those that feature violence, sex, crime and other acts of viciousness. This is especially important in the case of young people.

Dear friends, man came to the earth as a pilgrim, but has become a wanderer. Even in our spiritual quest, we wander from creed to creed, from one school of thought to another, and are filled with unrest. We move to temples and churches and places of pilgrimage, and meet with disappointment. For, not until we turn within, will we find that which we are seeking.

Truth is within! Wisdom is within! The source of all strength is within! Therefore, turn within!

A beginning has to be made somewhere. Every day, preferably at the same time and at the same place, let us sit in silence and pray, meditate, do our spiritual thinking. It is our daily appointment with God. We keep a number of appointments, every day. Alas! We neglect this most important of all appointments – our daily appointment with God. He is not far away from us. He is wherever we are. He is here: He is now! All we have to do is to close our eyes, shut out the world and call Him – and there He is in front of us. In the beginning we may not see Him: let us be sure, that He sees us. We may not be able to immediately hear His voice: but He hears us. The tiniest whisper of the human heart, the smallest stirring of the soul is audible to His ever-attentive ears. Speak to Him: open out your heart to Him: place all your difficulties before Him: and you will find wonderful things happen to you.

For Your Reflection

Spiritual Motivation In Capsules For You

1. A real beginning is made only when you commit yourself. Therefore, do not give in to hesitancy, the impulse to give up or draw back from the chosen path. Commit yourself here and now, to walking the way of the spirit.

2. Once you have made the commitment, you will find that God moves with you and guides your every step! You will find daily miracles happening in your life that help you progress on the path.

3. Whatever you wish to achieve, whatever you wish to accomplish, begin it now – and leave the rest in God's safe hands!

SECTION II

*Preparing To Walk The
Way Of Spirituality*

I have been reflecting on the words of a song by one of India's little known saints, belonging to the Sant M tradition, Sant Tulsi Sahib of Hathras:

> Cleanse the chamber of your heart, so that the Beloved may enter,
> Remove all the alien impressions, so that He can take His seat there.
> One heart, with so many desires, and always the lust for more,
> Where is the place for the Lord to enter and reside?

How true! How can we begin to walk the way of spirituality, how can we expect the Lord to be with us, to become a part of our life, until and unless we prepare to receive Him in our hearts?

Just imagine that a VIP is going to visit your house today. He may be a rich relative, a former acquaintance who has suddenly acquired power and position in life, or even your superior at work. You know how hectic the preparations are likely to be! We virtually transform our drawing room from its everyday state into a receiving chamber fit for royalty! We shift the everyday articles out, we rearrange the furniture, we clear books and papers out of sight, we change curtains and cushion covers – in short, our own family members sometime fail to recognise the familiar living space that they left in the morning!

This is all very well! Our guests need to be well received and well treated (whether or not they belong to the VIP category)! But Sant Tulsi makes a valid point when he reminds us that God is waiting to come and take His place inside our hearts; what preparations are we making to receive Him within?

The point that the saint is making is obvious: cleanse the chamber of your heart! Purify your inner instrument so that you are ready to receive the Lord into the temple of your heart.

In the pages that follow, I offer you some reflections on the preparation that we must make before we take to spirituality in daily life.

Sant Tulsi Of Hathras Meets Sheikh Taqi

Once, a dervish named Sheikh Taqi was returning from his Haj (Pilgrimage to Mecca) with a group of fellow pilgrims. They reached Hathras after darkness fell, and decided to pitch their tents for the night in an open area. In the morning, Sheikh Taqi discovered that Sant Tulsi Sahib was seated right opposite their tents, under the banyan tree. The two saints were delighted to meet each other, and their conversation has been recorded both in Sant Mat and Sufi literature.

During this conversation Tulsi Sahib tells Sheikh Taqi: "Huzoor, you go to Mecca and Medina, you go to many holy places; but you must remember there is no pilgrimage outside of the self. These outer pilgrimages will not benefit you much. The true pilgrimage is the inner journey; which begins from the heels of the feet and ends at the center of the crown. Hence, go within... Go within!"

Let me give you the words of this bhajan of Tulsi Sahib, which is like a sufi song!

Hear my words O Taqi, stay focused on the Satguru who has assisted you.

Do not succumb to negligence for this path if you desire to see the splendour of your Beloved.

His grace will guide you into His very presence, free of all dangers or fears along the way.

Go directly to your destination, for the Master has revealed to you

His instructions.

Rumi, Shams, Mansur and Sarmad arrived by this very path, and with firm resolve, they reached their goal.

Arduous is the way to the destination of love, but reaching there is not difficult. The one who resolves difficulties is with you and has given you His hand.

Says Tulsi, Hear me O Taqi, the inner secret is unlike anything you have known before. Keep it safe in your heart, for it focuses you on the Most High [God].

Chapter One

Detoxify Yourself

Let us reflect on this inner journey.

The first step is the stage of inner cleansing or purification.

Many of us are filled with impure energy. We are conditioned to think impure thoughts. We are driven by a permanent craving to satisfy our many desires, some worthy, some quite unworthy. And those desires are innumerable! No sooner is one desire fulfilled, than another arises to take its place. The truth is that at all times we are driven by our desires.

The tendency to accumulate material wealth, the craving for more and more, is the root cause of human restlessness. Greed, one of the seven deadly sins, binds people with fetters that shackle their capacity for self-fulfillment and inner harmony. As bestselling author, Dr. Wayne Dyer, tells us, it is just not possible to live one's life in joy and peace within the restricting structures of materialism, greed and accumulation. "The perpetual pursuit of more and more," he tells us, "only begets loneliness and unhappiness."

Attachment of any kind, as the Gita tells us, leads to suffering. *Raga*, or *abhinivesha* (clinging and attachment) as it is called, is an impediment – not only on the path of liberation, but also in the attainment of personal happiness. On the other hand, detachment is one of life's greatest lessons for those who seek the true joy of life.

If you wish to purify yourself, then detach from the world and its mundane desires. Surrender yourself in devotion and worship to God! Shift your energies from 'impure' to the 'pure'. This is not easy. You have to convince yourself, that your attachment to your near and dear ones is an illusion. The truth is that nothing, no one, belongs to you, and you belong to none. These attachments are ephemeral; they are like a mirage in a desert. Yet we cling to these illusions. We keep on saying: This is my house, this is my property and this is my child. No, nothing is ours! Nothing belongs to us! If it really belongs to us, we would carry it with us when we leave this world. And you know we carry nothing with ourselves when we depart!

Chasing shadow shapes and ephemeral desires, we tell ourselves that we are in pursuit of true happiness. But we are only deceiving ourselves. Happiness, true happiness, is an inner quality. It is a state of the

mind. If your mind is pure, clean and tranquil, you
are at peace, you are happy. If your mind is at peace,
and you have nothing else, you can still be happy. If
you have everything the world can give – pleasure,
possessions, power – but lack peace of mind, you can
never be happy. So it was that a holy man exclaimed,
"Nothing in the morn have I; and nothing do I have at
night. And yet there is none on earth happier than I."

Happiness does not depend on outer things.
Happiness is essentially an inner quality! Let me add
too: Happiness is your birthright! But happiness must
come from within you!

Six Tips for Spiritual Detox:
1. **Fast from doing things out of obligation. Feast
on doing things out of love.**
2. **Unplug from saying "Yes", when you should
really say "I'm sorry. I have to pass on that one".**
3. **Opt to spend time with just a few friends over
big group social activities.**
4. **Enjoy 'alone' activities that feed your soul.**
5. **Every time you set out to take on a new
activity, ask yourself: Is this productive or
fruitful activity? Choose fruitfulness over mere
'productivity'.**
6. **Let love for God always be the top priority of
your life...**

– Adapted from Faith Barista

The only bond, which is eternal, pure and strong, is the bond with your Guru. Your relation with your Guru is eternal. Rightly has it been called the Perfect Relationship. Your Guru is a link between you and God. If you are fortunate enough to find a true Guru – He will see you through the dark tunnel of death and lead you into the Realm of Light that we all seek to attain to, one day.

The first step is to be awakened to the fact that it is all within. One has to know one's self. The second step is to chant the Name Divine. The third step is to connect with God through the healing, cleansing power of prayer, about which I will tell you more, in the pages that follow.

Sit in silence and experience the inner peace. Once you get this experience, you will like to detach from the external world. You will like to keep to yourself. You will avoid meeting negative people.

Unfortunately, our minds are scattered. They are dispersed, tainted with desires, they look downwards. We need to purify our minds: we need to raise the level of our consciousness. We must learn to look upwards. We need to protect ourselves against the three pronged attack of *maya* – the desire for pleasure, wealth and power. Only then can we begin the process of inner purification.

> The cure of the part should not be attempted
> without the cure of the whole. No attempt should
> be made to cure the body without the soul, and
> if the head and body are to be healthy, you must
> begin by curing the mind. That is the first thing.
> Let no one persuade you to cure the head until
> he has first given you his soul to be cured. For
> this is the great error of our day in the treatment
> of the human body, that physicians first separate
> the soul from the body.
>
> – Plato

Those who wish to walk the path of inner
pilgrimage value inner peace, harmony and serenity.
They are eager and determined to probe the depths
of the true Self, and they have made a serious
commitment to walk the way of the seeker. And in
order to succeed on the chosen path, they make every
effort to conquer both outer distractions and inner
impediments.

In the Gita, we are given a memorable picture
of a tortoise. Once the tortoise draws in its limbs,
you will not be able to draw them out, even if you
cut the creature into four pieces! This is the kind of
determination you too, will need, if you wish to tread
the way of the inner journey that we are speaking of.

Sitting and concentrating the mind on a single object, controlling the thoughts and the activities of the senses, let the *yogi* practice meditation for self-purification.

– Bhagavad Gita

Exercise: Eight Steps to Spiritual Progress

1. We must pray, again and again. Pray with full consciousness. Pray to the Lord with utmost faith. Pray in the awareness that you are God's child and He will do only what is best for you.

    Pray to Him honestly, in simplicity, with longing and sincerity. Words and images do not matter in prayer: feelings are far more important. Therefore, pray with deep feelings.

2. Seek the guidance of a Guru, a spiritual mentor. Spending time in the presence of an evolved soul is the most powerful source of strength and inner wisdom. A Guru inspires us by his living example. He sees the potential in us that we ourselves are not aware of. Above all he encourages us to believe that we are also capable of achieving what he has! He provides tremendous powers of incentive and inspiration. He cures us of crippling negative emotions.

3. Start with *Karma Yoga* – before you set out in search of the inner self. Even those of us who feel diffident to tread the way of *abhyasa* can prepare themselves effectively by undertaking acts of selfless service. When we go out of our way to help and serve others, without claiming credit, without any thought of reward, we

automatically purify our *antah karana* or inner instrument.

4. Cultivate self-discipline. The Gita teaches us that tamas is overcome by rajas – the principle of action, energy and dynamism. When we cultivate discipline of the mind, it will automatically lead us to sattva – light and harmony. With this enlightenment, our spiritual progress can be really speedy.

5. Eat right. Sattvic food, food of non-violence will provide us with the right energy and the right frame of mind to pursue the path of the inner pilgrimage.

6. Offer all that you are, all that you have, all that you do, to the Lord, in a spirit of arpanam.

   Sri Krishna tells us in the Gita: "Whatever you eat, whatever you give in charity, whatever austerity you practise, whatever you do, O Arjuna, make it as an offering unto Me."

   This is the best antidote to conquering the ego and negating pride and arrogance. Whatever you do, offer it to God. Whatever you achieve, it is His grace, His doing. Therefore say to Him: I am not the doer. I am but a broken instrument. If there are any shortcomings, any mistakes that I make, they are mine. But all glory belongs to Thee! Stop saying, 'I did it.' 'This is mine.' 'I worked hard for it.' 'I earned it.' Instead say, 'Everything is Thine.' 'The energy is Thine.' 'Nothing belongs to me.' 'I am Thine.'

7. Cultivate the virtue of patience. Remember, haste makes waste. There are no shortcuts, no instant solutions, and no quick fixes on the path of the true seeker.

8. Remember, practice makes perfect. Ask any great athlete, any great singer, any great actor – and they will tell you that hours of effort and hard work have gone into their achievements. The inner light we seek to find is one of the greatest goals a human being can aim for. Therefore, give it all you have got! Pilgrimages, there are many. But if I have not entered upon the interior pilgrimage, I have wasted the golden opportunity of the human birth.

Harnessing The Power Of Prayer

One day in the Mother's house in Kolkata there were about three hundred novices and they were all out for the morning. One of the novices working in the kitchen came up to Mother Teresa and said, "Mother, we've got a problem; there's no flour left to make chapattis for lunch."

The situation looked bleak; three hundred plus mouths were coming to be fed in about an hour and a half and there was nothing to cook with. There was no food.

What would we expect Mother Teresa to do? Perhaps she would pick up the telephone and call some of her benefactors and mobilise them to find some way to feed her daughters. Instead, her spontaneous reaction was to say to this little novice, "Sister, you're in charge of the kitchen this week? Well then, go into the chapel and tell Jesus we have no food. That's settled. Now let's move on. What's next?"

Lo and behold, ten minutes later there was a ring at the door and Mother Teresa was called downstairs. A man she had never seen before was standing there with a clipboard. He said to her, "Mother Teresa, we were just informed that the teachers at the city schools are going on strike. Classes have been dismissed and we have 7,000 school lunches we don't know what to do with. Can you help us use them?"

God provided for the needs of his children.

– Michael Scanlan, *Let The Fire Fall*

Chapter Two

Cultivating The Attitude Of Gratitude

In the last chapter, we were speaking about the first three stages of the process of inner purification: The first step is to be awakened to the fact that it is all within. The second step is to chant the Name Divine; the third step is to connect with God through the healing, cleansing power of prayer.

As human beings, we seek to augment our finite energy by linking ourselves to God, who is the source of infinite energy. His power is inexhaustible, and He is ready to give some of it to us so that we may do what we have to do. Just by asking for His help, our deficiencies are set right and we are restored, rejuvenated and strengthened.

A peasant stood at the temple, gazing at the Lord for a long time. Other people came, offered their prayers and went away. But he just stood there, gazing at the beauteous face of the deity.

"Are you waiting for something?" they asked him.

"No," he replied. "I am looking at Him and He is looking at me!"

We should not only pray that God must remember us, but that we should always remember Him. Therefore, has it been said that prayer is practising the presence of God.

Prayer is man's attempt to reach out to God, to commune with Him in devotion, in the realisation that He is the source of all wisdom, truth, beauty and strength. He is also the Father and Mother of all of us. When we commune with Him in this awareness, we feel a transformation in our mind, body and soul, which touches our lives for the better. And remember, you cannot pray for a single moment without achieving something good out of it!

By myself, I can do nothing: that is the very first principle of spiritual life. The second principle is – He that is within you is greater than he that is outside.

To us, external forces appear to be strong and powerful. But they are nothing compared to that which is within you – the Lord, who is seated in the throne of your heart, for whom everything is possible.

When you raise your heart to God in prayer, it is very important that you are happy and grateful; in fact, in every situation and circumstance of life, a true aspirant should be ever thankful. He should be content with whatever he has. His *mantra* should be this: "Oh God, wherever You place me, I am happy."

> **Gratitude unlocks the fullness of life. It turns what we have into enough, and more. It can turn a meal into a feast, a house into a home, a stranger into a friend.**
>
> **– Melody Beattie**

Gurudev Sadhu Vaswani was indeed one of the happiest men I knew. One day, I asked him, "You have faced many difficulties and tribulations in your life. What is it that helped you to face such situations and remain unscathed, unfettered in spirit?"

His answer was simple. He only said, "I praise the Lord!"

I was a persistent seeker those days – I would not rest till I had found a satisfactory answer to my queries. Therefore, I asked him, "What do you do when you are ill, and your body is caught in the throes of pain?"

"I still praise the Lord!" was the answer.

"And when you are passing through the strain of suffering?"

Again he answered, "I still praise the Lord!"

In those beautiful words lay the secret of the Master's happiness. The simplest way to be happy, he taught us, was to praise the Lord in all circumstances, all situations of life.

When you are thankful to God for His infinite kindness and mercy, you are focusing on all that is best in your life, and the Law of Attraction will draw more of the same into your life. But let me also warn you, if you complain about unpleasant things, you will draw more of those negative forces into your physical experience!

Best-selling author Alan Cohen tells us: "Curse what you see and you will live in a world of pain; give thanks, and you will find more to be thankful about. The choice is yours!"

People often choose very selfish and narrow reasons to thank God. Businessmen offer thanks when they make a fat profit. Students offer thanks when they pass exams. In India, elaborate thanks are offered to God when a son is born!

However, a true seeker learns to give thanks to God for very different reasons. He knows that this human birth itself is the greatest of gifts that God has bestowed on him – for it is the means, the instrument by which he can seek his salvation. He knows that birth into this world is the necessary pre-requisite to gain ultimate freedom from the cycle of birth–death–rebirth.

> **Each moment of the year has its own beauty... a picture which was never seen before and shall never be seen again.**
> – Emerson

When you learn to thank the Lord in prosperity and plenty, you will also grow in the realisation that you owe thanks to Him in adversity and misery as well. For every disappointment in your life is His appointment. He upsets your plans, only to set up His own! When you learn to thank the Lord in all conditions, you will grow in the realisation that you are but an instrument of His Divine Will – and is that not a wonderful thing to be grateful for?

Offering thanks to God teaches us one of the most valuable lessons of life – to appreciate the here and now. We learn to stop wishing for what-might-have-been and yearning for what-is-not, and enjoy what is, now. So we offer thanks, we focus on the present moment, and experience the full wonder of the precious present moment.

The dynamic way of Thanksgiving is to make of your life an offering to the Lord. Affirm to Him that you are His, and that all your words, deeds and thoughts are dedicated to His glory.

Here is a little prayer that I often say:

> O Lord, I seek neither wealth nor power, nor the pleasures of this or the next world.
> I need Thee and Thee alone!
> Grant me the gift of longing – deep yearning – for Thy Lotus Feet!
> Grant me the gift of tears – that I may keep awake at night and meditate and, during the daytime, help as many as I can, to lift the load on the rough road of life!
> I thank Thee Lord, for Thy infinite mercy to me!

A heart filled with gratitude is one that promotes joyous living. And the positive gifts that thankfulness confers upon us are very many. It fills your life with peace, joy and serenity. It banishes negative thinking – for gratitude and complaints, gratitude and worry, gratitude and anxiety just cannot exist together!

The Roman philosopher Cicero said: "Gratitude is not only the greatest of virtues, but the parent of all the others."

If the only prayer you ever say in your entire life is thank you, it will be enough.

– Meister Eckhart

I read an old parable in which God invited all human virtues to attend a banquet in heaven. It was an all-ladies event, for virtues are personified as women – let men take note!

Hundreds of virtues, great and small, attended the banquet, and they were all on the most cordial terms with each other. Cheerfulness went round, talking to everyone; Friendship was busy bringing the guests close together; Hospitality saw to it that everyone helped themselves to the food they liked; Goodness beamed on everyone present.

Suddenly, God noticed that there were two ladies among His guests who appeared to be total strangers to each other. He took it upon Himself to introduce them. He took one lady by the hand and went towards the other.

"Generosity," He said turning towards the first lady, "I'd like you to meet Gratitude."

The two virtues, we are told, shook hands in astonishment, for this was the very first time that they had met each other!

This parable only shows that a lot of things go unrecognised, unacknowledged in this world of ours. We take a lot of things for granted – we fail to appreciate them, or return good for good.

Exercise in Gratitude

Meditation on Thanksgiving

The secret of a happy contented life is the attitude of gratitude.

Blessed are they who make everyday a day of thanksgiving, for they shall grow in the awareness of God's presence in their lives and in their hearts!

Count your blessings and thank God every living, waking, moment – for God's generosity to you is infinite!

Every accomplishment, every form of excellence, every success, small or big, belongs to God. If you are wise and intelligent, it is God-given. If your hard work and efforts are commendable, it is due to the grace of God. If you are truly conscious of this, and acknowledge His grace in all humility – why, this humility too is a manifestation of His mercy upon you!

When you learn to thank the Lord in prosperity and plenty, you will also grow in the realisation that you owe thanks to Him in adversity and misery as well. For every disappointment in your life is His appointment. He upsets your plans, only to set up His own! When you learn to thank the Lord in all conditions, you will grow in the realisation that you are but an instrument of His Divine Will – and is that not a wonderful thing to be grateful for?

Shall we try a simple meditation to cultivate the spirit of thanksgiving, the attitude of gratitude?

Step 1: Let us relax. Relax every muscle, every limb, every nerve in the body. Make it tension-free.

Relax your shoulders. Drop all the weight you are carrying with you – all your burdens, all your problems.

Now, let the mind be free – free from the worries of the past, free from fears for your future.

Live in the present moment – be conscious of the *now* and *here*!

Now, let us sit in a comfortable posture so that we will not need to change it for the next few minutes.

Now, take in three deep breaths. As you breathe deeply, be relaxed.

Breathe in...slowly, deeply...

Now breathe out...slowly...completely...

Step 2: Now tell yourself, as you breathe in: I am grateful to God for all the abundant blessings He has bestowed on me! I am grateful for my family and friends; I am grateful for my home and its amenities; I am grateful for my career or my studies or my vocation in life!

I am grateful to God for this beautiful planet and all the wonderful gifts of His creation! I am grateful for the air I breathe, the sun that lights my life, the moon and stars in their unsurpassed splendour and beauty!

Visualise a field full of spring flowers. Imagine that you are watching the glorious sunrise that happens morning after morning. Re-live the experience of the gentle breeze brushing your face and ruffling your hair. Imagine inhaling the scented night air as you look upon the moon and stars with awe and wonder!

Now stop to ask yourself: what have I done to deserve these marvellous gifts?

Therefore, say to God: I am grateful for the marvellous mechanism of the human body and the incredible instrument that is the human mind! I am grateful too, for the five senses that enable me to perceive this world, and the power of thinking that makes me what I am – a living, walking, talking, sensitive human being.

I am grateful to God for every breath I take, and the new life, the new energy that each breath brings into my being!

Inhale deeply, with each new breath you take. Feel yourself becoming new and fresh with every breath you take! Express your gratitude to the Almighty for every breath, every second of life that comes as a priceless gift to you from God!

Step 3: Now, feel the spirit of thanksgiving flowing through every nerve, every pore of your body. Repeat to yourself the *mantra*: Thank You God! Thank You God! Thank You God!

When you focus on the attitude of gratitude, you focus on all that is good and positive in your life. As all that is good and positive emanates from God, the person who practises the therapy of thanksgiving allows the most positive and powerful forces in the world to flow into him, and draws strength and healing there from. It is in fact, akin to being connected with a powerful spiritual dynamo! Feel the positive energy flowing into you, as you connect to the Super Power that is God through the expression of gratitude. Repeat to yourself the *mantra:* Thank You God! Thank You God! Thank You God!

The expression of gratitude is a rich and positive exercise. It is a mental and spiritual tonic. When you allow your thankfulness to be expressed, you are affirming God's goodness and grace. This always works to your own benefit – for you become hopeful, optimistic and happy.

Dwelling on the attitude of gratitude makes us open and receptive to the Lord's blessings. Feel the Lord's richest blessings being showered on you in abundance! Thank Him profoundly for all the gifts you are aware of – and for a thousand others which you have not acknowledged till now! Repeat to yourself the *mantra*: Thank You God! Thank You God! Thank You God!

Step 4: Feel the peace and contentment that enters your heart as you repeat the *mantra*: I believe in God's goodness, I believe that He has a plan for me! I am content to let that plan unfold in my life... I am content... I am grateful to God for all His blessings. I am content to accept His Will.. I accept, I accept, I accept....

Step 5: Now, let us offer our gratitude to God and the Guru. Visualise yourself before God; visualise yourself at the Lotus Feet of the Master, offering flowers of devotion and gratitude: what can you offer to the Beloved who asks nothing of you? Only this: that you will do what pleases Him most; that you will help everyone, appreciate everyone and love everyone. And that you will live in the spirit of thanksgiving every day, every hour, every beautiful moment of this life!

Count your blessings, keep on thanking the Lord. This induces the marvellous and restful feeling that God is in His Heaven and all is well with this world.

A Zen Master tells us that the real miracle is not to walk on water, in the air or on burning charcoal, but *just to walk on earth*. How wonderful for us to stop and breathe in the awareness that the world is a beautiful place; that being alive is a vital, joyous experience; and that life is the greatest miracle of all! Allow yourself to feel this miracle!

Become aware of the rhythm of your breathing. Open your eyes gently, and feel the positive energy of thanksgiving infusing your body, mind, heart and soul.

The Effect Of Satsang

A sister once came to see me in a very perturbed state of mind. She said that she had been greatly agitated, of late, by a personal crisis that had rocked her life. She needed to talk to me and was anxious for advice. I suggested that as it was nearly time for the evening satsang, she should attend the same, and then come to talk to me.

She agreed, and went away to join the satsang, which was about to begin. As I remember, it was a Tuesday, which, in our Sadhu Vaswani satsang, includes a session of meditation. Every evening when the satsang is over, we have a brief session of prayer and silence at Sadhu Vaswani's sacred Samadhi. After this refreshing and uplifting session, I sent for this sister myself, for she had indeed appeared very disturbed.

She came running up to me and said, "Yes, Dada?"

I gently reminded her that she had wanted to meet me urgently, over a matter that had been troubling her.

"Oh, yes, I remember," she said, with a smile. "But Dada, I really feel I don't need to trouble you and take

away your valuable time now. I have found the answer to my questions, the solution to my problem."

She explained that the moment she walked into the satsang, *she had felt a sense of peace and calm descending on her. As she heard the* kitran, *she felt the tears flowing from her eyes, unbidden. The day's* vachan *from the* Nuri Granth, *seemed as if it was deliberately addressed to her. She participated in the* aarti, *which she found to be a healing, purifying experience. In the meditation session which followed, she was actually able to hear her inner voice speak to her, and the terrible weight of anxiety and worry that had been pressing down on her, lowering her morale and her spirit, seemed to lift like a cloud. At the end of the session, she literally felt that she was a new person, ready to take on the blows and bullets of life. She had not only received inner guidance to approach her own problem, but was also filled with a sense of well-being, courage and confidence. In fact, till I sent for her, she had almost forgotten that she had come to me earlier that evening, in a distraught condition, seeking answers to questions that overwhelmed her. Such was the effect of* satsang *on her!*

Chapter Three

Seek The Fellowship Of The Holy Ones

Satsang (fellowship with the holy) is our route to Liberation, the safe passage to our eternal home. *Satsang* is as essential to our spiritual well-being as fitness and nutrition are to our physical health. The sad truth is, that while many people have become conscious of their physical health today, many of us are still indifferent to our spiritual needs, our spiritual welfare and the special 'nourishment' and 'therapy' and 'exercise routine' that the immortal soul within us requires!

People who are in the know of such things, tell me that fitness equipment like exercycles, treadmills, and rowing machines are now sold directly to fitness conscious individuals for use in their homes; whereas, a couple of decades ago, such machines were only to be found in gyms. Health drinks, low calorie food substitutes and meal replacements have also become extremely popular.

I am glad to know that people are now conscious and aware of the importance of physical fitness. My only desire is that they should become equally sensitive to their spiritual well-being! Our *shastras* tell us that this body we inhabit here on our earthly journey is actually a temple of the Lord: *Shariram Brahma Mandiram*. Can you see the logic behind keeping the temple in perfect condition, while the deity inside is neglected and uncared for? So let me remind you, this body is a very important and valuable instrument that is indispensable to us on this earthly pilgrimage; but it is an instrument that has been given to us, as an aid to seek Liberation. The body must help us perform those acts of good *karma* that will enable us to realise our true Divinity, and thus lead the *atman* to its true home, the Lotus Feet of the Lord.

Even those of us who are not too conscious of fitness and other such 'in' concepts, pay a good deal of attention to looking after the body. Every morning we get up, have a shower and clean ourselves thoroughly, before the daily work routine begins. We take great trouble to invest in clothes, shoes, soaps, shampoos and creams that will help us present a good appearance to the world. How many of us devote time to a spiritual routine every day?

I am sure you will agree with me: very few of us!

Satsang is nothing but the safest and easiest spiritual routine, that we can give ourselves. It cleanses and purifies our hearts. This cleansing of mind and heart is done through the chanting of the Name Divine, associating with men of God, as well as with like-minded aspirants who share our quest for Liberation, through *kirtan, bhajan* and recitations from the sacred scriptures, as well as listening to discourses that enlighten us. Just as we clean our body with soap and water, similarly we can purify our mind and heart by washing them in the waters of the spirit, the *amrit dhara*, that flows perennially in the *satsang*.

> **Still your mind in Me,**
> **Still yourself in Me,**
> **And without a doubt**
> **You shall be united with Me, Lord of Love,**
> **Dwelling in your heart.**
>
> *– Bhagavad Gita*

Have you ever wondered why some people go through constant suffering and misery? Whatever they do, seems to land them in trouble.

It is because they carry the negative vibration pattern of previous births. Such patterns can be changed and transformed only in the company of saints and sages. That is why it is said, in the stormy ocean of life we need the protection and the support of a holy one, who can clear our path and help us move towards more positive, happy and blissful life.

We live at a time when human nature seems to be at its worst. Evil has assumed frightening proportions, and the *vinaasha kaal* (disastrous times) that the holy scriptures speak of, seems close at hand. After all, what is this human nature we speak of? It is but the collective memory of our many previous births, and the residue of indelible *karmic* accumulation. It is very difficult to change human nature. It is next to impossible for us to change our own nature, which is grooved in the past. But what we cannot hope to achieve by our individual effort, a saint's grace can achieve on our behalf.

> **The rain does not fall in a certain land only; the sun does not shine only on a particular country. All that comes from God is for all souls. Verily, blessing is for every soul; for every soul, whatever be one's faith or belief, belongs to God.**
> **– Hazrat Inayat Khan** *(Sufi Scripture)*

Gurudev Sadhu Vaswani urged us to be in the company of saints and sages. Saints and sages radiate pure energy. These pure energies are the holy waters of the spirit. They purify and transform all those who come in contact with them. These pure energies can penetrate the subconscious mind and change its set pattern; they can even remove the *vaasanas,* the imprints of previous birth and its *karma.* That is why people seek out saints and sages so as to get relief from the negative patterns, which bring sorrow and misery into their life.

Perhaps many of you are not aware that we carry these negative patterns in our subconscious mind from one birth to another. A saint or a holy man can see the root cause of your suffering; a saint can understand why you suffer thus. In his company, by his grace, by his blessings, you can purify your past *karmas*, and actually write afresh the script for your destiny.

Once, I accompanied Gurudev Sadhu Vaswani on his visit to Jamshedpur. Here, an ardent admirer and devotee of Gurudev, took us to a beautiful lake. Gurudev Sadhu Vaswani remarked that the environment was beautiful and serene. I thought to myself, "Even in this pure environment there are some people whose minds are disturbed... they lack the spiritual sustenance and nourishment that can give them peace and tranquillity."

Let me tell you, even though our conscious mind may be at rest, our subconscious mind has its own undercurrent of turbulence, and this affects our lives far more powerfully than the workings of the conscious mind! The subconscious mind expresses desires of the past through dreams or through psychological compulsions that we don't really understand! This is the reason why good and virtuous people suddenly fall victim to sin. Innocent, smiling people, radiating joy, suddenly fall into depression. Sometimes, good leaders commit blunders, which bring them into bad repute. All these negative things happen, even among good people, because of the past *karmas*, and patterns of their desires formed in the subconscious mind. It is only a realised soul, a true Guru who can protect us from the negative influence of these subconscious forces.

Who is a Guru? A Guru is one who has not merely studied the *Vedas* and the Scriptures or one who writes a few books and gives discourses. A Guru is essentially a man of experience, of God-realisation. A true Guru is a friend of God. He walks with God. He talks to God. He lives and moves and has a perpetual fellowship with God. His every moment is spent in the presence of God. There is no difference, no separation, between such a person and God. To see such a one, is to see God Himself. Even if we were to go and meditate in the forest for several years, face hardships and practise austerities, or if we were to undertake a vow of silence or fast for years, or go on pilgrimages; it is nothing compared to spending a short time in the company of a true Guru!

To light a candle, you require another one that is already lit, or a matchstick. Similarly, to be able to kindle the light within, you require the company of a person who is already illumined. The Guru is an illumined soul; it is only he who can help enlighten another soul. That is why we have been told by wise men: seek to find God within you; if you cannot find God, seek out the company of a holy man who has found God within himself!

Have you seen those huge trees that grow by the roadside? During one of my regular morning walks, I noticed one such big tree with a huge trunk on my regular route. Just a week later, I saw that the same strong tree had fallen to the ground, uprooted by a cyclonic storm.

This can also happen (metaphorically) to a man who is strong and virtuous by character; a cyclonic storm of evil desire can devastate him. These desires are often hidden in our subconscious mind, and we don't know when and how they will manifest themselves and grab us without a warning. Such sudden storms are difficult to handle. This is why I urge you repeatedly: seek support in *sadh sangat*. The fellowship with the holy ones will give you the strength to face the storm and its turbulence. Alone, you would be destroyed. Being close to a saint, will strengthen you and revitalise your positive energy;

it will nullify those uncontrollable, evil desires. The pure and radiant energy you find in the vicinity of a saint will purify you, and protect you!

> **Lay not up for yourselves treasures upon earth, where moth and rust corrupt, and where thieves break through and steal:**
> **But lay up for yourselves treasures in heaven, where neither moth nor rust corrupt, and where thieves do not break through nor steal;**
> **For where your treasure is, there will your Heart also be.**
> **The Light of the body is the Eye. If, therefore, your Eye be Single, your whole body shall be Full of Light.**
> *– The Gospel according to* St. Matthew (6:20-21)

Man's life is so crowded with worldly activities, that he rarely has time for self-study and introspection. He seldom finds himself in that expansive, tranquil mood of silence and reflection, where he can listen to God, and chant the Name Divine in the heart within.

It is said that the worldly desires are like the salty waters of the sea. Such waters can never quench man's thirst. On the contrary, his thirst increases and his craving for fresh water grows even more acute! To drown yourself wholly in this worldly life is akin to quenching your thirst with salt water.

My humble request to all of you, my fellow pilgrims, is to spare some time for *satsang*. By all means do your work sincerely. Work is essential for a human being. It disciplines his mind and exercises his body. Work is a great boon. But we must remember, work is a means, it is not an end. Livelihood must never be confused with life. Do not make your work the objective of your life on this earth. The purpose of your life is to cultivate the soul. Hence, even while you are attending to your work, stay connected to the Source of all Life; stay in constant touch with God. If you give eight or nine hours a day to your work, it should not be difficult to spare one or two hours to your spiritual growth! This will help you achieve the kind of inner peace and bliss that work can never bring to you.

There is a verse in the Guru Granth Sahib which tells us, *'Jo Mange Thakur Apnay Te, Soi Soi Devay'*. It means – 'Ask and you shall get'. You have to ask Him to shower His grace on you. Sure enough He will fulfill your request.

Even as you ask for this grace, make it your practice to seek association with the devout and pious: in other words, start going to *satsang* daily. Participate in *naam kirtan*. Kindle that flame, which will make you seek the grace!

Before you begin all else, you must seek the grace of your Guru. The Guru is necessary on this path;

without his guidance your progress will be slow. Attain to the Guru's grace: and through the Guru, seek the grace of God! The Guru can certainly show you the path, but the effort must be made by the seeker. First there has to be the 'Intention'; then the quest, and then the Guru's grace, and finally your own effort, which will ultimately bear fruit by the grace of God!

The seeker's path is difficult; the seeker's path is long and weary! We often sing the song in *satsang*– "The sea is vast, My boat is frail: I trust in Thee, And all is well!"

We have much to do to reach our goal. We have to face storms. We have to cross treacherous oceans; we have to climb rocky mountains; we have to be tested by fire. It is tough to get past these tests. One thing can get us across safely: the Lord's grace. By His grace alone shall we reach our destination! And this grace is accessible to you through the grace of the Guru!

Man has to rediscover his heart. He has to reinvest himself with noble sentiments and higher emotions. The highest emotion is love. Let your heart expand and engulf the world with love! That love will bond you with the universe and its Creator.

> And when he sees Me in all and sees all in Me,
> Then I never leave him and he never leaves Me.
> And he, who in this Oneness of Love
> Loves Me in whatever he sees,
> Wherever he may live,
> In truth, he lives in Me.
>
> – *Bhagavad Gita*

Guru Nanak has said that the purpose for which you have come can be fulfilled only through your association with saints and sages. Therefore, take the Name Divine with love and hope and devotion. Remember too, that every breath is precious. Our lifespan is predetermined even before we come upon this earth. We have a limited number of days at our disposal. Every person is born with a set number of breaths. We take our breathing for granted, but if you really consider the truth of life, you will come to realise that every breath, every moment, is precious. There is no time to be wasted, for death can knock at our doors any minute!

This human life is precious, but we do not value it.

We count our money; we weigh our position and power most accurately; but alas, we fritter away precious hours and minutes of this rare gift of human birth, without realising their value! We boast that we can earn back the money we lose in the stock market;

but have you known anyone who can regain the days he has lost of his life? Can we put back the clock to buy more time from death?

Death, we are told, walks just two steps behind us, though most of us are blissfully unaware of its presence! If you wish to fulfill the purpose of your life before death overtakes you, you must take care of the company you move in. You must seek association with an evolved soul. You must seek the company of good people. The more you move in association of such people, the more goodness will flow into you.

Satsang has a positive effect on man. *Satsang* creates pure and positive vibrations which neutralise the negative emotions of man. When we go to *satsang*, we get to hear discourses of holy men, participate in the recitation of sacred scriptures and singing of soulful *bhajans*. All of this helps to raise the levels of positive vibrations and energises us. For a short time at least, we forget our mundane worries and get immersed in the pure waters of the Spirit. Our emotions rise above the senses, and we cry out, "O Lord! This is bliss. O Lord! You have given me this beautiful gift of life. Till now I have wasted it. But from now onwards, I will strive to achieve the goal of this human birth!"

Some of us are given to reading extensively from the scriptures; some of us perform elaborate rituals of worship; but our minds are not always under our control! Stillness and serenity of the mind is achieved only in fellowship with a saint. He alone has the *shakti* to transform you and make you anew.

You all have your share of worldly friends; keep them by all means; but do not refrain from seeking the fellowship with the holy men, who are friends of God. They are your canopy of protection. Seek shelter under them!

For Your Reflection

How can we gather to ourselves the true treasure of *satsang*? So let me give you a few practical suggestions:

1. Seek the company of people who go to the *satsang*. Association with them will give you the impulse to enter the world of the *satsang*, a world of spiritual quietude and prayer.

2. Set apart some time every day to refrain from worldly activities and focus on the inner world within you. Enter into nurturing activities like meditation, recitation from the scriptures, etc.

3. Keep yourself away from all unproductive talk, gossip and controversies. Do not criticise others, nor entertain gossip about them.

4. Do not miss your daily appointment with God. Fix a time for your meditation. Resolve that you will meditate for 15 minutes or half an hour or an hour daily. During this period you can chant the Name Divine, you can commune with God, meditate on some inspirational teachings, or pick up a sentence from a spiritual literature on compassion, oneness, etc. and reflect on it.

The King Who Wanted Liberation

Long ago there lived a King. A Pandit used to go to him every day and read the Srimad Bhagavat aloud to him. After every chapter, the Pandit would read the closing message, which said: he who religiously reads the Bhagavat or hears it, will himself witness the Light and will achieve mukti, liberation from the cycle of birth and death.

After a few months of daily reading, when the Pandit had completed reading the Bhagavat, the King asked him a question: "Tell me, have I witnessed the Light? Have I reached the stage where I will be released from the cycle of birth and death? Is true liberation now assured for me?"

To this, the Pandit replied, "That is a question which you alone can answer for yourself, your Majesty."

The King was not happy with this reply. "You have deceived me," he accused the Pandit. "Every evening, I have been hearing the Bhagavat Purana. At the end of each chapter you have said to me that he who hears the Bhagavat Purana will attain mukti and witness the Light.

Now, you have to prove what you have been reading. I give you one week's time to prove that I have attained liberation. If you fail to prove this, I will send you to the gallows."

The Pandit was taken aback. He had expected praise and reward from the King. Instead he had received a threat of death! Depressed, he returned home. Six days passed by, but he could not find any solution to the problem. How was he to prove to the King that after listening to the *Bhagavat Purana*, a man achieves mukti? The Pandit became worried and despondent.

His seven year old daughter, seeing her father's anguished face, asked him, "Baba, why are your eyes glistening with unbidden tears? What is your problem?"

The Pandit opened out his heart to his child. The girl heard him out. Then she said very innocently, "Is that what worries you? Don't cry, for I will come with you to the King's darbar tomorrow, and I will explain the situation to the King and hopefully convince him."

On the following day, the girl accompanied the Pandit to the King's palace. On entering the darbar hall, she ran to one of the huge, ornamental pillars and put her arms around it. And then, she began to cry at the top of her voice, "O please, please, will someone release me from the grip of this pillar? This pillar is holding me." The King witnessed the scene from his throne and thought that the girl was indeed stupid. Who has brought this foolish child to the court, he wondered. Surely, she was mad. For she herself was clinging to the pillar and shouting to others to come and rescue her!

Aloud, he said to her, "O foolish girl, just leave that pillar." The girl cried still louder, "O please, please, separate me from this pillar. Come someone, I have to go back home, but the pillar will not let me go. Have mercy on me and please release me from the clutch of this pillar."

Now the King was really angry. "Who is this stupid girl?" he thundered. "Who has brought her here to my palace? I shall punish them both severely."

On hearing this, the girl left the pillar with a smile. She humbly bowed before the King and said to him, "Your Majesty, you too are holding on to the pillar of your ego. You are unnecessarily blaming my father for not having achieved mukti. Leave the ego and you will surely witness the Light."

The King realised his mistake. He saw that liberation is not a gift which someone can present him on a platter. Mukti is to be earned. The saints, sages and the scriptures can only show us the path, but it is we who have to walk the path. It is we who have to achieve that inner freedom which is the way to liberation.

Chapter Four

Seek True Inner Freedom

The other day, I was taking a walk by the seaside with a few friends. The Arabian Sea stretched out before us in a vast blue expanse. The sky was clear and birds were circling overhead. Suddenly we saw a formation, a flock of birds gliding gracefully across the skies. "How I wish I were a bird in the sky," remarked a young girl who was with us.

"You are such a bright young child," I said to her. "Why do you want to be a bird in the sky?"

"I want to be really free, I want to fly," she exclaimed. "Yes, I want to be free as a bird. I want to enjoy the freedom of the open skies."

I was reminded of my own teenage years, when my ambition was to join the Merchant Navy and take to the vast, wide, blue seas!

Every one of us wishes for that kind of freedom. Freedom, which is infinite and limitless!

"My child, if you want to be truly free, then you must know what true freedom is," I said to her. "It is the freedom of the inner self, the freedom you feel from within!"

It is unfortunate, that we look only for outer freedom, whereas true freedom lies within.

As I watched the birds in the sky, I was reminded of the words in that beautiful book, *The Imitation of Christ.*

"If you wish to make progress in virtue, live in the fear of the Lord, do not look for too much freedom," the voice of Christ tells us in this beautiful book. "My child, renounce self and you shall find Me. Give up your own self-will, your possessions, and you shall always gain. For once you resign yourself irrevocably, greater grace will be given to you…" And again, "If you desire to attain grace and freedom of heart, let the free offering of yourself into the hands of God precede your every action. This is why so few are inwardly free and enlightened — they know not how to renounce themselves entirely."

Isn't that a beautiful thought — to attain inward freedom through utter renunciation? How many of us are capable of giving up something to attain true freedom?

May I ask you, what is your idea of true freedom? Is it to live and act and do as you please? Is it to fulfill all your aspirations and desires? Is it to indulge your every whim and fancy? Is it to throw off all restrictions and regulations that keep you chained, confined to a routine that you resent? Or is it something that transcends all this?

The desire to be free, to feel free to pursue one's goals and desires is an innate human aspiration.

> **The different parts and pieces of a chariot are useless unless they work in accordance with the whole. A man's life will bring nothing to him unless he lives in accordance with the whole universe.**
>
> **– Lao Tzu**

Deep within each one of us is an innate desire for freedom. For some of us it is merely felt as a material desire to be free from financial restrictions, to be able to possess whatever we crave for. This may be a new car, a better job or even an expensive holiday abroad. For others, the desire is more mature, more elevated: we wish to achieve true peace, joy or love. Whether it is freedom from want or freedom from worldly cares, the desire to be free is simply part of human nature.

So what prevents us from achieving this freedom?

We all know of convicts and offenders who are locked in physical prisons behind metal bars under the law of the land; naturally they crave to be released from confinement, to be free like the rest of us. But there is also another confinement that many of us are subject to. I believe that many of us are locked in a mental prison of our own making; we feel restricted, confined, by our own oppressing thoughts and emotions and crave to be free from those crippling negative energies.

To be still, to taste that beautiful moment of calm, to feel the central core of peace and bliss that is within, is to be truly free and truly happy!

Is it not true that we all long for such moments of absolute freedom, freedom from the demons within?

Remez Sasson, the inspirational writer, tells us that all of us are trapped, imprisoned by the conditioning of our own incessant thinking. Freedom from the compulsion of constant and endless thinking is real freedom.

Our minds are constantly grappling with thoughts from the moment we wake up in the morning until we fall asleep at night. We do not have even a moment's freedom from our thoughts in our waking hours. Thoughts create more thoughts and also receive thoughts from the external world around us. This habit is so strong and deeply embedded that nobody even thinks of overcoming it.

Can you really consider yourself free in such a state? You may be a free citizen living in a free country; you may be financially independent; you may exercise your choice in daily decision making; and yet, and yet, your mind keeps you chained to an incessant flow of thoughts and mental images, many of which are useless and futile and some of which are actually negative and depressing. Outwardly, you are free; but deep within, you are enslaved by your own thought processes.

So ask yourself: what is confining you, restricting you in such a state? It is your own mind. Therefore, the Gita tells us: Man is his own friend and man is his own foe. In the measure in which we think good thoughts, positive thoughts, we become our own friends. In the measure in which we think negative thoughts, thoughts of defeat and despair, we become our own foes. Positive thoughts induce magnetism; negative thoughts weaken your magnetism. A cheerful attitude strengthens your magnetism, discouragement weakens it. Hope reinforces your magnetism, despair undermines it. Faith re-emphasises your magnetism, doubt dilutes it. Love empowers your magnetism, hatred takes away from it.

> **Between stimulus and response there is a space. In that space is our power to choose our response. In our response lies our growth and our freedom.**
>
> **– Viktor E. Frankl**

No one will 'grant' you spirituality, no one can present spiritual strength on a platter to you. Your spiritual energy has to develop from within. It is you yourself who must grow and evolve in spiritual strength in order to make a success of your life on earth and in the dimension beyond life.

The universe works like an echo: Whatever thoughts you think, will rebound on you. Therefore, be careful of the thoughts you think. Free yourself from the bondage of crippling negative thoughts, before you seek external freedom. Our thoughts are all-powerful. How many of us can really control them?

We must realise once and for all: no one else is to blame for our present condition. We have built it with our own thoughts and desires generated in the near or distant past. Therefore, I tell my friends again and again: "Change your thoughts, and you can change your *karma*. Change your *karma* and you will change the conditions in which you live."

You are the architect of your own destiny. You are the builder of your own fate. Every thought, emotion, wish, action, creates *karma*: we have been creating *karma* for millions, perhaps billions of years. If our thoughts, emotions and actions are benevolent, so-called good *karma* results. If they are malevolent, evil or difficult, bad *karma* is created.

When we become aware that our destiny is created by our own thoughts, words, actions and desires, then there is always the possibility that is open to us, to correct and improve ourselves by changing our thoughts and actions for the better!

In this connection, I would like to share with you the Sindhi experience; I may even refer to it as the Sindhi saga of freedom. As many of you know, the Sindhi community is, technically speaking, a stateless community in free India; this is because the land of our birth, the *Sindhu desha*, went wholly into Pakistani territory after Partition. Again, as all of you must know, many of my people who came into freedom and independence, walked into independent India, practically penniless, with virtually no possessions except the clothes they carried on their backs!

Today, the (Hindu) Sindhi diaspora is a unique example of a community that was driven away from its native land, became refugees in their own country, and rose like a Phoenix from the smoldering ashes of Partition, to become one of the most successful and philanthropic people in the world. How was this possible? Let me give you the words of Gurudev Sadhu Vaswani:

"...I believe there is a rich treasure in the traditions, folklore and literature of Sind...In the Sindhi soul, there is an immensity, an elemental strength, an aspiration to the Infinite, such as is suggested by the vast deserts of *Sindhu desha*... her poets and mystics, her *fakirs* and *dervishes*, her singers and contemplatives, achieved interior freedom... In the simplicity and humanity of her poets and mystics is the seed of a spiritual culture..."

Spiritualism, mysticism, immensity of vision and aspiration to true freedom – the Master has indeed captured the essence of Sindhi literature in a few memorable words!

He would often tell his Sindhi friends that though they had left their lands, their property, their homes and wealth, they had brought with them a far more valuable treasure – the treasure of their culture, traditions and their spirit of freedom!

During the troubled days following the traumatic partition of India, Gurudev Sadhu Vaswani urged the refugees from Sind to be strong within. He exhorted them to be self-sufficient and refrain from begging for government help. Again and again, he repeated those magic words which became a *mantra* of positive thinking for all of us: "Within you lies a hidden *shakti;* awaken that *shakti* and all will be well with you." I remember, too, his unforgettable call to the shattered community, "Believe and achieve!"

To believe in ourselves, to believe that we are the architects of our own destiny is true inner freedom!

Exercise In Self-Analysis

Are you really free?

It is good to subject yourself to your own review, once in a while. Such a personal self-examination can be a real eye opener, and benefits you in your spiritual growth.

All of us make mistakes at one time or another; all of us do what is exactly right on certain occasions. As the saying goes, "You win some, you lose some." But whatever we do, it is important that we act with awareness and learn from each experience, good or bad. "Ponder upon your own conduct," says a Hebrew proverb, "and you will bring much good to yourself."

Set aside at least one day of the month, to review your life and actions in a mood of calm detachment. What was it that prompted you to do such and such a thing or avoid doing such and such a thing? Was the action worthy of you? Looking back, did you feel proud of what you had done? Did you act out of compulsion or was your choice made freely?

Remember, good choices make us wiser and better human beings. We learn to make good choices only from experience. And experiences are often acquired through bad choices!

Periodical exercises in self-analysis help us grow in wisdom to make the right choice more often. Should you find that you have done things which you are ashamed of, it is essential that you must overcome such weaknesses in the future.

Have you offended someone? Seek their forgiveness.

Have you neglected to offer a helping hand? Make amends for your negligence.

Have you made someone happy with your words or actions? Resolve to do more in the same vein; determine to make more and more people happy.

Wisdom is not always something you have to learn. Often it resides within you.

Freedom is not always doing whatever you please. More often than not, it is the choice you make to do what is good and right.

SECTION III
The VIBGYOR Of Spirituality

What does it take to walk the path of spirituality? How can we bear witness to the truth of the *atman* in deeds of daily living?

In simple terms it means imbibing and internalising certain qualities associated with spirituality, and putting them into practice to the extent possible in our everyday lives. I refer to these qualities as the VIBGYOR of Spirituality – for they are seven in number, even as the colours of the rainbow are seven in number. They are:

1. Truth

2. Purity

3. Humility

4. Child-like Trust

5. Selfless Service

6. Practice of Daily Silence

7. Love

Have you seen and marvelled at the magnificent beauty of a rainbow? It arches across the horizon when raindrops refract the sunlight and remind us that the Universe operates according to God's well laid out principles which are also scientific and systematic! Before Newton discovered it, people did not know that visible light was made up of seven distinct bands of colours. It was Newton who taught us that the raindrops, acting like a prism, refract or bend the light, so that the colours separate and show up as seven different bands – violet, indigo, blue, green, yellow, orange and red.

Newton used a prism to show that the different bands of visible light actually split up into rainbow colours; he projected the resultant rainbow onto a wall. This brought a further query: Was it the prism that was colouring visible light? To prove this point, he then used another prism to refract or bend the bands back together again. This caused all the colours to merge together into what we call visible or white light.

The magic of the rainbow, indeed, the miracle of visible light, is God's marvel! Newton revealed the same to us in terms of scientific principles and order. This great scientist firmly believed that God was the Masterful Creator whose existence could be seen in the sheer grandeur of all creation. "…'Tis inconceivable that inanimate brute matter should (without the mediation of something else which is not material) operate upon and affect other matter without mutual contact," he wrote to a friend. "This most beautiful system of the sun, planets and comets, could only proceed from the counsel and dominion of an intelligent Being… This Being governs all things, not as the soul of the world, but as Lord over all; and on account of His Dominion He is wont to be called "Lord, God" or "Universal Ruler"…The Supreme God is a Being Eternal, Infinite [and] Absolutely Perfect…"

No one who sees a rainbow can ever fail to respond to its marvellous beauty! And through the ages, the colours of the rainbow have always held a mystical and deeply symbolic significance for the thinking, sensitive individual. Emanuel Swedenborg, a great admirer and follower of Issac Newton and a distinguished scientist and philosopher in his own right, gave up his academic research which had brought him considerable fame and fortune, when he was given a direct revelation of the spiritual world – a revelation which he believed, came directly from God. He regarded this event as the birth of the New Age when it would be possible for us *"to enter with the understanding into the mysteries of faith"* by means of the spiritual truths which were being revealed to mankind through him. As his biographer puts it, "For the first time, a highly trained scientific intellect was used to describe spiritual laws and principles by observing the life of the spirit". Let me say to you, Swedenborg made no attempt to preach or propagate his theories. He believed that the truth would be made manifest to all people when they were ready for it!

The VIBGYOR of the rainbow are the colours of light made visible to us through the marvel of the universe! They symbolise the spiritual truth, that we must not merely absorb, but reflect and transmit God's Divine qualities through deeds of daily living. Indeed, the rainbow symbolises enlightenment in a celestial phenomenon of visible beauty that is a joy to behold! It reflects the inner awakening of enlightenment caused by the radiant light inherent in truth and wisdom – an inner light that can dispel the darkness of doubt and despair.

In the pages that follow, I urge you to reflect the colours of inner awakening – the VIBGYOR of spirituality – in deeds of daily living, so that the radiance of this inner light may spread all around you, touching the lives of you and your people with the magic of the eternal principle of Divine Truth!

He Who Tells The Best Story...

A clergyman was walking down a deserted street when he came upon a group of about a dozen boys, all of them between 10 and 12 years of age.

The boys were shabbily dressed and were chewing gum. They were staring intently at a dog, as they circled around the creature, silently. The dog was a lame, stray animal, obviously a street dog, a mongrel. Concerned lest the boys should hurt the dog or harm the animal in any way, the clergyman called out sharply, "Hey kids, what are you up to?"

One of the boys stopped chewing his gum and replied, "This dog is just an old neighbourhood stray. We all love him and want to keep him, but only one of us can take him home. So we have decided that whoever tells the biggest lie will get to keep the dog."

Needless to say, the reverend was taken aback. "Honestly!" he exclaimed, "I'm quite distressed by your attitude. You boys shouldn't be having a contest telling lies!" There and then he launched into a ten minute sermon against lying, beginning, "Don't you boys ever attend church? Haven't you been told that it is a sin to lie?" He ended with the resounding assertion, "Why, when I was your age, I never, ever, told a lie!"

There was dead silence for about a minute. Just as the reverend was beginning to think he'd touched their conscience after all, the smallest boy spat out his chewing gum in disgust, gave a deep sigh and said, "All right guys, he wins. Give him the dog."

Chapter One

Walk The Way Of Truth

The great injunction of our ancient scriptures is this: *Satyam vada ; Dharmam chara* (Speak the Truth, abide by Righteousness).

Scriptural scholars tell us that these words were actually part of the final farewell uttered by the Guru to his disciples who were on the point of 'passing out' of their *gurukul shiksha* to step out into the wide world beyond the bounds of the Guru's *ashram*. In fact these injunctions were part of the final 'convocation' ceremony of ancient times, uttered as the Guru's parting advice to the young men whom he had taken such pains to educate all these years!

The Upanishads too, declare, for their part: *Satyameva Jayate* (Truth alone triumphs). *Satyat Nasti Paro Dharma* (There is no *Dharma* greater than truth), declare the *puranas*.

Truth is God. Our scriptures pay tribute to this fact by referring to God as *satya priya* (lover of truth) and *satya swaroopa* (embodiment of truth).

(306)

Mahatma Gandhi often said: "People say God is Truth. I believe that Truth is God!" For Gandhi, the logical equivalent or manifestation of God was to be found in Truth. Truth is God, he declared. Truth is Rama, Narayana, Ishwara, Khuda, Allah and God. He frequently quoted, with fervour, the Sanskrit proverb: *Satyat Nasti Paro Dharma,* and regarded it as the very foundation of his value system. The pursuit of truth, the attempt to realise truth in one's thoughts and action, he said, is the substance of the religion of man. "Devotion to truth," he wrote, "is the sole justification for our existence." Little wonder then, that his autobiography was entitled: *The Story of My Experiments with Truth.*

When he was a student, they put a question to Mahatma Gandhi: "Tell us what is more precious than silver?" he answered: "Gold is more precious than silver." "Is there anything that is more precious than gold?" he was asked. And He answered: "Truth is more precious than gold and there is nothing that is more precious than Truth."

Gurudev Sadhu Vaswani emphasised the same when he said to us: "Truth, though she take me through the fire; Truth, though she lead me to the scaffold!"

And Truth is not a feeble thing that you and I need to save and protect. Let us not underestimate the power of Truth, for our scriptures also assert: *Satyameva Jayate!* Truth alone triumphs! And the truth that will ever triumph is the knowledge of the Divine being that is manifest in all of us, the immanence of God, and the awareness that we are not just frail beings, but immortal spirits lit by the spark of His Divine fire. *Ishwarah sarva bhutanaam hriddhe arjuna tisthathi*, Sri Krishna tells us in the Gita. "The Lord dwelleth in the hearts of all beings, O Arjuna!"

The disciples questioned Jesus concerning the Way of Life: "How should we fast? In what manner should we pray? How should our alms be given? What dietary law should we observe?" Jesus said, "I will instruct you in all these matters, but first you must put off your love of the lie, the false way of life followed by the children of this plane of existence, and be converted, changed so that you hate that which you have previously loved, and love that which you have previously hated. Then I will be able to show you all things, for there is nothing hidden which will not be manifested when you have put on the mind of Truth."

– Sayings of Jesus

Our great *avatara purushas* too, have taught us through precept and practice, that Truth is greater than all else.

Consider the fourth *avatara* of Maha Vishnu, namely the Vamana *avatara*. The young brahmin *brahmachari* walks into the *yagna shala* of the demon emperor Mahabali to beg for *biksha*. Enchanted by the Divine youngster, Mahabali tells him, "Ask whatever you wish for. I will deny nothing to you." To symbolise this promise, he offers *argya* – water poured on the *brahmin's* hands to formalise his promise.

Shukracharya, the Guru of the demons, is distressed at the sight of Vamana. Desperately, he tries to warn the demon king that he should retract his promise. Mahabali realises that his doom is upon him; but the great emperor cannot and will not back out, either to save his kingdom or even to save himself. "Can there be a greater evil than going back on my plighted word?" he asks his Guru. "And how fortunate am I that Sri Hari Himself is asking for alms at my hands! If this spells doom for me, I embrace this doom with wide open arms. To surrender my all at His Holy Feet is the Ultimate *mukti* for me!"

They who know the truth are not equal to those who love it, and they who love it are not equal to those who delight in it.

– Confucius

The Srimad Bhagavat tells us that at this point of ultimate surrender, Mahabali uttered these words:

"There is nothing more sinful than untruthfulness. Because of this, Bhudevi, Mother Earth once said, 'I can bear the heavy burden of any sinner, but I cannot support a person who is a liar'."

Today, we utter all kinds of lies, all shades of lies, including white lies and lies to escape wrath and punishment. I doubt if any transaction can ever be concluded without uttering one falsehood or the other. Consider the heavy burden that Mother Earth must be carrying today!

Are we truthful? Do we live a truthful and transparent life? If we are truthful, many of us would be forced to concede that our life is full of lies and falsehood. Social psychologists talk about the "games" people play, the "roles" that they assume in their daily life. Under the roles and games we play, our real personality is hidden from the world. We wear a mask of goodness, we dress well and perfume our bodies and pose to be honest and clean.

It is human nature to try to find in others what we lack. We are untruthful. We suspect others of being the same. It is also human nature to conceal one's own faults from one's own self. We are not able to face our own faults. When we are not true to our own self, how can we be true to others, how can we be true to our Guru?

God is Truth and if you want to go nearer to God, then you should bear witness to the Truth in deeds of daily life.

> **The high-minded man must care more for the truth than for what people think.**
>
> – Aristotle

To travel the path of truth is not only difficult, it needs a tremendous amount of discipline, courage, steadfastness and determination. But the rewards of following this path are spectacular and what is more important, eternal.

How may we follow the practice of truth in everyday life? Let me offer a few practical suggestions:

1. Become aware of why you do not speak the truth: is it out of fear? Or is it due to desire for gain? Or perhaps, out of ill-will and the wish to hurt others? Address the root cause, and do not let negative emotions like fear and greed and ill-will dictate your attitude. When you conquer these negative emotions, you learn to speak the truth in utter freedom.

2. Realise that the duty to speak the truth should not become a license to hurt another: therefore, practise truth along with kindness.

3. Speak the truth at the appropriate time: helpful suggestions and honest utterances should not be uttered when your listeners are not prepared to take them.

4. Do not rehearse half-truths or lies as excuses to utter to friends: if there has been a lapse on your part, admit the truth.

5. Learn the art of sincere apology. Learning to say sorry is one of the most difficult acts of truth. It involves being honest about yourself and being honest to the other person as well.

6. Not just outright lies, but also exaggerations and omissions amount to falsehood: therefore, in all important matters, learn to speak the truth, the whole truth and nothing but the truth.

7. Remember that gossip, slander and rumour are some of the worst forms of falsehood. Refrain from these at all times, and at all costs.

8. Hypocrisy and pretence are also akin to falsehood. Be aware of who you are and what your limitations are. Do not pretend to be what you are not.

9. Practise honesty in all your transactions, especially as they relate to money matters. Avoid malpractices in all business dealings.

10. Offering or accepting bribes is also a form of dishonesty. Refrain from corrupting others; equally, do not seek illicit gains for yourself by accepting bribes.

Exercise in Introspection

1. Do not belittle your efforts at being honest or ethical. Reflect on your past deeds which have given you peace and satisfaction. Build on those feelings and aim to achieve the same every time.

2. Are you one of those people who believe that there is a 'bandwidth' for honesty, integrity and truth? You must learn that there can be no compromise, no dilution of principles such as these. Ultimately, each of us is answerable to God, who not only sees what we are doing and saying, but is aware of our innermost intentions.

3. Are you one of those people who use truth economically? Let go of such a miserly attitude. Start off with at least one day in the week when you speak nothing but the truth. This does not mean that you should be insensitive, or hurt others by rude remarks. It only means that you do not succumb to the temptation to utter lies.

4. Assess your own reactions to truth-telling. How do you feel when you have spoken the truth and acted with integrity? Less prone to guilt? Or a sense of inner strength and peace? Ask yourself: can I do it more often? Can I do it at all times?

5. What are the occasions, situations in which you are constrained to resort to falsehood? Was it out of fear of authority? Was it to boost your ego? Was it to project a better image of yourself? Was it to evade taxes? Was it for monetary gain? Reflect on the consequences of your choice. Realise that right action can put not just you, but everyone you deal with in a win-win situation.

6. Gossip is nothing more than telling tales and carrying tales. Invariably, gossip is about someone who is not present to present his or her side of the story. Gossip, to right thinking people, is one of the most vicious forms of falsehood. Do not labour under the illusion that there is such a thing as 'harmless gossip'. It may not harm the other person, but it is most certainly harming you!

7. If you have indulged in dishonesty or untruth or gossip, it is not too late to make amends. Wrongs can always be set right. You can apologise to people whom you have hurt by your gossip or slander; you can replace what you have wrongly taken away; you can compensate for losses that others might have incurred because of your dishonesty. Make amends without delay, and see the difference it makes!

Are You Still Holding Her?

Tanzan Hara was a famous Zen monk of the Meiji Period. He was also a Buddhist scholar and became the first lecturer in Indian philosophy at Tokyo University.

As a young pilgrim monk he had often travelled across the country with other monks to reach distant centres of learning. On one such trip, he was walking with a close friend, an older monk, when they came to the banks of a rapid river in spate. They saw, however, that the river was quite shallow, and decided to wade across the river. Just then, they saw a beautiful young lady who was hesitating to wade through the stream, and begged Tanzan to help her. "There is no need for you to worry," said Tanzan, "I'll carry you across. Just hold on to my shoulders tightly. Alright?" and lightly holding the girl he carried her across.

They reached the other side safely and the girl blushingly thanked Tanzan; but he noticed that his friend had gone ahead, and in his haste to catch up, he did not wait to hear her. He caught up with the older monk and the two of them walked about a mile in silence. Tanzan's friend appeared to be displeased for some reason. Suddenly the friend could contain himself no longer and bluntly said, "You're a disgrace. Do you think monks should carry young girls about?" He looked angry.

Tanzan, pretending not to understand, looked round about him and said, "What? Where is this girl?"

"Don't go on pretending. You held a beautiful girl close to yourself just a short while ago."

"Ha, ha, ha, ha, ha you mean that girl. I carried her across the river and put her down long ago! Have you been carrying her in your mind all this way?"

Hearing this, the friend was at a loss for words.

Chapter Two

Practise Purity In Thought Word And Deed

In ancient India the two great ideals of purity and prayer were brought together in the one great concept of *brahmacharya*. Do not think that *brahmacharya* is limited to just celibacy. *Brahmacharya* can also be practised in married life. *Brahmacharya* is not asceticism in; nor is it stoicism. *Brahamcharya* is literally, moving with God! To move and live in *Brahman* — that is to be a true *brahmachari*. He must be a man of purity and prayer. These two make the body and spirit vital. They rejuvenate the outer body, breaking the barriers of weakness. They link man with God: and he finds a great *shakti* (energy) flowing through him. He becomes a channel for the outpouring upon others of the spirit of Light!

Dear friends, this physical body is but a dwelling which we inhabit for a fleeting while. A time will come when we have to leave behind this physical form and move onward, forward.

The *jignasu*, the true seeker is always conscious of this truth. He keeps his senses under his control, he maintains the purity of his physical form. He knows that life is a priceless gift that we have received through the grace of God. Therefore, it is fitting that we devote this life to the service of God.

There was a devotee of the Lord, an aristocrat who was often invited to attend the King's *darbar*. One day, at a special gathering held at the royal palace, he too was present with the wealthiest and wisest men in the kingdom. The King, in a mood of generous extravagance, presented each of his guests with a magnificent robe. The guests were delighted by his generosity and thanked their sovereign profusely.

As our man was leaving the *darbar* hall, he was seized by a fit of sneezing. His nose began to run, and he looked in vain for a handkerchief – alas, he was not carrying one that day. Instinctively, he wiped his running nose on the long, flowing sleeve of the garment that the King had just bestowed on him.

A few courtiers who saw this, rushed to the King. "Oh sire, this man has insulted your Highness, brought disgrace upon your dignity," they complained. "You bestowed an expensive robe on him – and he wipes his nose with it! This is gross abuse of your priceless gift! It is intolerable!"

The King was furious. He sent for the man and said to him harshly, "Take off the robe that I gave you and leave my court at once. You are exiled from my presence and you shall not set foot in my court ever again!"

The man was deeply affected by the unexpected turn of events. In his anguish, he thought, "The King is a temporal ruler, who has bestowed a worldly gift on me. This garment is ephemeral, subject to wear and tear. Just because I wiped my nose on the robe, the King has banished me from his court. Ah, but what of the precious garment that the King of kings, the Emperor of emperors has bestowed on me?"

Indeed, the Lord has bestowed a precious robe on each and every one of us – rich or poor, saint or sinner, we have all received such a robe. That priceless robe is the human body. Alas, in what manner do we abuse this body! Let us learn to respect this precious gift, let us treat this body with the dignity it deserves. Every *jignasu*, every seeker, maintains the purity of this physical form. He guards his body from falling a prey to desires and passions. For physical discipline is an essential first step on the path of spiritual discipline!

> **I will not let anyone walk through my mind with their dirty feet.**
>
> – Mahatma Gandhi

If you wish to maintain the purity and sanctity of the temple that is your body, spend some time in meditation everyday. Without this practice, we cannot attain purity or sanctity of life. Therefore, as I said, the *jignasu* retires to a quiet corner, where he prays, "Oh Lord, keep me always in the blessed grace of Your Divine presence. Guard me, protect me from evil passions and desires, For he alone is safe, who seeks Your protection. All the rest drown in the deep waters of the *sansar sagar* – this vast ocean of *maya* that we call life!"

Gurudev Sadhu Vaswani was brilliant at his studies and rarely missed the top rank in his school days. At the matriculation examination, he secured a scholarship which took him to college. His classmates in the college often wondered at the unsullied purity of his life and his utter guilelessness and they all loved and respected him as one belonging to a world remote from their own.

One day, a few of his friends took him out for an evening walk. They were out for mischief. They took him to the house of a beautiful courtesan and, leaving the two together, disappeared for a while.

The courtesan gazed at him and she was inflamed, for he was truly handsome.

As she drew closer to him, the fragrance of her scented garments filled his nostrils. But he continued to sit still as a statue carved out of stone.

And she said to him in a bewitching voice, "Will you not step into my inner chamber?"

And he said, "Am I not already in the inner chamber?"

She did not understand the meaning of those words. Laying bare a part of her body, she said to him, "Look at me! Am I not truly beautiful?"

He looked not at her. But with eyes half-closed, he said to her, "Beloved sister! The beauty you behold in the mirror, again and again, will fade away sooner than you imagine, for it is merely the beauty of flesh and skin. And flesh can draw only flesh to itself, and flesh becomes food for flesh and is consumed in the fire of passion. But there is another beauty which shall not fade! It is the beauty of the Unseen in you. Think of that beauty! Gaze upon it until your appetites are burnt and your body becomes a radiant temple of the Spirit."

The courtesan had never seen such a young man in all her life. She was speechless, lost in wonder.

Then, looking at her with his dawn eyes, he said, "Come, sister! Let us sing together the Holy Name of God!"

Amused, the courtesan joined in singing God's sacred Name. It was at that moment his friends entered the room, giggling, sure they would behold their immaculate friend in the arms of the harlot. The joke was turned against them. And from that day they knew Gurudev Sadhu Vaswani was no ordinary person, that his life was incorruptible, stainless and pure as the flowing waters of the River Ganga, that he was of the race of those who visit the earth from time to time but who do not belong to the earth. They belong to the Kingdom of the Light, the Kingdom of the Spirit, the Kingdom that is higher than the stars and deeper than the seas.

> **When you express "purity" which is the truth about yourself, you feel a love for yourself that is expressed by self-respect, self-esteem and self-confidence!**
> – Tae Yun Kim, *Seven Steps to Inner Power*

How may we practice purity in thought, word and deed? Gurudev Sadhu Vaswani spoke of five aspects of our life, which needed purification: and, it applies to all of us, and not just aspiring *sadhakas* or seekers!

1.   The very first is *Vaak* – voice, utterance,
     sound, speech. Voice is the outer expression
     of thought. *Vaak* must be purified if you wish
     to grow in the perfect life.

     Utter what you believe to be true. Speak out
     the truth – but not in bitterness. Purify your
     utterance by means of love. Do not wound or
     hurt the feelings of others.

     Is it that someone's mode of worship does not
     appeal to you? Do not defile him as 'idolater'
     or 'infidel' or 'pagan'. Respect his views – but
     follow your own.

     I wonder if you have noticed how the *vaak*,
     the utterance of a saint, a realised soul, a
     pure and lofty master comes with a special
     meaning, a special music which goes straight
     to the heart? Such a one may speak in English,
     Hindi, Sindhi, German or Hebrew – but he
     speaks the language of love. Such *vaak* is pure.
     It has *shabda shakti* – so it touches the chord
     of the heart. The soul vibrates in response to
     this voice, and experiences joy.

     Men of few words know the value of words
     as well as the worth of silence. Such men find
     it easy to practise the presence of God. They
     only utter those words which God puts into
     their mouth.

So, let us keep our *vaak* pure. Let us speak only that which is true, that which is pleasant and that which is useful.

2. Next to *vaak* is *Prana*. *Prana* too must be purified, for it is our "life breath" – our respiration by which we live.

   Many of us control speech, but are unable to control *prana*. When breath is properly controlled, drawn in and let out, it helps to keep body and mind healthy, relaxed and pure. Of the benefits of *pranayama*, I have already spoken to you in earlier sections.

   When *prana* is not controlled and purified, we get bad dreams. When we practise *pranayama*, even our dream-state, our subconscious life becomes good and pure.

3. Next to *prana* is *Chakshu* which is interpreted as sight. If only we realised how many sins are committed due to untrained, uncontrolled sight! A volume could be written on "modern degradation through sight" – degradation brought about by watching impure, unhealthy, unwholesome 'entertainment' and reading sensational novels.

   A story is told to us of a Hindu devotee who plucked off his eyes and became sightless to escape sins of sight! Did not Jesus too echo the same idea, when he said, "If thy right eye offend thee, pluck it off?"

When the sense of sight is pure, no object is coveted and things are felt to be but passing apparitions of the One Glory. Beauty becomes the glimpse of the Beloved who invites us, through the things that are seen, to the threshold of the Unseen, so that we may commune with Him!

4. Next comes *Shrotrah* – hearing. This too, must be purified.

   To listen to gossip, idle chatter, cruel criticism and malicious talk is to indulge in sin through hearing. The rule enjoined by our ancient sages is to hear only the good, the pure, the wholesome and the true.

   And so in books of the past we read how great was the value attached to hearing the Name of God. *Nama smarana* is one of the greatest sources of purification. So let us train ourselves, that we may hear, the harmony, the Divine Music of the Universe. So let us purify ourselves, so that we may hear God's voice giving us His message in the heart within.

   The singers of the *Upanishads* heard the *mantras*, the *deva vani* of the Divine! For us too, there is the call of the *satguru*, the call of the Higher Self, which we can hear, when we rise above the assault of the senses.

5. And finally comes *Balu*, which means 'vital sense' or 'bodily vigour'. One of the saddest things in modern life is the lack of recognition of the sanctity of the vital force, the creative force in us.

The Buddhists have a beautiful theory that *sanskaras* build up the man: and *sanskaras* are induced by man's contact with the environment. So it was in the ancient past, that the student of sacred knowledge (*Brahma Vidya*) and the seekers after higher life, were asked to observe *brahmacharya*. So were the senses trained, so was the body built up, pure and strong.

One by one the senses must be disciplined, and thus prepared to walk the way of perfection.

Purity does not mean crushing the instincts but having the instincts as servants and not the master of the spirit.

– Eric Liddell, *The Disciplines Of The Christian Life*

The secret of self-discipline is purity: heart-purity, not purity of outer actions alone. We must cultivate purity of motive, thought and impulse: for purity is essential to the seeker on the path. As the *Upanishad* declares:

The knots of the heart must be snapped, the bars of desire must be broken, the heart must be pure!

God has given us a triple-treasure: 1) will; 2) thought; and 3) imagination. Let us keep them pure and undefiled. Let us submit ourselves to the best form of discipline — self-discipline. For without self-discipline, we will only drift as dead leaves in the autumn-wind!

The life of the flesh is full of 'pleasure' (a pleasure that is actually poisonous), of bodily sensations, of excitement and enjoyment: it is a life dear to the lowest 'self' in us. Eat, drink and be merry — is the motto of this life. And this life does not think of life beyond death.

The life of the Spirit is a battle with appetites and desires. And he who battles with desires, must often shed tears. Sometimes – perhaps often – he falls, but he rises again. It is a life of tremendous difficulties, a life of pain and struggle. But it is also a life of search and quest. It is a life in which the cry of the heart ever rises upward: it is a life of struggle, but it makes us heroic. And when the period of conflict is over, we are one with the pure, the holy, the Divine! Can there be a higher goal than this? Can we ask for anything more?

In the life of the flesh, we have pleasure, but darkness surrounds us. In the life of the Spirit, we struggle and fall: but we rise, again and again, until, at last, we touch the Divine! This is what spirituality is all about.

For Your Reflection

Practising Purity of Thought

Whenever an unclean thought comes to you, immediately, in that very instant, say to yourself, "I was made for greater, nobler, loftier things: I shall not be a bundle of unclean, impure desires," and start repeating the pure Name of God.

The Name of God is at once pure and purifying. It purifies those that sing it with deep love and longing of the heart.

Inward beauty is reflected in the joy and peace that prevail in a person's life. When I talk of inward beauty, I mean the order and the harmony that prevails in the mind. It is the beauty of good thoughts, high aspirations and fervent prayers. If our thoughts and aspirations are pure, our desires are also noble and beautiful. In short, we are beautiful within! Inward beauty is also reflected in our person – for the face, as they say, is the index of the mind.

We cannot take this inner beauty for granted. For impure thoughts come to us again and again. Even when we are seated in a holy place, evil desires, evil thoughts strike us unexpectedly. If we let these thoughts and emotions stay with us, they become ugly blots and stains on our consciousness.

Socrates used to pray again and again, "God, make me beautiful within!" If you wish to keep your mind uncluttered and grow beautiful within, build your life in purity! Every impure impulse, impure thought and impure emotion, spoils your inner beauty and robs you of happiness.

Drop It!

Once, a great king decided to renounce his power and possessions and seek initiation from the Buddha as a monk. The entire assembly of bhikkus had gathered around the hermitage to witness the initiation ceremony.

The king arrived, dressed in an ochre robe. His head was shaven, and he had dispensed with all his ornaments. He walked with bare feet through the assembly of monks – and in his right hand, he carried a priceless diamond, as an offering to the Master. In his left hand, he carried a rare and beautiful white lotus – in case the Buddha refused to accept the ostentatious offering of the diamond.

Buddha, seated with closed eyes, said to the king, "Drop it!"

The king, aware of the unsuitability of the offering, immediately dropped the diamond. Buddha's voice commanded again, "Drop it!"

This time the king dropped the lotus.

Again the voice commanded, "Drop it!"

The king was baffled, for he had nothing to drop now. He continued to walk towards the Master. But Buddha said once again, "I say to you, drop it!"

The king understood. In one of Buddha's discourses, he had heard the Master say, "Yena tyajasi tat tyaja" – Leave that (the ego or the I thought) through which you have left everything!"

He understood that he was still in the grip of the ego; he was still entertaining the thought that he had dropped the diamond and lotus at the Master's command. He lacked the true humility that is the mark of a seeker.

At that moment, he surrendered himself totally to the Buddha and dropped his ego. The Master opened his eyes and acknowledged him with approval – for at that moment, the king had surrendered himself to the Master in all humility.

Chapter Three
Glow With The Radiance Of Humility

The word 'humility' derives from the Latin *humus*, which literally means the earth; therefore, it is a quality associated with being 'grounded', down-to-earth; in spiritual terms, humility is not just a behavioural attribute; it is closely linked to egolessness, absence of pride in the self.

Many years ago, my Beloved Gurudev told us the story of a seeker of God. In quest of the heaven-world, he moves, from place to place, and, after much weary wandering, finds himself standing at the gate of the heaven-world.

The gate-keeper asks him, "Who are you?"

And the seeker answers, "I am a scholar and a teacher."

"Wait here a while," says the gate-keeper, "I shall go in and report your arrival."

Soon, the gate-keeper returns with the answer, "I cannot let you in, for the Master says there is no place for teachers in the heaven-world."

I hope my teacher-friends are not upset by the course this story is taking. This story is about a teacher who had not yet found his true vocation. As Sadhu Vaswani used to tell us, "So many teachers, are vain. They parade their little learning. How can there be a place in the heaven-world for those who live in a world of vanity?"

A scholar came to a saint and said, "O seer of the secret! Teach me to live the Life Divine!"

The saint said to him, "Go and unlearn what thou hast learnt and then return and sit before me!"

He who would be a seeker, he who would walk the path of discipleship must walk the way of humility. He must give up the opinions he has formed, the standards to which he is accustomed, the judgements he pronounces on others whom he considers as 'inferiors'. The things the world worships – rich food, fine houses, costly clothes, the applause of men, honours and titles, name and fame, degrees and designations – are as nothing to him.

> **Humility is not thinking less of yourself, it's thinking of yourself less.**
>
> **– Rick Warren**

But let us return to the story.

Disappointed, the seeker is about to turn away, when he hears the words, "O teacher! The dust of dead words clings to thee! Wash thyself of this dust in the waters of silence!"

The teacher follows the advice given to him. Every day he sits in silence and listens to the words of the saints and sages. Gradually, his 'self'-consciousness drops; he becomes humble. And one day, as he sits in meditation with a true longing in his heart for the Lotus Feet of the Lord, he hears the words:

"Blessed is the life of a helper and a servant! If you would enter the heaven-world, breathe out this aspiration that you may be a servant of all, a servant of teachers and pupils, of the lonely and lowly ones, of all men and birds and animals, a servant of God and His creation!"

The seeker breathes out this aspiration, again and again. He lives his life in tune with this aspiration. And, one day, he finds himself back at the portals of heaven. This time, the gates of heaven are wide open. The angels are there to greet him, saying, "Blessed indeed are you, O servant of God and His suffering creation! Enter in and behold the Master's face – pure and fair, beyond compare!"

Yes, the Kingdom of God, the *ashram* of the Guru, the path of discipleship is for the humble at heart. Unfortunately, many of us are proud, vain and lost in ego! When we are lost in ego, we become blind to wisdom, and can only wander from darkness to darkness!

> **I claim to be a simple individual liable to err like any other fellow mortal. I own, however, that I have humility enough to confess my errors and to retrace my steps.**
>
> **– Mahatma Gandhi**

I referred to a teacher who was proud of his accumulated academic knowledge and qualifications; let me hasten to add – we human beings have one thousand excuses to be vain and arrogant; beauty, youth, wealth, career, designation, even the salary we draw, the clothes we wear, the number of people who are at our beck and call, our efficiency, our ability to 'manage' others, the homes we live in, why, the very cars we drive are reasons enough to blow up our ego to enormous proportions!

When I took leave of my near and dear ones and sought refuge at Gurudev Sadhu Vaswani's feet, the very first lesson he taught me was the lesson of humility.

"The God that rules millions is the ego," he said. "Enthrone God in your heart – the God of Love – if you wish to cease wandering!"

When I asked him how I could enthrone in my heart the God of Love, his answer was simple: "Be humble as ashes and dust!"

My Master said to me that his lonely heart was not in search of the proud of purse, the proud of power or learning, for the world was full of such people. He sought the company of the humble ones, the simple ones, of those who had reduced themselves to nothing, who had emptied themselves of all 'self' – so that they could be used by the Lord to do with them whatever He would.

"We are proud of our power and inventions," Gurudev Sadhu Vaswani said. "And yet, what are we? Grass that floats on a stream!"

"What is the mark of him who has attained?" I asked him one day. In his hand was a pencil. With it he drew the figure of a zero – 0 – and he said, "This is the mark of him who has attained: he becomes a zero."

And, on a green card, he wrote a brief message for those who had gathered for his *darshan* that day. The words were so penetrating that they have stayed in my heart, to this day: "Blessed be thou, if thou bend until thou break, becoming nothing, a zero! In the *yoga* (union) of two zeros is the One Infinite!"

> **Humility is the foundation of all the other virtues; hence, in the soul in which this virtue does not exist there cannot be any other virtue except in mere appearance.**
>
> **– Saint Augustine**

Gurudev Sadhu Vaswani often said, "I am not even a speck of dust. I am not an English zero, but a Sindhi Zero, which is just a dot." Such was the humility of this great man. Let us introspect and find out what we think of ourselves. Would we ever think that we are nothing? Would we ever consider ourselves the dot which is almost invisible? Something tells me that for many of us, the answer must be in the negative. We are egoistic. We have a larger than life ego. It is this ego which makes a few of us deny God.

A renowned philosopher of Germany, in one of his books writes: "Have you not heard that God is dead? Hasn't this news reached you yet?" I have also noticed this – that men who deny God think very highly of themselves. They consider themselves above God.

All life is a gift from God. In fact, neither you nor I, nor any of the millions upon millions of species in this planet, can exist without God. We are bound to God just as a child in the womb of the mother is connected to her life-blood by the umbilical chord. If we are separated from Him even for a brief moment, we would simply drop down dead.

Why is it that we are sometimes apt to think that God is not with us? Why? Why do we feel lonely and helpless? If God is an ocean of Love and He is always with us, why does He allow us to doubt His Love and His Divine Power? Why do we experience this feeling of being abandoned and orphaned? The reason is, that there is an invisible veil between God and us. It is the veil of the self, the veil of the ego.

Gurudev Sadhu Vaswani often said, "When the ego goes, God glows." If only you would erase the ego, you will see God. Gurudev Sadhu Vaswani always assured us that it was easy to find Him, for He is nearest to us. In this connection, he quoted a saint, "Learn the art of vanquishing the ego." Give up your ego. Forget your 'self' and you will realise God. This is *sachha gyaan* – true knowledge.

> **As long as you are proud you cannot know God. A proud man is always looking down on things and people: and, of course, as long as you are looking down you cannot see something that is above you.**
>
> **– C. S. Lewis**

The truly humble are also the truly happy. And what we need to be truly happy, is not a change in outer circumstances, but deliverance from slavery to the self, the petty ego. This petty ego sits as a tyrant on some of us, robbing us of the bliss i.e. our heritage as children of God. For let me say to you, God built this world in beauty, and we were meant to live our lives in the fullness of freedom and joy. Man was meant to live like a song-bird, unfettered, free. Alas, man finds himself cribbed, cabined, confined. He has become like a bird in a cage – he is trapped in the cage of self-centeredness!

Not until self-centeredness goes may man become truly happy and free: and the prison of self-centeredness opens with the key of humility. Especially important for the seeker on the path is humility: for it sets free the swan bird of the soul, and the soul can soar into radiance and joy!

The way to the heart of the Guru, the way to true blessedness and grace is the way of humility.

Significant are the words which the humble shepherd boy sings in John Bunyan's *Pilgrim's Progress*:

> He that is down need fear no fall;
> He that is low, no pride;
> He that is humble ever shall
> Have God to be his guide.

The truly humble man must die to the world, must die to the ego. His self must be annihilated, before he can be filled with the Guru's grace.

It is not just ordinary mortals like us, who are afflicted with the ego. Great people also have their ego. If you have a small ego, it is easy to vanquish, and your suffering will also be small. But if you have an enormous ego, it is going to cause you a great deal of pain and suffering before it is done away with!

It is the same with 'surgery'. The removal of a small growth like appendicitis or tonsillitis only involves a minor surgery. But if it is a major growth, it will require a major surgery! Earlier in this book, I told you the story of Shuka Muni, a realised soul, an evolved seer, who also had to be cured of his massive ego before he attained enlightenment! He must serve as a warning to all of us who are proud of our learning and accomplishments.

A *Pandit*, well versed in the *shastras*, once came to meet Gurudev Sadhu Vaswani. "Is it not true that a deep study of the *shastras* can help the seeker on the path?" he asked the Master.

Gurudev Sadhu Vaswani answered, "The *shastras* are often studied as an intellectual exercise, and often their students quarrel among themselves over the interpretation of the texts. The darkness of a room is not dispelled by uttering the word 'Lamp'! So too, the darkness of the ego cannot be removed by the word-meaning of the spiritual texts. This darkness will not be dispelled until the 'inner light' is unveiled. And the inner light is unveiled through that illumined one whom we call the Guru."

We read many books – but to the pilgrim on the path, books may be a burden. We study the lives of saints – but of what avail is this study if our daily lives do not bear witness to it? Every morning, we read from the scriptures – but are we any better than parrots who recite again and again, the Name of God? We go to the *satsang* every evening without fail – but are we better than a temple bell which, at the exact hour, calls the devotees for worship?

The one great barrier between us and self-realisation is the ego. Alas, instead of putting it down, we strengthen it; we hug it to ourselves as if it were our dearest friend. Our actions, our thoughts, our flights of imagination only feed the ego – until the ego becomes our master and lord.

Let us break the tyranny of the ego!

The ego is a thief; the ego is our most dangerous enemy; it is the force that separates the soul from God. It is the impenetrable wall which hides us from the Light with dark shadows of 'I', 'Me' and 'Mine' falling on us, obstructing our vision.

Of what are we proud? Youth, beauty, wealth, power – all, all are transient. Sant Kabir sings:

> One enemy or the other
> Always treads upon your heels:
> Lust may be driven out, but anger lingers;
> And greed will stay when anger goes;
> And then, when greed is gone,
> Vain glory, vanity and the wish to be honoured
> Fills the emptiness left in the mind...

On the spiritual path, the ego has to be annihilated. Therefore, the Guru must become a butcher!

Only when all association with *aham* – 'I' ness – is dissolved – enlightenment, illumination and union with the Divine can be achieved, and we can walk the way of spirituality.

For your Reflection

Practising Humility in Everyday Life

1. Are you easily offended? Does your temper flare up frequently? Are you constantly irritated by what people say or do? If your answer to any of these questions is yes, learn to control your responses to people and situations.

2. At least for a few hours every day, resolve that you will not take offence at any criticism or negative remark that you receive from others. Accept it in the right spirit and see whether it can help to make you a better person.

3. Keep your eyes open for situations in which you try to push hard to get your own way. Let go of personal preferences and allow empathy and understanding to guide your response.

4. Meet people with the awareness that they are your brothers and sisters. Do not cling to your power, your status or the advantaged position that life has bestowed on you. People may be your subordinates; but they are not inferiors. Always retain the awareness that all of us are equal in the eyes of God.

5. Do not go around looking for faults and weaknesses in others, even if your job is to spot such errors and rectify them. Focus on

the rectification of the faults and deal with people as a good teacher would – patient, understanding, ready to guide and not prone to judge or condemn.

Three Days More

Suiwo, the disciple of the famous Master Hakuin, was himself a good teacher. During one summer seclusion period, a pupil came to him from a southern island of Japan.

Suiwo gave the new student a tough assignment: "Try and concentrate so that you may be able to hear the sound of one hand waving."

The pupil remained with Suiwo for three years but could not pass the test. No matter how hard he focussed, he simply could not hear the sound of one hand waving.

Dispirited, he came in tears to Suiwo one night. "It's no use Master," he said. "I am unable to pass the test. Now, I must return south in shame and embarrassment, for I cannot solve my problem."

"Do not despair, dear child," said the Master. "Wait one week more and meditate constantly."

One week passed. Still no enlightenment came to the pupil. "Try for another week," said Suiwo. The pupil obeyed him, but in vain.

"Still another week," ordered the Master. Yet this was of no avail. Utterly despondent now, the student begged to be released, but Suiwo requested him to undertake another meditation of five days. This too, was without result.

Finally, he said to the pupil: "Meditate for three days longer, and if you still fail to attain enlightenment, you had better kill yourself."

On the second day the pupil was enlightened.

Chapter Four

Cultivate Child-Like Trust In God

Hand over yourself, in loving child-like trust to the Lord. It is important that we become carefree and trusting just like a little child. It is then that no worry, fear or anxiety can ever come close to you!

When man surrenders himself to God, He takes upon Himself his entire responsibility. All we need to do is to hand ourselves over, in child-like trust to the Lord. And the angels of God will go ahead of us to clear the way. No obstacles will be too difficult, no barriers will be impossible for us to cross!

True faith is belief that whatever may happen, God loves me, He is always there for me! It is akin to the absolute, unconditional, complete trust that the child has in its mother.

A mother and her child were alone at home one night. When they were about to get into bed, the mother switched off the light and the room became dark. A sudden fear gripped the child. The woman opened the window, and up in the sky, the moon shone bright.

"Mother, is the moon God's light?" asked the child.

"Yes dear," replied the mother.

"Will God switch off His light when He goes to sleep?' asked the child anxiously.

"No, my dear," said the mother. "God never goes to sleep, and His light is never switched off."

"Well then," smiled the child. "As long as God is awake, I'm not afraid!"

God loves us, just as much as a mother loves her only child. He has a plan for each one of us; and His plans are perfect. If what we ask in prayer goes contrary to God's plan, that prayer is not granted – and of course, this is for our own good. Suppose a child were to come up to its father and ask for a matchbox or for poison or a razor – will the father give any of these things to him? On the contrary, he would say, "No my child, I will not give it to you because it will harm you."

So too, there are certain things that God in His Divine Wisdom, denies to us. He never ever makes a mistake. He knows what is good for me, what is good for you, and He will grant us only that which is good for us, and nothing else. For each one of us, He has an individual plan, and it is a perfect plan. If what I ask for subscribes to that plan, He grants it to me, not otherwise.

> **When we are children we seldom think of the future. This innocence leaves us free to enjoy ourselves as few adults can. The day we fret about the future is the day we leave our childhood behind.**
>
> **– Patrick Rothfuss**

Swami Vivekananda was travelling aboard a steamer that was taking him to America to attend the *World Congress of Religions*. Although a kind benefactor had purchased the ticket for his voyage, no arrangements had been made for his stay in the United States. There would be no one to receive him on his arrival in that strange, new land. He did not know where he would go when he disembarked, nor where he would stay. However, he *did* know one thing for certain: that the Great Providence, who had always taken care of him, would not let him down in that distant land to which he was now being sent.

As the Swami stood on the deck communing with the Lord of love in the heart within, a fellow passenger came to greet him. The Swami's radiant face and piercing eyes had fascinated the American, who was eager to get to know him.

"What takes you to America?" he asked Swamiji, when they had shaken hands and introduced themselves to each other.

"I go to attend the World Congress of Religions which is to be held in Chicago," the Swami replied.

"I am from Chicago," the man said. "May I know where you will stay when you are in Chicago?"

This was more than Swami Vivekananda knew. "I do not know," he said, adding, with his dazzling smile, "May be, I shall stay at your place?"

The words were uttered in such child-like simplicity that they went right to the heart of this wealthy man from Chicago. Without a moment's hesitation, he said, "It will be a joy and privilege to have someone like you staying in my house. I shall endeavour to keep you as comfortable as I can!"

May I say to you, when we make our lives complicated with power and possessions, we move further and further away from the simple joys and pleasures of life. We fail to notice the green grass and the fresh morning flowers. We don't have time to hear birds singing or watch our little ones smiling.

We drift away from the state of child-like innocence and simple joy —which is our basic nature.

> **It takes a very long time to become young.**
> **– Pablo Picasso**

Have you not been inspired by that oft-quoted saying: Faith can move mountains!

You will agree with me that these are words that have inspired courage, confidence and optimism in hundreds and thousands of hearts since they were uttered, millennia before today...

Being reminded of Hillary, Tenzing and the conquest of Mt. Everest, I hope my readers are not setting out for the Alps, the Rockies or the Himalayas, to command them to move in the Name of God!

Let me quote an anonymous saying to curb excessive enthusiasm on your part: "True, faith can move mountains: but don't be surprised if God hands you a shovel."

In other words, we must learn to pull and pray; for prayer with your personal effort is the true way of achievement. As a wise man tells us, "Your faith must allow God to be God." While you can certainly call for His grace and help, you cannot sit back and expect Him to do your homework. If that is what you understood by faith – leaving it all to God while you sink into inertia and passivity – you need to relearn your concept of faith. In this, as in so many other things, it is good to remember that much loved proverb: God helps those who help themselves! As Edmund Hillary put it so well, "It is not the mountain we conquer but ourselves."

There is a beautiful story of which the great German poet Goethe was very fond. Peter asked Jesus, "How is it that you can walk on the waters, and we cannot?"

Jesus answered, "Because I have faith!"

Peter said, "We also have faith."

"Then follow me," said Jesus, and stepped on the water. Peter followed. They had not gone very far when a huge wave arose in the waters.

Peter cried, "Master, save me: I am sinking!"

"What is the reason?" asked Jesus.

And Peter said, "Master, I saw a huge wave and fear entered my heart."

Jesus said, "You feared the wave: You did not fear the Lord of the waves!"

With child-like faith you can witness miracles in your daily life – this is the message conveyed by Jesus.

To pious Hindus, the 'moving' of a mountain is not an unfamiliar thing. Did not Maha Vishnu oversee the uprooting of the mighty, legendary Mandaranchal mountain to be used as a 'whisk' to churn the ocean during the *samudra manthan*? Did not Sri Krishna lift the Govardhana Giri effortlessly to protect the *gopas* and *gopis* from the fury of Indra? And did not that great devotee of Sri Rama, the incomparable Rama *bhakta* Hanuman move the Sanjivani Hill to the battlefield in Lanka to administer the healing medicinal herb that saved Lakshmana's life? Have you ever seen children listen to these *puranic* tales with wide-eyed wonder?

We know very well that God 'moved' these mountains. These incidents from our sacred *puranas* tell us that nothing is impossible if you have faith.

Let me narrate to you a Welsh legend. There was a tiny village standing near a small hillock in Wales. The villagers were proud of the historical legends associated with their tiny village. It was believed that Noah's Ark had landed on the flat top of their hillock, called Mt. Garth. However, their pride in their village took a severe beating when two government cartographers arrived in their village, and set out to measure Mt. Garth. After a preliminary survey, they brusquely told the villagers that their hill could not really be called

J.P. Vaswani

a mountain, for it was not even 1000 ft. in height. The trouble was, the hillock was 'short' by about 100 feet or so.

Enterprising villagers, their friends and family members from far-flung areas, put their heads together. They would not allow two government geographers to deprive their village of its historical importance, by denying the name of 'mountain' to their own Garth. A plan was finalised – the villagers would *raise* the height of the mountain *physically* by piling up hard soil, rubble and stones on the flat hill-top.

The seemingly impossible scheme was executed and the government 'cartographers' were forced to conclude that Garth Hill was, in fact, a mountain.

So you see, the innocence and faith of the villagers actually caused a humble hill to become a mountain! But jests and stories apart, all of us are confronted by 'mountains' which thwart our progress and development, and become serious obstacles which impede our efforts.

What are these mountains? They are mountains of negativity – despair, defeatism, pessimism, low self-esteem, lack of self-confidence, guilt, inferiority complex, worry and anxiety!

To quote William Shakespeare, "Our doubts are traitors, and make us lose the good we oft might win, by fearing to attempt." If there is a mountain, climb it! In the words of the Negro singer, go over it; go around it; or cut a tunnel through it!

Bhakti yoga is the path of utter devotion, supreme love for God. It is pure and selfless love, which is far above worldly love. It does not involve bargaining with God over results; it is above all selfish motives. It is intense devotion and attachment to the Lord. It has to be felt, experienced – not talked about or discussed. It is like the absolute, unconditional trust that the infant has in its mother. It makes the aspirant simple and child-like in his absolute trust in God.

> **People were bringing little children to Jesus to have Him touch them, but the disciples rebuked them. When Jesus saw this, He was indignant. He said to them, "Let the little children come to me, and do not hinder them, for the Kingdom of God belongs to such as these. I tell you the truth, anyone who will not receive the Kingdom of God like a little child will never enter it." And He took the children in His arms, put His hands on them and blessed them.**
>
> **– St. Mark's Gospel**

What are the qualities of an aspirant who has developed child-like trust in the Lord?

- He has a soft, loving, tender heart.

- He is free from pride, lust and anger, greed and egoism.

- In his great love for the Lord, he strives for perfection – and ceaselessly works to overcome his defects.

- He is free from all cares, fears and worries. Like a child, he feels himself safe and secure in the Lord's Divine protection.

- He treats everybody alike; he does not see people as 'enemies' or 'friends'; all people are his brothers and sisters. His love extends to all alike – for in each and every human being, he perceives the form of the Lord.

- His faith in the Lord is firm, unwavering and absolute. His strength and courage are derived from this faith. This faith roots out all anxiety and fear from his mind.

- He is firm in the conviction that all that happens to him, happens for the best – for it comes as God's Will. Happiness and sorrow are also forms of God's Grace.

All of us can cultivate such child-like trust in the Lord. We only need to hold firmly to the truth that we are God's children and that He is our dear Father who is too loving to punish us, and too wise to make a mistake. We must remember too, that God helps those who help themselves and that our efforts and endeavours must operate in tandem with His Divine Will.

I don't need to remind you of this, that if we regard ourselves as His children, it goes without saying that the rest of mankind are our brothers and sisters, as indeed is the whole of creation. Therefore, we must share whatever we can, with those whose need is greater than ours.

To those who are unable to live on their income, this may appear a difficult thing to do. But even they will find that in the measure in which they share what little they have with others, they will be richly blessed. Out of the little that remains to them, they will get more, much more than they expected. This is what we, in the Sindhi language, call *barkat*.

I know a lady in Australia who sets apart a tenth of her earnings for just such a purpose – and she has not been the poorer for it. Once, when she sent a certain amount to be spent on the service activities of our Sadhu Vaswani Mission, she wrote to me: "It is with gratitude that I pass on to you this amount from my 'Lord's Tenth' fund. This money has nothing to do with me, except that I send it to wherever the Lord directs. So this gift is from Him and the recognition and thanks are due to Him…"

This is one of the laws of life — the more we give, the more we get out of the little that remains. Therefore, I tell my friends again and again: surrender all you are and all you have in God's safe hands. When you allow Him to take over, you have nothing to worry about!

He who hath surrendered himself hath found the greatest security of life. And we need wander no more. All his cares and burdens are borne by the Lord Himself. How beautiful are the words of the Gita:

> They who worship Me
> Depending on Me alone,
> Thinking of no other —
> They are My sole responsibility!
> Their burdens are My burdens!
> To them I bring full security!

The more we meditate on the Lord's words, the more we shall grow in that true life which is a life of self-surrender. The life of child-like trust and true faith is a blessed, carefree life. It is a life free from the shackles of earthly "experience". To be truly free is to be born anew, to become a pure child of God. Such a one lives with God and walks with God and speaks to Him and hears Him speak.

Exercises in Being Child-Like

Just for Today...Tips to Celebrate the Child in You

1. Just for today, take time out to do something that makes you really happy! Allow time to laugh, joke and say nice things to people you interact with.

2. Just for today, set aside cold reason and logic and listen to the voice of your intuition. Be open to imaginative ideas.

3. Just for today, be happy and content with whatever you have. Be willing to rest content with the present moment with all its joys and rewards.

4. Just for today, don't try to win others' praise and approval; don't try to cultivate a 'good' image. Just for today, be yourself – simple, natural, spontaneous.

5. Just for today, put aside cynicism and negativity: choose love, trust and hope.

6. Just for today, look at the world with the eyes of a child. Marvel at its wonders, its natural miracles, its fascinating happenings. Rediscover the sense of wonder that was yours in childhood.

7. Just for today, don't forget that you are God's child – and He loves you more dearly than you can ever imagine!

I Am My Brother's Keeper

There is a moving story about Sadhu Sundar Singh, who was once travelling across the Himalayas with a companion. It was winter, and a severe blizzard was raging. The conditions were indeed very trying. As they trudged ahead, they saw a man lying still, by the narrow mountain path. To all appearances, he seemed to be frozen lifeless in the lonely terrain.

The Sadhu stopped to revive him and to offer whatever help he could. But his companion was adamant that they should move on. "It's no use wasting your time over him," he argued. "He is past reviving. If you stop to help him, you will be in trouble too, for it is suicidal to stop anywhere in this weather. We must push ahead so that we can reach the next village before it is dark."

But the Sadhu did not have the heart to leave the dying man to his fate. Resolutely, he began to rub and chafe the man's hands and feet, hoping to give some warmth to his cold limbs. His companion was so annoyed that he walked away from there, without even looking back.

Ten minutes of vigorous rubbing did nothing for the stranger. Finally, Sadhu Sundar Singh lifted the man on his back and began to trudge painfully through the falling snow.

Call it a miracle if you like – or call it good karma *which fructifies instantly. The warmth of the exercise made the* Sadhu's *body temperature rise, and this gradually revived the stranger. The strain of carrying the man also helped the Sadhu to withstand the cold and the two mutually sustained each other.*

When they had travelled a couple of miles, they saw another body lying by the wayside. It was the Sadhu's *companion, who had refused to stop earlier. He was indeed frozen to death. Alone, he had not the warmth to fight the storm.*

Chapter Five

Offer Selfless Service To Humanity

Dharam to hai pyaar
Dharam to hai mohabbat
Dharam to hai prem
Dharam to hai sulah
Dharam to hai shanti
Dharam to hai seva.

Religion is love
Religion is pure affection
Religion is peace
Religion is service!

The hands that serve, help and heal are holier than those that turn the beads of the rosary. Service is truly sacred – for it helps you realise God.

Gurudev Sadhu Vaswani was once asked, "What is your religion?" His reply was truly significant. He said, "I know of no religion higher than the religion of unity and love, service and sacrifice."

For him, indeed, to live was to serve, to live was to love, to live was to bear the burdens of others – to live was to share his all with all.

One evening, as we were taking a walk on the roadside with Gurudev Sadhu Vaswani we saw a poor man lying underneath a tree. His clothes were tattered and torn; his whole person, his body and limbs were covered with filth. Gurudev Sadhu Vaswani stopped at the sight of this man. He asked for a bucket of water to be brought. And when it was brought, this prince among men — he had but to lift up a finger and hundreds of us would rush to find out what his wish was — with his own hands he cleansed the body of the poor beggar and passed on to him his own shirt to wear! The poor man pointed to the cap on Gurudev Sadhu Vaswani's head, and without the least hesitation, the Master passed on the cap to him. On that occasion he spoke certain words, which I can never, ever forget. He said, "This shirt and this cap and everything that I have, is a loan given to me to be passed on to those whose need is greater than mine."

Mark the word *loan* — everything that we have is a loan given to us, to be passed on to those whose need is greater than ours. Nothing belongs to us; nothing has been given to us absolutely; everything has been given to us as a loan — our time and our talents, our knowledge, our experience, our wisdom, our prestige, our influence in society, our bank accounts, our property and possessions, our life itself is a loan given to us to be passed on to those whose need is greater than ours. In these simple words of the Master, as it seems to me, are enshrined the seeds of a new humanity, a new world order, a new civilisation of service and sacrifice.

> **The best way to find yourself is to lose yourself in the service of others.**
> *– Mahatma Gandhi*

The following *subhashita* (gem of speech) is attributed to Sage Ved Vyasa:

All the wisdom that is taught through innumerable books may be summed up, in half-a-verse, thus: "To serve humanity is meritorious, and to harm anyone is sinful."

Service, it has been rightly said, is the rent we have to pay for being tenants of this body. Every morning, as we wake up, we must ask ourselves this question: What can I do to help? What can I do to make a difference? For indeed, each one of us can and must make a difference. There are so many tasks to be accomplished by us – there are hungry ones to be fed; there are naked ones to be clothed; there are elders to be cared for; there are children to be taught. There is so much work to be done! And every one of us – from the youngest to the oldest – can make a difference.

"There is not much that I can do on my own", is what many of us think. We are mistaken. The tragedy for many of us is not that our aim is too high and we miss it – but rather that our aim is too low and we reach it!

As Herschel Hobbs says, "The world measures a man's greatness by the number who serve him. Heaven's yardstick measures a man by the number who are served by him."

Walking the way of spirituality is to live a life of love, compassion, the spirit of caring and sharing and service. It is also the shortest and quickest route to God. The way of service is closely allied to the way of brotherhood—for we need to assert, again and again, "I am my brother's keeper!"

And who are our brothers? Our brothers and sisters are all those who suffer and are in need of help—men, women, birds and animals. We must become channels of God's mercy, help and healing, so that His love may flow out to them through us and our actions. When we become instruments of God's love, there is no limit to what we can accomplish. In God's Divine plan, we can become the sanctuary of the weary and heavy-laden; we can, with our efforts, become a source of sweet, refreshing waters in the wilderness that is this world.

> **Everybody can be great...because anybody can serve. You don't have to have a college degree to serve. You don't have to make your subject and verb agree to serve. You only need a heart full of grace, a soul generated by love.**
> **– Martin Luther King Jr.**

There is a simple question that all saints ask of us: How can we claim our love to God if we do not love our fellow human beings? How can we call ourselves human beings if we watch our brothers and sisters suffering and struggling?

God is Absolute Love—and if we love God, we must be imbued with the longing to serve our fellow men. I believe that true service is a spiritual activity, which at its best, is born out of the Love of God. It was a true saint of God who said: Prayer without work is as bad as work without prayer!

God cannot be satisfied with our adoration and devotion if they come only from our lips—for words and alphabets cannot make a prayer. It is our hearts and our own lives that must bear witness to our devotion—and what better way to achieve this than through the service of our fellow human beings?

It is possible that some of you may be really overcome by doubts and anxiety when I talk about service to humanity; you may think to yourself, "After all, we are not millionaires. We are people with limited means at our disposal. How can we aspire to serve suffering humanity?"

God can use the least of us in great acts of service, when He so wills. When Jesus fed the five thousand people who had followed him into the hills, he did not make use of his chief disciples, the apostles as they were called later. In fact, they were full of tension and anxiety, and planning to send the crowds away. Instead, Jesus turned to a small boy whose mother had packed a simple lunch for him. But this boy was willing to give all he had in perfect trust to the Master. I am sure there were many wealthy people in the crowd who had better food with them, but I doubt if they had the faith, trust and devotion of the little boy, who was willing to give his lunch away when the Lord asked him to.

This is the great gift of service – it blesses him who receives and him who serves!

"What do we live for if not to make the world less difficult for each other?" asks the distinguished writer and novelist, George Eliot. Most of us are inclined to be self-centered, and to live narrow, selfish lives – but it is only in selfless living that we can discover the best that we are capable of. And do not restrict 'giving' to the giving of alms, giving money to the poor! You were surely made for higher things—so give of yourself, give of your time, talents and energies to lighten the loads of the weary and the heavy-laden!

Albert Schweitzer was always pained to hear people say, "If only I were rich, I would do great things to help and serve others." He would point out to them that all of us could be *rich* in love and generosity, and that we could always give our loving interest and concern to others—which is worth more than all the money in the world!

Nowadays, we use the word 'philanthropist' to describe a multi-millionaire who donates vast sums of money to charitable organisations. Many of us do not know that *philanthropist* is derived from two Greek words, *philas,* which means loving, and *anthropos,* which is man. In other words, the root meaning of philanthropist is a loving man. Aren't we all capable of becoming philanthropists? Of course we are— if we give of ourselves, from a heart filled with love.

"If you want others to be happy, practise compassion," the Dalai Lama tells us.

In loving and compassionate service, in selfless and caring service lies the secret of true spirituality.

Of course charity begins at home, but it need not stay put there! Extend your service to the society, the community in which you live. Let your community reach out to others — and you will find that the whole world is soon linked by the spirit of selfless service!

"Let everyone who comes to you return to their life feeling better and happier," Mother Teresa would often say to her helpers. If we all tried to follow this simple precept, wouldn't we leave the world a better and happier place?

And the ways to do this are numerous. To quote the poet H.W. Longfellow:

> No man is so poor as to have nothing worth giving;
> as well might mountain streamlets say they have
> nothing to give the sea because they are not rivers!
> Give what you have. To someone it may be better
> than you dare to think!

Can you read? Then read to a blind student. Can you write? Then write a letter, fill a form for someone who is not so lucky. If you are not hungry, share your food with someone who is. If you are happy, contented, at peace with yourself, reach out to those who are not as fortunate as you.

We all have something to give! Let us give with love and compassion, and we will make the world a better place!

How can I refrain from quoting those beautiful lines that have never failed to inspire me!

> I shall pass through this life but once.
> Any good, therefore, that I can do
> Or any kindness that I can show to any fellow creature,
> Let me do it now.
> Let me not defer or neglect it,
> For I shall not pass this way again.

Don't hold back! Don't underestimate yourself and your abilities! Don't imagine that you cannot make a difference! We may feel that our effort is but a drop in the ocean—yet every drop counts in the ocean of service!

You can make a difference. Let me give you the words of Bertrand Russell:

> It may seem to you conceited to suppose that you can do anything important towards improving the lot of mankind. But this is a fallacy. You must believe that you can help bring about a better world. A good society is produced only by good individuals, just as truly as a majority in a presidential election is produced by the votes of single electors.

We regard ourselves as responsible citizens. We pay our taxes and our bills on time; we exercise our franchise and fulfill our democratic duties; we try to obey all traffic rules; we steer clear of breaking the laws of the land; we try not to interfere in other people's affairs . . .

But this is not enough! Doing our duty is alright –
but we need to do our duty *and a little more!* The
opposite of love is not hate but indifference, or
apathy — to the needs of those around you. We need
to contribute our share — our mite — to the welfare of
the world; to what Sri Krishna called *lokasangraha.*

Little drops of water make the mighty ocean!
Little grains of sand make this beautiful land. So too,
when we all perform little acts of service, little deeds
of kindness, the world will be a better place.

> **The best antidote I know for worry is work.
> The best cure for weariness is the challenge of
> helping someone who is even more tired. One
> of the great ironies of life is this: he or she who
> serves almost always benefits more than he or
> she who is served.**
> – Gordon B. Hinckley, *Standing for Something:*
> *10 Neglected Virtues That Will Heal Our*
> *Hearts and Homes*

Swami Vivekananda put forward the highest
concept of service when he coined the term *Daridra
Narayana* – the Lord in the form of the poor – and
asked people to serve Him. "Where would you go
to seek God?" he asked. "Are not all the poor, the
miserable, the weak, Gods? Why not worship them
first?"

Swamiji had the compassionate heart of a mother. When a famine was raging in Bengal and his followers could not get money to carry out relief work, he seriously thought of selling the Belur Math property, which he had just purchased to set up the spiritual centre of the Ramakrishna Mission.

So intense was his compassion, so noble his spirit of service that he once said to a friend, "The thought comes to me that even if I have to undergo a thousand births to relieve the misery of the world, aye, even to remove the least pain from anyone, I shall cheerfully do it. Of what use is my personal *mukti* alone? I shall take everyone along that path with myself!"

An ancient legend tells us that someone asked Sri Krishna, "Tell us Lord, which is Your favourite Name among the *Sahasra Nama* – thousand Names – by which we call You?"

The Lord replied, "It is *Deena bandhu* – friend of the weak and the oppressed. That is the Name I love best."

The Bhagavad Gita imposes on the devout believer, the duty of *yajna* or sacrifice. Mahatma Gandhi interprets sacrifice to mean service. He points out that the Gita also tells us: "He who cooks only for himself is a thief." There is no higher law than the law of *yajna*, the law of service. "True *yajna* is an act directed to the welfare of others, done without desiring any returns for it, whether of a temporal or spiritual nature," Gandhiji says. "This body therefore, has been given to us only so that we may serve all creation with it."

Gurudev Sadhu Vaswani was indeed a great soul, who was, "Born To Serve". Everyday, Gurudev Sadhu Vaswani sat underneath the trees he loved, and gave to the poor and broken ones who came to him. He gave them money, he gave them food, he gave them clothing. Above all, he gave them the benedictions of his loving heart.

Literally, till the last day of his earth-pilgrimage, he served the poor and broken ones. In their faces he beheld the face of God. Every human being, every creature, was to him an image of the King of Beauty. To bring joy into the lives of the starving, struggling, sorrowing ones was one of the deepest aspirations of his life.

A man came to him, one day, and giving him a bundle of notes said, "Dada! Here is some money for your temple." What did Gurudev Sadhu Vaswani do? He utilised the amount in feeding the poor, saying, "The noblest temple is the heart of a poor man, who gets his food and who blesses the Name of God!"

Gurudev Sadhu Vaswani never longed for the joys of the heaven-world. He did not aspire to *mukti*, salvation, liberation from the cycle of birth-death-rebirth.

The question was put to him more than once, "Is there anything higher than *mukti*?"

He answered, "I do not ask for *mukti*. I fain would be born, again and again, if only that I might be of some help to those that suffer and are in pain!"

The Master knew how to walk the way of true spirituality.

Does not the Lord tell us: "Whatever you give to the least of men, you give unto Me?" We will do well to remember that the Lord lives in the lowly and the humble. When we serve them, we serve Him. So it was that Sadhu Vaswani said, "Service of the poor is worship of the Lord."

Gurudev Sadhu Vaswani also said: "If you would be happy, make others happy." These beautiful words are carved on the pedestal of his statue, which greets everyone who enters the city of Pune, at the Sadhu Vaswani Chowk, where the Pune cantonment meets Pune city.

The Chinese have a number of proverbs and aphorisms, rich in the wisdom of life. One of these proverbs tells us: "If you want to be happy for an hour, take a nap. If you want to be happy for a day, go out for a picnic. If you want to be happy for a month, get married. If you want to be happy for a year, inherit a fortune. And if you want to be happy for a lifetime, go out and serve others."

Serve others – for life is too short; so let us be quick to love and prompt to serve. The day on which you have not served someone in need, a brother here, a sister there, a bird here, an animal there – the day on which you have not served a fellow being is a lost day indeed!

A lot of us tend to believe that the little that we can do, counts for nothing, against the vast canvas of the world's misery and suffering. But just as little drops of water together make the mighty ocean, so too, little acts of kindness and compassion can and will make a difference.

> **True leaders understand that leadership is not about them but about those they serve. It is not about exalting themselves but about lifting others up.**
>
> **– Sheri L. Dew, *Saying It Like It Is***

When we start living and working for others, then our lives too, become richer, more rewarding, more meaningful. We are able to tap our inner *shakti* to its highest potential; we become more energetic; we become more creative; we solve problems easily. Above all, we grow in the consciousness that all life is One, all life is Reverent, all men are brothers – and that birds and animals too, are our brothers and sisters in the One family of Creation. Is not this the highest form of consciousness – this awareness of the Unity of all life?

How may we cultivate the spirit of selfless service? Let me offer you a few practical suggestions:

1. Serve Silently

The very first rule of service is: Serve Silently! Do not serve for show or publicity. Let the right hand not know what your left hand gives away.

I am afraid that today, we serve with cries and clamour. We seem to have confounded service with show and noise. There are so many people who do a little act of service, and spend a sleepless night, only to get up anxiously in the morning and scan the newspapers eagerly to see if their little act of service has been reported in the press!

This, my friends, is not true service! I am sometimes deeply saddened when I think of the shadows we run after – name, fame, greatness, popularity and publicity. The true strength of a nation is not in popularity and publicity – the true strength of a country, the true strength of a community, the true strength of a society is in those who serve silently!

2. Serve Humbly

The second principle of service is: Serve Humbly!

Serve with humility – and this is no easy task. Many of us are apt to imagine that the act of giving – of our time, money, effort or resources – is an act of superiority. We feel that we are conferring a great favour – doing *meherbani*, as they say in Hindi – on those whom we seek to serve. I think, it should be the other way round. We should be grateful to those who give us the opportunity to be of service to them.

We have received countless blessings from God. We are in receipt of so many favours from the marvellous universe we live in. We owe a debt of gratitude for these innumerable blessings conferred upon us. This debt we will be able to pay back only if we go out and serve the less fortunate ones – the aged, the infirm, the handicapped, the halt, the unwanted, the unloved, the hopeless and the homeless ones. We should be deeply grateful to them, for they are giving us the opportunity to serve them – and so, to give back at least a fraction of all that we have received from the Lord.

Let us serve humbly – therefore, let us seek no reward for our service – not even a simple word of thanks. For expectation of any return – in any form – makes our service conditional.

3. Serve Lovingly

The third rule of service is: Serve Lovingly! Love is what the world needs most today. Love does not merely make the world go round – it is what makes the ride worthwhile, as Franklin Jones has said. And true love is love-in-action; for love that does not express itself in action, does not exist at all!

There are very many wealthy people who speak harsh words to the people they serve. They may give a poor man money and tell him, "Don't show your dirty face to me again!" or they may lose their temper and yell, "Don't be so lazy! Don't expect me to prop you up all the time!"

Friends, this is not true service. The people we seek to serve are not apart from us – they are a part of us. This sense of identification is very essential for true service. When you serve others, you must identify with them.

I am told that a tree called the *Upas* tree grows in certain parts of Indonesia. It grows very thick and it secretes poison so that all forms of vegetation around it are killed off. There are people like the *Upas* tree – they criticise, condemn others; but will not lift a finger to help others improve themselves.

4. Serve Unconditionally

The fourth principle of service is: Serve Unconditionally! Service should not become interference. If you wish to reform the world, begin with yourself. A true server realises that he must mend his own life, before he begins to set others right.

Many people take to service with an ulterior motive; their service comes with strings attached. They expect the beneficiaries of their generosity to follow their ideology, their beliefs or subscribe to their way of thinking. It is said that some service organisations even try to convert people to their religion, in lieu of services rendered. This is surely inimical to the spirit of true service, which, at its best must be spontaneous, unconditional. Jesus would never countenance our service as an offering to him if we insisted on serving only Christians. Krishna would not accept our service if we offered it only to Hindus. Service should be a labour of love; and love knows no barriers of caste, creed, race or religion.

Aristotle was taking a stroll, accompanied by a few friends. They were accosted by a poor man, who appealed to them for charity. The man was known to have a bad reputation.

Aristotle gave alms to the poor man. This met with the disapproval of his friends.

"You should not have helped him," observed one of them. "You know his reputation. Why do you encourage such people?"

"I did not offer my charity to the man," explained the great philosopher. "I gave it to humanity."

Who are we to judge the worth of needy ones?

This noble spirit of serving without judgement, serving without interference, serving unconditionally was beautifully exemplified in the life of my Gurudev Sadhu Vaswani. He once said:

If I meet a hungry man, let me not ask why he is hungry, when so many others feast at their banquet tables. Let me give him food to eat.

If I meet a naked man, let me not ask why he shivers in the cold of wintry nights, when so many have their wardrobes filled to over flowing. Let me give him garments to wear.

And if I meet a man lost in sin let me not ask why he is lost, but with a look of compassion, with a song or a syllable of love, let me draw the sinner to the spirit.

Let me draw by awakening the longing that lies latent in all.

Let me lead some out of darkness into Light!

"Blessed are those who give without remembering – and take without forgetting," says a wise man.

5. Cultivate the Soul

The fifth principle of service is: If you would serve aright, Cultivate the Soul! Cultivate the Soul! Therefore, know that you are only a tool, an instrument. God is the One Worker. Cultivate the Soul! Therefore, do not confound the means with the end. Renouncing all egoism and selfishness, become instruments of the eternal *shakti* that shapes the lives of individuals and nations.

The essence of Vedanta may be summed up in the one concept: All Life Is One. If such oneness is accepted, the question arises, who is serving whom?

The concept of oneness does not take away from the ideal of service. When a speck of dust enters the eye, does the hand not rush to soothe the eye? So too, do human beings help one another, even while they are aspects of the One Life Supreme.

Hindu philosophy teaches us that our true self is the *atman*, the spirit. The body is just the garment we wear, while we are upon this earth. Thus all activity is outside – work done for the sake of work. For the pious and the devout, all work is an offering to God. All work is His work. You and I are only instruments of God.

Gurudev Sadhu Vaswani always emphasised the spiritual value of service. For, he believed that the soul stagnates in idleness, even as fresh water grows foul without motion. But he also believed that true service should express love – love for the world around us, the people, birds, animals, and all aspects of creation. For out of such love is true service born.

Talking of *karma yoga*, Gurudev Sadhu Vaswani teaches us to worship God through service. He also points out the stages in this worship:

1) Offer your service as a duty. Do your work as a disciplined soldier. Do it as your duty. Think not of the fruits of action.

2) Work for the welfare of the world. Look around you! The world is in suffering: the world needs helpers. Serve and be ready to suffer in service of suffering humanity.

3) Work as *yagna* – an offering to God. Dedicate your life to God. If your life is not a dedication to the Divine Life, it becomes disintegration. The life dedicated to the Divine is indeed, a happy life. It is a life of true service – and through it we grow in reverence for the poor, realising that service of the poor is real worship of God.

Thus does service become a prayer. For to serve is to pray. You no more think of "doing good to others". Your service becomes disinterested devotion to the Lord.

Let us close with the inspiring words of St. Francis's prayer:

> Lord, make me an instrument of Thy Peace,
> Where there is hatred let me sow love
> Where there is injury, pardon;
> Where there is discord, let me bring truth,
> Where there is doubt, faith;
> Where there is despair, let me bring hope,
> Where there are shadows, may I bring Thy Light;
> Where there is sadness, let me bring joy.
> Lord, grant that I may seek rather to comfort than be comforted;
> To understand, than be understood;
> To love, than be loved;
> For it is by giving that one receives,
> It is by forgetting self, that one finds,

It is by forgiving, that one is forgiven,
It is by dying that one awakens to eternal life.

Selfless service is the bridge that will take you from the life of the world to the life of the spirit.

Exercise: Positive Affirmations on Loving Service to Others for every day of the week

Day 1: I am not apart from others. The others are a part of me. Whatever I do for others, I do for myself.

Day 2: I have been blessed with so much! I have so much to offer others. Let me do so in a spirit of generosity, caring and sharing.

Day 3: This world is a vale of suffering for many; let me do all I can to mitigate the suffering of others.

Day 4: I aspire to be God's servant; and the best way to do this is to serve my fellow human beings as best as I can.

Day 5: I aspire to treat others the way God treats me – with understanding, patience and kindness.

Day 6: I believe that my life gains meaning and value in the measure that I help others.

Day 7: I aspire to touch others' lives positively, so that I may bring smiles everywhere I go.

The Language Of Silence

It is said that King Louis VI of France had a friend who had been his classmate during childhood. Later, as their ways parted, Louis became the sovereign, and the friend became a monk, and a devoted disciple of St. Francis. One day, King Louis felt like meeting his childhood friend. Out of respect for the monastic way of life, the King himself went to the monastery where he resided, rather than send for him to visit the palace. There was great excitement in the monastery as the King arrived. How would the King greet his friend? What would the monk say to the King?

The King and the monk were closeted together for over two hours. For two hours they sat with each other, without speaking a word to each other. In silence they sat and in silence they parted. After this meeting with his childhood friend, King Louis bowed down to him and took his leave. The monks asked the King's friend, "What did you say to him? What did you two talk about all this time?" The King's friend replied, "Whatever we had to communicate to each other, we communicated in silence. The profoundest and greatest truths are communicated through silence."

Chapter Six

Cleanse Yourself In The Waters Of Silence

Silence is the language of the soul; it is the unspoken, unwritten vocabulary of prayer and devotion; the music of stillness; the mirror of your innermost self. I like to think of still, profound silence as our personal, intimate appointment with God. And for those who wish to walk the way of spirituality, silence is the first and simplest step on the path.

Silence is two-fold; there is outer silence, which is freedom from noise, freedom from the shouts and tumults of daily life; and there is inner silence; it is freedom from the clamour of the senses and desires; it is the cessation of all the mental acrobatics that we are constantly engaged in; it is the quietening of all the conflicting passions and sensations that dominate our mind.

Such a silence, interior silence, in short, gives us the peace that passeth, nay surpasseth understanding!

Silence is not just the absence of sound; silence has its own being; it is with you, within you, wherever you are at this moment; you can reach out and be with it, right now, if you choose. As Francis Bacon observed, "Silence is the sleep that nourishes wisdom."

He who does not know how to be silent will not know how to speak.

– **Ausonius**

I have always believed that God speaks to us through silence. God is not from you afar. He is not locked up somewhere in a far-off temple; you do not have to go to a *tapobana* (forest of meditation) or a mountain-peak to find Him. He is *here* – He is *now* – He is in the heart within you. You can speak to Him, commune with Him as with a friend or with a member of your own family. Establish contact with Him in silence – and be prepared to LISTEN – for in the depths of silence will you hear His Divine voice – not in the clamour and noise of this world.

We are unable to see God, because He is beyond our sense perception. We are able to see what our eyes see; we are able to hear what our ears hear; we are able to feel what our physical hands and feet can touch. God is beyond and above these finite, limited human senses. This is why we are unable to see God, hear God and touch God. God transcends the senses, the mind and the intellect.

Yet, we shall be able to experience God, if we turn our senses inward. For this, the practice of silence is necessary. Silence takes us beyond words, thoughts and actions. It reveals to us truths of life, and in that silence-created space, devotion is born. Silence not only heals and rejuvenates us, but communicates to us things which are beyond the grasp of our earthly senses. In silence, it is possible for us to see God, may be even to hear His flute-like voice!

The most essential ingredient in prayer is not words but the deep silence of communion.

May I tell you about the therapy of silence? Aldous Huxley noted, "The twentieth century is 'The Age of Noise'. Physical noise, mental noise and the noise of desire!" In this age of deafening noise, silence has extremely high therapeutic value, for it has always been a spiritual tonic from time immemorial. As the health of the mind impresses the condition of the body, a calm and still mind is the identity of a fit person with a sound mind in a healthy body.

> **I think the first virtue is to restrain the tongue; he approaches nearest to God who knows how to be silent, even though he is in the right.**
> *– Cato the Elder*

In this age of noise, it is imperative for all of us to make efforts to step out of the daily din and clamour and enter into the silence within. It is said that the *yogis* meditating in the caves of the Himalayas lived for an average of 150 years. This only proves that silence is more nutritive to the human psyche than all the health food and supplements in the world. A Californian doctor states that a mortal can survive a good, healthy life span of over 100 years if he simply practices the right combination of silence, meditation and prayer. Not only does silence help our spirit and body, it improves mental clarity and cognitive function.

It was St. John of the Cross who said, "Speaking distracts, silence and work collect the thoughts and strengthen the spirit."

In silent prayer and meditation, one can connect with that which is greater than our individual self – our Infinite Source, the Absolute which for want of a better word we call God! When one establishes a link with God, one feels rejuvenated. There is a prevailing sense of positive, calming relaxation. The healing of the body becomes an ongoing automatic process.

Dear brothers and sisters, pilgrimages there are many. But if I have not entered upon the interior pilgrimage, I have wasted the golden opportunity of the human birth.

We live in a world of deafening noises. Particles of noise cling to our souls: they need to be washed in the waters of silence. Silence cleanses. Silence heals. Silence strengthens.

And silence reveals. Silence will bring you face-to-face with yourself.

We have referred again and again to the Socratic query: Who are you? Other people have told you many things about yourself — some complimentary, some otherwise. But all that is not really you. You must now try to find who you are. This is the biggest challenge of life. You must discover yourself. It is not easy to do so — but it can be done through the therapy of silence.

The observance of silence and the occasional choice of solitude can also be beneficial to the practice of *satya* or truth. When we speak little, the opportunity to utter falsehood is also reduced.

> **In silence man can most readily preserve his integrity.**
>
> – Meister Eckhart

Beautiful and serene is the silence of the spirit! When we enter its realm, we experience peace, harmony and a sense of well-being. Our ego gives way to Divine love. Our stress and tension melt away. In this condition, we can listen to our inner voice, which can help us solve the most difficult problems of this life.

Have you seen a plant that has not been watered? Its leaves grow pale, its flowers wither, and it droops miserably. The moment you nourish the plant, the leaves will regain their lost freshness and greenness. Gradually, the flowers will recover their beauty and fragrance, and the plant will be restored to life. What you have done is to water the roots, to work this miracle of recovery. Silence waters the very roots of your life. When you open the windows of your heart and soul to receive the silence of the spirit, you lift your consciousness to bathe in the waters of Divine healing.

Alas, in the mechanical rush of the modern world, we have lost touch with the cultivation of silence and solitude. Our lives are getting increasingly complicated; the list of things to be done gets longer, while 24 hours seem to get shorter! At the end of the day, we feel drained, exhausted, emotionally and mentally weary. Where can we find retreat from this spiritual exhaustion? The Roman philosopher Marcus Aurelius has the answer: Nowhere can man find a quieter or more untroubled retreat than in his own soul.

It seems to me that many people today are terrified of silence, afraid of being alone. I know several couples who do not like to spend a quiet evening at home, by themselves. They invite friends over, or go over to clubs or to restaurants so that they do not face solitude. I even know a few people in whose homes the TV is always switched on – even when no one is watching it! They tell me it is comforting to hear the sound or noise from the TV!

Why are we afraid of solitude and silence? Possibly because we cannot bear to look deep within ourselves! This is why many people say they don't have time for silence or meditation. But they will realise, when they go deep within themselves, that the Infinite is within – and we have nothing to fear!

Socrates was one of the wisest men of the ancient world. Many were the youths whose lives he influenced for the better.

Socrates counselled his disciples to keep their mouths shut – and speak only when absolutely necessary.

"O wise one, how may we know when it is right to speak?" they asked him.

"Open your mouths to speak only after you have asked yourself three questions, and received an affirmative answer to each of the three," replied Socrates.

What were the three questions?

The first question we must ask ourselves before we speak is – is it true? If we are not sure about the veracity of what we are saying, it is better that we do not utter a word. When we utter words carelessly, we ourselves become transmitters of untruth.

The second question to ask is – is it pleasant? Many are the empty remarks and vain statements that people make in idleness to hurt others. It is better that these unpleasant words remain unspoken.

The third question according to Socrates is – is it useful? Is our statement going to benefit the listener? Will our words bring comfort to someone? Are we likely to help someone with what we say? Only in that case should we go ahead and speak.

An Eastern account of Jesus attributes the following statement to him, "A day will come when you will have to render account for every idle word you have spoken".

We will all do well to remember this; we must pay – not merely for an untrue word, not merely for a bitter word, but for every *idle* word we have uttered!

Is it true? Is it pleasant? Is it useful? These are the three questions we must ask ourselves before we speak.

> We need to find God, and He cannot be found in noise and restlessness. God is the friend of silence. See how nature – trees, flowers, grass – grow in silence; see the stars, the moon and the sun, how they move in silence... We need silence to be able to touch souls.
>
> – Mother Teresa

Did you know that in its strictest form, a *mantra* is not an expression with meaning? It is a sound, a *shabda* with its own special and unique vibrations. Of course, when we utter the sacred Name aloud, the sounds create their own waves. But when they vibrate in silence, within us, they have a tremendously beneficial effect on our being. In fact, according to the Hindu tradition, our ancient sages who sat in deep meditation for a lifetime heard these sounds in the silence within their souls; the sounds they heard – *shruti*– have now become the *mantras* which we use.

Nowadays, we attach meaning and value only to that which is uttered in words: silence, and the eloquence of silence is lost on most of us. Therefore, it requires practice to appreciate and absorb the vibrations that a *mantra* produces at a much deeper level than words. Rather than look for any *meaning*, we must learn to *experience* the vibrations at a profound level.

A whole book could be written on the fascinating subject of the inter-relation of *mantra* and meditation. Suffice it to say that *mantras* heard within, produce healing, soothing vibrations, so that we attain a level of experience that is deeper than mere thought.

Gurudev Sadhu Vaswani who has been the inspiration, the guide, the guardian and the leading light of my life, offered us a simple, straightforward *sadhana* which each and everyone could practise effortlessly: the three S's – the *sadhana* of Silence, *Sangha* and Service. He urged us to practise silence everyday; he emphasised the spiritual fellowship that was available to us at the *satsang*; and, above all, he urged that our life, our wealth, our talent and our time were all but a loan given to us by the Almighty, to be poured out in selfless service to those less fortunate than ourselves.

Spend a little time in silent communion with God, everyday. Attend the *satsang* regularly. And do whatever you can to alleviate the suffering of others, to make others happy!

Silence, *sangha* (fellowship) and service! If only we could follow these simple techniques of *sadhana* we would indeed find our lives transformed!

Silence is always a special form of prayer and communication for the seeker on the path. Silence speaks to us when we listen carefully with the ears of the heart. In the eloquent stillness of silence, we can hear the Divine music of God. When man meditates in silence and delves within, with the grace of God, he hears the eternal melody of the flute. This Divine melody, wafting on the breeze of the realm of the spirit, brings unbidden tears of ecstasy to his eyes; he is immersed in the ocean of bliss. Gurudev Sadhu Vaswani in his sacred writings says, "The Lord is playing the flute, He is singing the song of love, and it is a Divine calling to my spirit."

Gurudev Sadhu Vaswani has described three types of silence. The first is, *Karam Mauna*. It means forgetting all your work to observe silence. Do not be hindered by the work and the distractions associated with it. Do not allow these hindrances to venture inside you. Keep them away. Be aware and watchful.

Once there lived a saint. A friend had written him a letter, to which for some reason he could not reply immediately. However, one day, while sitting in silence in order to meditate, he suddenly remembered about the letter to which he had to reply. Immediately he got up and wrote to his friend, "This is my last letter to you. I sincerely request you not to write any more letters to me in the future, as, your letters distract me from my meditation." Avoiding the actions which are a hindrance to silence, is termed as *Karam Mauna*.

The second is, *Smriti Mauna*, or neutralising distracting memories. Sometimes the past happenings creep into the mind and disturb us. It is a common experience that when we sit in silence, long forgotten events and incidents appear on the horizon of our consciousness. It is especially the unhappy incidents that trouble us, making us feel remorseful. This is very common among elderly people. We are forgetful of the current events and happenings. We do not remember what happened yesterday, but when we sit in silence, the incidents of early childhood, events that occurred several years ago, suddenly crop up. This should be avoided. Therefore, before you sit in silence, command your mind to forget the past and to meditate on the present.

The third is, *Trishna Mauna* – silencing the desires. Man is wrapped up in many layers. The first layer is of desires. Our interior world of consciousness is much larger than the external world of pleasures and desires. Hence, when we sit in meditation and step into the vast ocean of consciousness, waves of desires obstruct our way, and we get drowned. Therefore it is necessary, that before entering into the subconscious, we should put up the 'No Entry' board to all desires. This is the third type of silence we should practise.

The inner journey requires these three silences, namely, *Karam Mauna*, *Smriti Mauna* and *Trishna Mauna*.

Many of us are trapped by the blaring noise, the glaring lights and the mechanical routine of a demanding society. We are surrounded by the buzzing of alarms, the ringing of telephones, the clatter of keyboards, the loud volume of the TV, the high decibel levels from loudspeakers, horns, engines, cars, buses and trucks. The glare of the TV screen and artificial lighting are constantly hurting our eyes. We get up like mechanised robots and go about our daily routine listlessly.

Let me say to you, you must learn to exercise your soul! Turn to nature to nurture you. Learn to spend at least a little time everyday in outdoor activities – it can be something as simple as walking or just sitting on a garden bench. Being in touch with the healing forces of nature helps to restore calm, peace and a sense of harmony to your life.

Today, very few of us take time to sit quietly and commune with nature. I know people in Mumbai and Chennai who do not go to the seaside even once a year. I know many Bangaloreans who have never taken a walk in the City's famous Cubbon Park. I know people in Pune who have never explored the green and lovely hill tracks which surround the city.

That is indeed a pity. When you turn to nature, you rediscover yourself. When you turn your back on the noise and commotion of the city life, you are able to capture the beautiful silence of the soul within you.

The demands and distractions of modern life only take us away from ourselves. This is why Indian philosophy and culture insist on silence, withdrawal, stillness and meditation whereby you can discover the Divine within yourself.

Truth is within! Wisdom is within! The source of all strength is within! Therefore, we must turn within, in silence!

Exercise in Silent Awareness

This exercise in silence calms the restless and agitated mind and helps in increasing the power to concentrate on work, studies and spiritual development.

Let us relax. Try to relax every muscle, every nerve, every limb, of the body – make the body tension-free. Relax the mind as well: let it be free of fear, anxiety, frustration, worry, depression and disappointment. Even as a towel is wrung to drain it of every drop of water, so let the mind, pictured in the form of a towel, be drained of all tension, drop by drop.

We are now ready to embark on a spiritual journey that, with God's grace, will take us into the depths within and give us that which surpasses understanding.

Be relaxed and let the face wear a soft smile.

Let us for a brief while forget the world, forget its worries and vexations, its tensions and tribulations and feel that we are in the presence of God. God is always with us. We are not always with God. We forget Him again and again. Therefore we must practice the presence of God. Everytime we find our thoughts straying away from God, let us bring the mind gently, lovingly back into the Divine Presence.

To do this, let us offer a silent prayer: O Lord, may our senses be free from the drag of sense objects. May our minds sit still in the Divine Presence as a bee sucking honey out of a flower. May our intellect, the *buddhi*, be illumined with the Light of the *Atman*. May our entire being be filled with Light. Light, Light. Light in front, Light behind, Light to the right, Light to the left, Light above, Light below, Light within, Light all around. Light, Light, Light...

Do not interfere with the breathing: merely watch it. Watch the breath as it comes in and flows out at the tip of the nostrils.

This is an exercise in awareness. We do not have to control the breath; we have only to watch it. Be relaxed and let the face wear a soft smile. And be alert!

Remain silent for about five minutes.

The period of silence is over. Rub the palms of your hands together, softly place them on your eyelids, and gently open your eyes.

Only Time Can Tell

Long, long ago, there was an island in the midst of the ocean where all the feelings lived. Happiness, Sadness, Knowledge, Wisdom, Love, Indulgence and several others lived side by side in a good-neighbourly atmosphere. Love too, lived with them.

Suddenly, all the feelings were told without any warning that the island would sink to the bottom of the ocean very soon. They were warned to leave the island immediately. So, all the feelings prepared their boats to leave the doomed island. However, Love decided to stay behind. She said that it was her wish to try and preserve the island paradise until the very last possible moment. But the following day, when the island was almost totally under water, Love decided it was time for her to leave. She began looking around for someone to ask for help.

Just then she saw Luxury passing by in a grand boat. Love waved to her frantically, asking, "Luxury, can you take me on your boat?"

"Sorry," Luxury replied, "my boat is overloaded with gold and silver and there's just no room for you anywhere!"

Love saw Vanity, who was passing in a beautiful vessel, and called out to him for help. "So sorry, my dear, but I can't help you," Vanity said, "You are all wet and you will damage the silken upholstery on my beautiful boat."

Next Love saw Sadness passing by. Love said, "Sadness, please let me go with you." Sadness answered, "Love, I'm so sorry, but I just need to be alone now."

Then, Love saw Happiness and cried out, "Happiness, please take me with you." But Happiness was so overjoyed that he was escaping from the island, that he didn't even hear Love calling out to him.

Feeling unwanted and abandoned, Love began to cry, when she heard a voice say to her, "Come Love, I will take you with me." Love could not make out who it was, but it was an elderly person. Love felt so blessed and overjoyed that she forgot to ask the elder his name. When they arrived safely on land the elder went on his way.

Love realised how much she owed the elder and when she met Knowledge she asked who it was that had helped her. "Don't you know, it was Time," Knowledge answered.

"But why did Time help me when no one else would?" Love asked him. Knowledge smiled and with deep wisdom and sincerity, answered, "Because, my dear, only Time is capable of understanding how great and valuable Love is."

Chapter Seven

Make Love The Mantra Of Your Life

Have you ever asked yourself: What is the secret of a happy, peace-filled, rewarding, fulfilling life?

Gurudev Sadhu Vaswani, in one of his books, writes about the secret of a happy life. He tells us, "When you enter the portals of Heaven, God will not ask you about your caste, status or wealth. He will not ask you about your educational qualifications, your designation or your business acumen. He will ask you whether you have learnt the art, the life skill of loving your fellow human beings."

Love is the light that illuminates the dark ways of life. Love is Heavenly. Love is beautiful. To grow in the life of the spirit, we must learn the art of selfless love. And let me tell you dear friends, this is an art that you can learn very easily. Learn the art of speaking gently, lovingly and sweetly. Learn to offer a helping hand to everyone who needs it. Learn to be humble and treat others with respect. Look upon all creation as one family with God as the loving Father of us all – and you have mastered the art of true love!

Today, people talk of hard skills, soft skills, communication skills and technical skills. May I say to you, life skills are more important than professional skills! Love is far more essential to a successful life than vocational degrees. For love purifies your life and makes it sweet and meaningful.

What is love? What is the way of love? The way of love is selflessness. It is the way of sacrifice. Love has no place for ego or selfishness. Love is an ever-expanding positive energy. It was Rabindranath Tagore who said, "Love is an endless mystery, for it has nothing else to explain it." I cannot define or explain love to you! You have to feel it in your heart; you have to experience its healing, purifying powers, for it blesses both those who love, and those who are loved.

Have you ever prayed to God, to show you the way of love? Have you asked Him to bless you and shower you with that beautiful emotion called love?

Do not pray for material goods. Do not ask for petty favours. Ask for something which is more valuable, everlasting and blessed. God in His infinite mercy and kindness, will bless you with love that is pure and self-energising.

If you wish to walk the way of spirituality, if you wish to know God and understand Him, you must love Him more and more.

The more you love Him, the more you will know Him.

The key to knowledge is — LOVE!

Darkness cannot drive out darkness: only light can do that. Hate cannot drive out hate: only love can do that.

– Martin Luther King Jr.

There are a hundred and one ways of doing the same thing. Are you a professor teaching in classroom? Are you a lawyer arguing a case in a court of law? Are you a doctor attending to patients? Do the best you can! There are many ways of doing the same thing. Some are right, some are wrong. But only one is the best! And because you are doing everything for the love of God, because you are doing everything as an offering unto the Lord, you must do your work in the best way possible.

It was an Arabian poet who said: "Are you a mason building a house? Build it in the aspiration that some day perhaps the Beloved will come and dwell in your home. How much love would you not put into the building of such a house!"

"Are you a weaver working at the loom, weaving a piece of cloth? Weave the cloth in the hope that the cloth will be worn by the Beloved. How much love would you not pour into your weaving!"

There was a painter who painted pictures of fascinating beauty. One day as he was painting, a friend happened to drop in. The artist was painting a beautiful portrait of Sri Krishna. The friend stood spell-bound. The painting captivated his heart.

"Do you like the picture?" enquired the artist.

"Yes, I not only like but I admire the picture. You could not have painted such a beautiful face of the Lord until you loved Him!" said the friend, with deep admiration.

"Love Him!" echoed the artist, "Of course I do. And the more I love Him, the better will I paint Him and the more fascinating will the picture become!"

Just imagine a world – very much like the world we live in, but which is free of all disorder and chaos; a world in which everything is done with love, for love's sake, for helping other people; a world in which everything comes to pass in the right way, at the right time, in a perfectly harmonious manner. As we visualise such a world, we will find the love and joy and peace of God flowing into our lives like a perennial river.

The secret of a new life, the spiritual life, the life beautiful, is love of God!

> **If you judge people, you have no time to love them.**
> — **Mother Teresa**

Very many years ago, a young man came to meet my Gurudev Sadhu Vaswani. He was utterly desolate and downcast, and he said to the Master, "I am just thirty years old, and I am an utter failure! I have lost my job. My ancestral property is mortgaged. My wife has left me, and I am unable to support my old mother. I am utterly frustrated with life. What shall I do?"

Gurudev Sadhu Vaswani said to him, "You are not the pathetic weakling that you take yourself to be! You are not poor and broken! You are like the prodigal son who has drifted away from his rich father and does not know how infinitely rich he is."

The young man was bemused. "Excuse me," he stammered. "Who is this rich father you are speaking of? My own father passed away five years ago—and he only left behind debts which I am yet to pay off!"

Gurudev Sadhu Vaswani smiled and said to him, "I am speaking of our Heavenly Father. He is the Father of us all. And He is the source of all supply. He is the source of all that you and I will ever need or desire. He is the source of prosperity, plenty and peace. He is the source of happiness and harmony. He is the source of love and joy, strength and wisdom, power and security. All you need to do is turn to Him in love and prayer – and you will lack nothing!"

Alas—that is exactly what we cannot or will not do!

The Swiss psychiatrist Carl Jung states, "Civilisation today has become sick because man has alienated himself from God."

I think the greatest affliction of modern civilisation is that we are moving away from God, and the awareness that we are all His children.

Some young atheists even say, "We have no need of God. There is nothing man cannot do on his own. Man has been able to set his foot on the moon. Man's rockets go flying past the distant planets. Man has been able to station satellites in space. Who needs God today?"

God is the source and sustainer of life. And man cannot live a healthy life physically, mentally, morally, spiritually, so long as he cuts himself off from God. It is very easy to drive the spirit out of the door — but once you have done that, life loses its flavour; the 'salt of life' grows flat.

May I share with you the prayer that I offer every day at the Lotus Feet of the Beloved? I urge you too, to turn to God as often as you can. Think of Him during your daily routine. Pray to Him ever so often: "I love You God! I want to love You more and more! I want to love You more than anything else in the world. I want to love You to distraction, to intoxication. Grant me pure love and devotion for Thy Lotus Feet, and so bless me that this world-bewitching *maya* may not lead me astray. And make me, Blessed Master, an instrument of Thy help and healing in this world of suffering and pain."

Keep love in your heart. A life without it is like a sunless garden when the flowers are dead.
– Oscar Wilde

There is a simple question that all saints ask of us: How can we claim our love to God if we do not love our fellow human beings? How can we call ourselves human beings if we watch our brothers and sisters suffering and struggling?

I have always asserted that Hinduism is not a religion, but a way of life. And the Hindu way of life embraces the whole of God's creation in its entirety! For Vedanta teaches us that there is but One Life in all! The One Life sleeps in the mineral and the stone, stirs in the vegetable and plant, dreams in the animal and wakes up in man. Creation is one family; therefore let us not forget that birds and animals too, are our younger brothers and sisters! It is our duty to guard them and protect them!

Our hearts need to be saturated with love, for love is the light which will illumine the way of spirituality. For this, developed brains are not needed; we need enlightened hearts that can behold the vision of fellowship, unity and brotherhood. Love is what we need to build a new life of the spirit, a new humanity, a new world of brotherhood and peace. We must eliminate the dark forces of greed, selfishness, prejudice and mistrust—and cultivate the power of Love which is also the power of Joy and Peace!

We all want peace—peace of mind, peace in the family, peace in the community around us, peace between countries, peace in the world, peace with our environment. As I said, there is scarcely a soul upon the earth that does not yearn for peace. But how many of us are prepared to pay the price?

I will tell you what I think is the price we must pay: We must love one another. I will go one step further: We must love one another or perish!

We must love one another; we must pray for each other; we must be prepared to sacrifice for each other; we must put aside selfishness and narrow national interests and work for the goal of world unity.

To walk the way of spirituality, we must love our neighbours; we must not stop with that; we must love our enemies too.

Make no mistake about this: To an Indian, "Love thy neighbour" means loving the people of Pakistan; to an Israeli, "Love thy neighbour" means loving the Palestinians; to Christians, it means loving the Muslims and Hindus and Sikhs!

Let me remind you therefore, of the words of the apostles:

> Bless them that curse you, and pray for your enemies. Fast on behalf of those that prosecute you; for what thanks is there if you love them that love you? ... Do ye love them that hate you, and ye will not have an enemy!

Can we, as human beings do this?

If we could, we are asserting the Divinity in us – and we are truly advancing on the way of spirituality!

True love is a feeling that touches mind, heart and soul. It is perhaps the feeling which is the highest that any human being is capable of: for I believe that love is of God; in fact I believe that love is not just an attribute of God – Love is God and God is Love! That is why I urge my young friends not to fall in love – but rise in true love!

I am afraid many of us have a rather shallow and superficial conception of love. We look upon love as something romantic — a thing of the heart. We regard it as something intangible, ephemeral, something which we can't even find words to describe.

Native American Indians look upon love as a kind of wisdom. They believe that love is the first wisdom given to us, and we derive all else from that knowledge. The famous writer Carlyle echoed the same idea when he wrote: "A loving heart is the beginning of all knowledge."

> **We can only learn to love by loving.**
> – Iris Murdoch

Love is not out there somewhere. It is with you, within you. The more you offer love to the world and the people in it, the more it will come back to you! Indeed, it was a wise man who asserted: "Love grows by giving. The love we give away is the only love we keep. The only way to retain love is to give it away."

I have always been a great believer in the strength and sustaining power of true love – love which transcends the physical and the material, love that is Divine and universal, and moves out to all people, to all of creation! We must all love one another – or perish!

In love, I believe, is the solution to all the problems of life; if life is a battle, love is its victory; if life is a story, love is its theme; if life is music, love is its melody; and if life is a flower, love is its fragrance!

The world's greatest need today is love-in-action! This love manifests itself in sympathy, service and sacrifice. If you wish to show true love, you must pour your life out in sympathy, service and sacrifice, to all humanity.

Someone asked me, "How can we know and feel the kind of love you speak of?" And my answer was: "You will know it when you become love!"

How can we grow in the spirit of such true love? So let me offer you a few suggestions:

1. People often talk of 'falling' in love; you must rise in love – in love with God, and in love with your fellow human beings, as also with brother birds and beasts.

    Therefore, establish a firm and loving relationship with God, first and foremost.

Make God your father or mother, your friend or brother. Let everything you do strengthen this relationship with God.

When you have established such a relationship, you will find it natural to offer the love of your heart to everything and everyone around you.

2. Speak softly; speak gently; speak with loving kindness. Treat everyone with love and respect. Greet God in everyone you meet.

3. Do not see the faults of others. When you find fault with others and criticise them harshly, you are drawing negative forces to yourself!

4. Love your family, love your friends and neighbours; but love those who hate you and criticise you as well! Breathe out love to those who ill-treat you and speak harshly to you! For every blow you receive, give back a blessing. This is not an impossible, impractical precept I'm preaching to you: it is a sound, wholesome approach to life that will bring lasting peace and happiness to you!

5. Whatever you do, whatever you say, whatever you think, whatever you give – do it for the pure love of God! When you live life

as an act of love and devotion to God, you will find that you can never do anything which will displease God! Your life will become the life beautiful, the life of love and purity.

6. The law of love is the law of service and sacrifice. Therefore, go out of your way to help others. And rejoice in everything that the Will of God brings to you.

Love blesses the one who offers it and the one who receives it. Love can keep you healthy and happy, and help you face the problems of daily life in the right spirit!

Let me repeat: Love is not an attribute of God: Love is God!

Love is never blind – for love sees not only with the eyes, but the mind, the heart and the spirit. Love goes about with wide open eyes, looking for opportunities to be of service to those in need.

We are told that a holy man was pained to see suffering and misery, wherever he turned. In deep despair, he cried out to God: "O Lord! They call You the God of Love and Mercy. How can You bear to see so much suffering and yet do nothing about it?"

From the depth of his consciousness, he heard God's voice tell him: "I did do something. I created you!"

God has created us and poured love into our hearts so that we may alleviate the pain and suffering we see around us.

Let us not curse the darkness. Let us kindle the light of love in our hearts!

Exercise: Positive Affirmations of Love

Love is never blind, whatever the novelists may say! Love sees with the eyes of the heart.

Love is unconditional. It does not come with strings attached. Love is not a bargaining tool or a blackmail weapon. It cannot be subject to conditions or stipulations.

A loving relationship is the greatest gift a human being can be blessed with.

God's love for us manifests itself in a thousand ways, every minute, every hour, every day! Make sure your heart is always open and receptive to receive and appreciate those gifts.

Just for today, don't try to 'influence' or 'persuade' or 'reason with' people you meet; instead, offer your loving support and understanding to them. You will find that this brings out the best in them.

Today, choose one person who means the most to you. And just for today, look at everything you do from that person's perspective. Just for today put that person's interest above your own.

Unconditional love should not leave you vulnerable or insecure. It should make you joyous, strong and ready to offer even more love.

If you wish to love others, you must love yourself!

Get to know yourself better. Count your blessings. Assess your strengths. Develop a healthy sense of self-esteem.

Learn to love the good qualities that you are capable of manifesting – learn to love truth, purity, humility, sacrifice, service, honesty and gratitude. Choose one quality each day and focus your loving attention on it. Love other people who express that quality and learn from them.

Make a list of all the things, the people, the qualities you love most. Now, set your priorities. What or whom do you wish to love more than all else? Make a resolution to devote more energy and effort to fostering those relationships that mean the most to you.

<u>Afterword</u>

Spirituality For Busy People

Many brothers and sisters tell me: "Our worldly duties are wearisome and exhaust all our energy. We do not have the time or the effort to devote to spirituality. How can we aspire to tread the path you tell us of?"

I have added this Afterword for their benefit. It sums up in brief, what I have tried to tell you through the pages of this book. Do not make the mistake of assuming that spirituality is only for people who have nothing to do! In fact, 'busy' people perhaps need spirituality more than the rest of us, so that their 'busy'ness does not overwhelm their lives!

And whatever gave you the impression that spirituality is time consuming or exhausting? It is a refreshing, revitalising experience!

The more I have thought of it, the more it has seemed to me that what humanity needs today, is something more than rites and dogmas. Humanity today needs reassurance. People, today, need to know that they are not alone, that they have not been abandoned, that there is one who loves them and cares for them as they are, in spite of what they are. Philosophy and theology have so much to tell us of God. But what people need today is an experience of God. There is a difference between eating dinner and reading the menu. There is a difference between reading a travel book and actually visiting the land described therein. There is a difference between watching an advertisement on the TV screen and actually owning the product advertised. So it is with actually experiencing God, making God a reality in your life.

Every minute, every second comes to us as a gift from God. Every breath, every inhalation and exhalation is an offering of love from God. One way to realise this is to stop doing whatever you are doing, close your eyes, take a slow, deep breath. A slow, deep breath is one in which an inhalation lasts at least five seconds, as does an exhalation. A total breath lasts at least ten seconds.

If you breathe in and breathe out like this six times, it will take you no more than a minute. If you do this ten times in a day, whenever you can spare one minute at a time, it will take only ten minutes; but let me say to you, being aware of the breath, being conscious of the *prana* that sustains your life, can change your life!

I urge you to do it right now! As we take in the breath, let us say inwardly: "I open the door to God, to enter my life." Take in the breath and say to yourself inwardly: "I open the door to God to enter my life." Take out the breath and say to yourself, if you like, aloud: "Thank You God, for entering my life." Do this nine times more. Soon, you will realise that God is, that He is watching you: that He is watching over you. And this can change your life!

As I said, Philosophy can be very revealing. But it cannot change you. It can only touch the superficies of life. Hence the value of the message that was given by the seers and sages of our ancient land, the rishis and saints who lived here in the days of yore. They taught the people how to live the true life, the new life, a life of simplicity and sympathy and service, a life of new awakening, of self-effacement and self-realisation. They taught the people how to keep the mind fresh and to take the time and effort to live the life beautiful, a life dedicated to the highest that we are capable of becoming!

It is this message that the world needs today. The ultimate fact for these great ones was not matter or force, but the *Atman*, the Spirit – not determinism but the spirit of joy, *ananda*. Out of *ananda*, the universe was born and to *ananda* the universe is moving, even as the streams move on to blend with the sea. I breathe out an aspiration that the memory of these great ones may shine and shine as a light to many whose minds wander in these days of cruelty and confusion, of tension and terrorism. I bow down to their beautiful image in my heart and I pray that their message may reach the farthest end of the earth and continue to be a source of inspiration to generations unborn.

What is this message? The message, in simple words is: "O man, you are not what you take yourself to be. You are not the body, nor are you the body-mind complex. The body is a garment you have worn. The body is a house. You are the one who dwells within the body, the indwelling one. And the mind is an instrument which you have brought with yourself to be able to do your work on the physical plane. Within you is a temple — the temple of the heart. In this temple dwelleth God Himself. He is not afar: He does not dwell on a distant star. Closer is He to you than breathing, and nearer than hands and feet. Blessed are you if you set out in search of Him.

The ways are many. Some of them I have described to you in the pages of this work. A simple and easy way is the way of Love. To know God, you must love Him…

Gurudev Sadhu Vaswani was in London. He was walking on the roadside when suddenly it started to rain. He sought shelter underneath a tree. An Englishman was standing there already. He looked at Gurudev Sadhu Vaswani and said to him: "It seems to me that you are from India. And India is considered to be the motherland of religious consciousness. Can you tell me in three words, what is the true spirit of religion?"

Gurudev Sadhu Vaswani said: "The first word is love: the second word is love: the third word is love." Yes, the true spirit of religion is love. Religion is not rites and ceremonies, creeds and dogmas. Creeds are broken reeds, and dogmas divide. The true spirit of religion, and the secret of spirituality is Love. And what is Love? Love, true love is to reckon oneself as nothing and the Beloved as the All. The truly spiritual man knows that he is nothing, the Guru and God are everything. When our earthly pilgrimage comes to a close, when the body drops down dead, and we enter the Great Beyond, no one will ask us how much wealth we amassed, how many crores we collected, how may degrees and diplomas we acquired, how many lectures we gave or heard; they will ask us if we have learnt the word of letters four, L-O-V-E; how much love we had acquired and shared with those in need!

Love and humility go together. They are but two sides of the same coin. Where there is love, there is humility.

A German scholar made a study of several saints. He said that saints were of different temperaments, from different backgrounds. Some of them were learned, some of them were illiterate. Some of them were rich, some of them were poor: some of them could sing, some of them could not sing: some of them had strong muscular bodies, some of them were weak: some of them were orators, some of them could not give lectures. But they all had one thing in common. They were men and women of utter humility. This is the distinguishing mark of a saint, a truly spiritual man. You may come across many who appear wise and learned. They may deliver inspiring discourses and give brilliant interpretations of the sacred texts. But if they have not conquered their pride, annihilated their ego, they have not attained sainthood.

Saint Francis of Assisi was a saint of the purest ray serene. One day, they asked him: "You are not learned: you are not wealthy: you are not handsome: why is it that the whole world runs after you?"

St. Francis said: "There is nothing in me. Whatever I am, it is all due to the grace of God." And they asked him: "Why is it that of all men, God chose you as one on whom to pour His grace?" He said; "God set out in quest of the most wretched and the most lowly amongst men, so that He could demonstrate what His grace could achieve and He did not find a man more wretched than I."

I am often asked: "What was the path Gurudev Sadhu Vaswani asked you to take to attain to God?" My answer is: "He taught us to walk the little way, the *Alpa Marga*."

In wonder, they ask: "What can that be? We have heard of *Bhakti Marga, Gyana Marga, Karma Marga, Raj Yoga, Hatha Yoga* and other *Margas*. But we have not heard of the little way, the "*Alpa Marga*". Tell us something about it.

The little way is the simple way. It is the humble way. It asks us to do little, simple tasks with love and devotion and offer them to the Lord. He who wishes to walk this way must learn to become humble. In utter surrender, he must say to the Lord: "O, Lord, I am nothing, Thou art all." *Na ham, na ham, Tu ho, Tu ho!* The pilgrim of the little way is not bothered about what other people think of him. He is not even hurt if someone humiliates him. He remains calm even when he is criticised. If we are criticised, we get angry and our reaction is to hit back. When we get angry, we immediately give tit-for-tat. Our reaction is an eye for an eye, a tooth for a tooth. The pilgrim of the little way believes in forgiving and forgetting. He knows that what is hurt is the ego and he is out to annihilate the ego.

In his efforts to annihilate the ego, he finds that it is not possible for him to do so. He feels the need of a Guru — a person who is egoless, who walks with God, who talks to God, who has his entire being in God. The pilgrim on the path feels that by himself, he can do nothing. At every step, in every round of life, he needs the help of a self-realised, God intoxicated person whom, for want of a better word, we call Guru.

I am asked: "What should be the daily life of a pilgrim on the Path? How does he spend his hours? What is his daily programme?" As he wakes up in the morning, he breathes out an aspiration of purity, love, joy, peace, humility, an aspiration for life: "What does it profit a man if he gain the whole world and lose his soul?" Or "Apart from Thee, I need nothing, O Lord." Or "I love You, Lord. I want to love You more and more." Or *Deena Bandhu Deena Naath, Meri Dori Tere Haath.* "I surrender the thread of my life in your safe Hands." He repeats this aspiration as often as he can during the day, even in the midst of his work. He thanks the Lord for the gift of a new day.

He takes a shower and spends some time (if possible half an hour) in meditation and prayer. The Law of Meditation is regularity. Even if he has urgent work to attend to, and is not able to find time for meditation, let him but spare three minutes and practise what I call a mini meditation session. Let him spend the first minute on relaxation by concentrating on his breath. Let him inhale vitality and exhale tension. In one minute, he can easily take ten inhalations and ten exhalations. Let him spend the second minute in giving attention to a spiritual aspiration such as the one with which he woke up in the morning. Let him spend the third minute by breathing out peace to all beings: "May all beings – men, birds, animals, insects, etc. – be happy and full of peace and bliss."

He takes a brisk walk for half an hour. Walking is said to be the best of exercises. The practitioners of Zen and Tao have even perfected the art of Walking Meditation!

But to return to our pilgrim on the path, our spiritual aspirant: he takes breakfast, consisting of fruit and fruit juice and feels grateful to Mother earth for providing delicious fruits which nourish his life.

He attends to his daily duty, then takes a break to have his lunch which may be something light.

He relaxes for 15 to 30 minutes and gets back to his work.

The evening, he devotes either to *satsang* or reading some positive literature.

He takes dinner which may consist of soup and bread or a *chappati* and cooked vegetables.

Before going to bed, he goes over the events of the day and finds there have been some acts of omission and commission in his life that day. He prays for strength and wisdom not to repeat the mistakes again. He sleeps deeply and soundly, waking up early in the morning, fresh and vibrant, looking forward to a new day.

What is spirituality? In simple words, it is knowledge of God, not an intellectual knowledge but an illumined personal experience of the Supreme. Everyone knows that God exists. But that knowledge of the existence of God is book knowledge, indirect knowledge, theoretical and borrowed knowledge. Mahatma Gandhi said, "For the last 30 years I have been striving to see God face to face." It is this personal encounter with the Divine that is needed. Sri Ramakrishna had it and he could say to Swami Vivekananda: "I see Him more clearly and intensely than I see you!" Such spirituality will bind the nations and bring together the people of the world and transform them into a world community.

May I quote the words of the Alwar saints: those who have experienced it, cannot analyse it; those who analyse it, cannot experience it. Spirituality is such a thing: if you think you have it, you have lost it; if you actually have it, you are not aware of it! That is, you will not go around saying, "I am a deeply spiritual person." Or, to put it differently, spirituality is an endless journey. If you think you have reached the end, in reality, you have not even begun. We talk of spirituality as though we are experts on spirituality. Spirituality is boundless, unable to be fenced in. We cannot capture it: it captures us. As much as we may try to hold it fast, it will always escape our grasp. We can only be pilgrims on the Path.

And every pilgrim on the Path will find these practical suggestions helpful.

Practical Suggestion 1

Always keep in mind the Golden Rule which states that You must do unto others, as you would have others do unto you. You must not do unto others what you would not wish them to do unto you. You are truly spiritual when you see yourself in others.

Practical Suggestion 2

Take care of your thoughts. Very often we pay scant attention to our thoughts. We say: "What does it matter? It was only a thought. But thoughts lead to words and words to actions; and actions form our character. Therefore, I say to my friends again and again, take care of your thoughts.

Practical Suggestion 3

Do not be in a hurry to give a promise . But if you have given a promise, you must be in a hurry to fulfill it. Your life must bear witness to the ideal of Truth. For Truth is God.

Practical Suggestion 4

Let prayer become a habit with you. Pray, pray and continue to pray. So many of our prayers remain unanswered, because we give up praying. We become impatient and lose faith. We feel that as God is not going to act for us, we must act for ourselves. We forget that God acts at the right time. If He has not yet acted, it only means that the right time is not yet. This applies not only to material requirements but, also, to mental and spiritual needs.

Practical Suggestion 5

Accept whatever comes to you. Do not seek the 'pleasant': do not shun the 'unpleasant'. Rejoice in everything that happens. All that has happened, all that is happening and is yet to happen – all, all is for the best! "Meet every situation in life with the favourite prayer of St. Frances de Sales: "Yes, Father! Yes, and always Yes!"

Practical Suggestion 6

Whatever you do – it may be a lowly act such as sweeping a room or a noble deed such as saving a life – do it wholly for the love of God. "Whatever you eat, whatever austerity you practise, whatever you give in charity, whatever you do, do it, O Arjuna, as an offering unto Me," says the Lord in the Gita. Can there be a simpler way of communing with God than this, that we offer unto Him every little thing we do, every thought we think, every word we utter, every aspiration we breathe? This is the right way to practise the presence of God.

Practical Suggestion 7

Remember Death every day. We live in a world of uncertainty. There is only one thing of which we can be certain – that every passing day draws you closer to that moment when, leaving everything you hold dear and near behind – your wealth, friends, family, country – you will have to enter into the Great Beyond. Gurudev Sadhu Vaswani said to us that we must not have any worry at all – except this one worry, that we have to set out on a long, endless journey but have made no preparations for the same.

Remembering death will also reinforce the fact that you are not the body you wear. The body is only a cage. It will drop down. The bird will fly away.

Practical Suggestion 8

You must develop a good sense of humour. A sense of humour helps you to meet the vicissitudes of life in your stride. It lends you poise, it gives you balance and it helps you bend without breaking and these are essential traits of a happy and contented person. I have often been asked, "Which do you think is the most important of the five senses?" My reply has always been, "None of these, but the sixth one, the sense of humour." With your sense of humour you can confront the most difficult of situations and can come out unscathed.

Practical Suggestion 9

If you have wronged a person, do not waste time in making amends. Have you hurt someone? Have you cheated him? Have you spread scandals against him? Have you exploited him for selfish purposes? Then, waste no time in setting right what has gone wrong.

On the other hand; has someone wronged you? Forgive him, even before forgiveness is asked. And your mind will be at peace and the world around you will smile.

Practical Suggestion 10

Help as many as you can to lift the load on the rough road of life. Gurudev Sadhu Vaswani said:

> Did you meet him on the road?
> Did you leave him with the load?

On the road of life are many who go about carrying heavy loads. The loads are not merely physical. There are many who carry on their hearts the loads of worry, anxiety, fear. Lighten their loads. Be a burden bearer! The day on which we have not helped a brother here or a sister there, a bird here or an animal there – for birds and animals , too, are God's children and man's younger brothers and sisters in the one family of creation – the day on which we have not helped someone in need is a lost day, indeed.

Let me say to you, spirituality is a gift of God: It cannot be earned. It cannot be acquired or possessed. For it is a reality given freely and spontaneously. All we can do is to keep the door of our heart open, and entreat God to enter therein. "When wilt Thou enter the home of my heart?" should be our constant prayer.

"Where is the dwelling of God?" asked the Rabbi of Kotzk of a number of learned men who visited him. They laughed at him and said: "What are you asking? God is Omnipresent. He is everywhere." The Rabbi then gave his answer and said: "God dwells wherever man lets Him in!"

May I, with folded hands, appeal to everyone of you, whose good fortune it is to aspire to walk the path of Spirituality: "Let Him in! Let Him in! Let Him in!"

100 Stories You Will Never Forget

Price: ₹ 200

Many Paths: One Goal

Price: ₹ 350

Does God Have Favourites?

Price: ₹ 125